AF608110

Public Affairs and Democratic Ideals

Public Affairs and Democratic Ideals

Critical Perspectives in an
Era of Political and Economic Uncertainty

CURTIS VENTRISS

Published by State University of New York Press, Albany

Printed in the United States of America

For information, contact State University of New York Press, Albany, NY
www.sunypress.edu

Library of Congress Cataloging-in-Publication Data

Name: Ventriss, Curtis, author.
Title: Public affairs and democratic ideals : critical perspectives in an era of political and economic uncertainty / Curtis Ventriss.
Description: Albany : State University of New York Press, 2021. | Includes bibliographical references and index.
Identifiers: LCCN 2020024649 | ISBN 9781438481258 (hardcover : alk. paper) | ISBN 9781438481265 (ebook)
Subjects: LCSH: Public administration—Evaluation. | Public administration—Moral and ethical aspects. | Public administration—Citizen participation. | Government accountability. | Democracy.
Classification: LCC JF1351 .V46 2021 | DDC 352.7/48—dc23
LC record available at https://lccn.loc.gov/2020024649

10 9 8 7 6 5 4 3 2 1

Dedicated to Lisa Ventriss and Alex Ventriss

❧

. . . Where trust in society and its institutions is battered, and where interests fail to gain the recognition they feel entitled to, there is an explosive mixture ready to be set off. Individuals cannot stand too much uncertainty in their lives, and the direct measures of uncertainty are the rapid and fluctuating loss in value of money people use for exchange (the aggravating discrepancies between income and what one has to buy, the erosion of wealth one has painfully accumulated) and fluctuating unemployment. It is these circumstances that the traditional institutions and democratic procedures of a society crack, and the irrational, emotional angers and desire for a political savior come to flood tide . . .

—Daniel Bell

And so the question becomes whether the ideals [of democracy] themselves must be given up or drastically revised, or whether there are ways of rearticulating them that retain their moral force.

—C. Wright Mills

If they can get you asking the wrong questions, they don't have to worry about the answers.

—Thomas Pynchon

Contents

Foreword

For me, this book has had a long history. Some of the issues I have examined in this book, in fact, go back to my undergraduate days. Other issues raised mirror the era in which I grew up, as I explain in more detail in chapter 9. But it was my two mentors in graduate school, more than anything else, who had the greatest impact on my thinking, particularly in exploring, as Theodor Adorno (1967, p. 10) so candidly put it, "the societal play of forces that operates beneath the surface of political forms." These two mentors respectively were John Dyckman (1922–1987) and Alberto Guerreiro Ramos (1915–1982). John Dyckman, an economist, was one of the leading scholars in planning and international development who served for many years as the chair of the Department of City and Regional Planning at the University of California, Berkeley. He later became the first James Irvine Chair of Planning at the University of Southern California. His last appointment was as a professor of geography, Johns Hopkins University. By contrast, Guerreiro Ramos was a prominent sociologist and administrative theorist who wrote seminal works in Brazil before coming to the United States. After being forced to leave Brazil after the military coup in the 1960s, he resided briefly at Yale University, but spent the rest of his career at the University of Southern California. He is best known for his book, *The New Science of Organizations: A Reconceptualization of the Wealth of Nations.*

With that said, this book is in response to many of the questions they posed to me when I studied with them. They believed it was crucial to ask "foundational questions" that explore the underlying assumptions of economic, political, social, and cultural norms of the modern polity, especially as it related to both public administration/management and public policy. Moreover, they both strongly encouraged me to examine issues that went beyond a procedural/managerial perspective—as valuable as this approach may be in addressing some important societal issues. That is, they encouraged me to not just limit my inquiry of public affairs to strategies of collaborative policy networks, participative deliberation, economic efficiency in service delivery, professionalism, and the like (as important as they are to the study and practice of public affairs), but to undertake a substantive exploration of those political and economic presuppositions that have shaped civic and political life.

Needless to say, I am not claiming in this book to be exhaustive or contending that my analysis is in anyway definitive concerning the challenges that we face in both fields. Rather, I argue here that the issues I have raised—and their respective theoretical and practical nuances—are largely neglected in the mainstream literature of public administration/management and public policy. To cite only one brief example, there has been little, if any, discussion of how the modern state might confine what constitutes, or should constitute, legitimate questions and policy approaches in addressing major social issues of the day. In short, I hope this book ignites an ongoing debate about certain fundamental issues, assumptions, and approaches that are often taken as a historical given, or that are regarded as so obvious and self-evident that they are seldom scrutinized for their validity and continued relevance. In this regard, I have raised concerns about the role and purpose of civic participation, the economic crisis of 2008 and its impact on governance, the role of the state, the fixation on procedural and utilitarian rationality to public affairs, and the important centrality of publicness.

I argue that these issues are especially important in this era of political and economic uncertainty.[1] For example, this uncertainty is partially reflected in the views of many citizens who are frustrated by what they perceive as an increasingly dysfunctional governing system unable to respond to major societal problems, an acerbic political discourse that has contributed to a troubling political polarization and tribalism, and a lack of any serious collaboration among key policy actors in finding meaningful political consensus on an array of policy issues. For example, in the United States, this political unease is presently juxtaposed with a heightened sense of economic uncertainty of increasing income and wealthy inequality, stagnant wages for middle-income families since the 1970s, the impact of globalization on local and regional communities, uneven economic growth between urban and rural areas, and limited social mobility. This political and economic uncertainty has contributed, to some degree, to a distrust of public institutions by many Americans and in other countries (Mounk, 2018). What is key here is the following: as the political environment has become more and more consumed by a growing uncertainty of whether we can effectively resolve these daunting challenges, it has taken its toll on the body politic both in the United States and elsewhere. Among other things, it has—at least to some extent—contributed to the emergence of a pseudo-democratic populism that channels such economic and political uncertainty into fears, anxieties, and a numbing cynicism among certain segments of the citizenry in the United States (and in other countries). Coupled with voters who feel neglected by political and economic elites, these citizens will likely become a permanent and disruptive political fixture on the landscape (Eatwell & Goodwin, 2018). Given these stark realities, I think that for those in public management/administration and public policy the time has come to directly confront the validity of certain basic assumptions and to start asking different kinds of questions—questions that could in both fields make many rather uncomfortable and, I suspect, at times defensive.

As I write this, some of the more deleterious implications of widespread political and economic uncertainty have been vividly displayed during the COVID-19 pandemic and the consequential societal and economic distress that has instilled fear, frustration, and anxiety among the general public. This widespread uncertainty is especially acute in a time of economic and political discord—a situation, as previously noted, that can metastasize into an attitude of declining confidence and trust in public governance. As public fear and anxiety continued to spread during the Covid-19 pandemic, again, the most vulnerable in society became the most adversely impacted. According to Derek Thompson (2020), the COVID-19 will, unquestionably, "supercharge" (his term) the prevailing forces of inequality in society.

That said, what I contend in this book is that in addressing political and economic uncertainty, particularly in this time of societal discord, public distrust, and political polarization requires, among other things, a critical examination of not only the embeddedness of market values in political and economic decision making, but also how this ubiquitous embeddedness has impacted the broader moral, societal, and institutional fabric of society. The risk of ignoring or dismissing this kind of examination is to fall prey to what Karl Polanyi asserted is a misguided view of reality that ultimately results in "an inability to solve the problems of our civilization" (1944, p. 126).

As I argue in more detail in chapter 6, this distortive view of social reality can lead to what I refer to as economic and political involution that impedes our ability to critically scrutinize those underlying societal plays of forces that have contributed to our most vexing economic and social problems. We become enamored, in other words, with a steadfast conviction that it is with market-centered correctives, when all is said and done, that offers the most efficacious way to ameliorate society's most pressing issues. Simply stated, this involution has a propensity to further exacerbate a myopic fixation on the centrality and merits of such technocratic market/managerial perspectives. That is, regardless of how well-intentioned these managerial perspectives seem to be, we have a penchant (consciously and unconsciously) to see contentious societal issues as just another administrative problem to be resolved. As a corollary, this fixation runs the risk of leaving untouched any serious inquiry of those hegemonic assumptions that legitimize those powerful governing political and economic actors who strongly influence, if not dictate, the dominant market narrative of key policy initiatives (Bartels, 2016).

Although the United States has employed both needed public health measures and aggressive fiscal and monetary policies to abate the deleterious economic and health fallout of the COVID-19 pandemic, certain significant (and controversial) questions merit posing. First, how can we in a market economy such as the United States, driven largely by finance capital, the voluminous expansion in the market supply, debt creation, and buttressed by strong consumer demand, successfully implement a policy that on one hand would mandate stringent health restrictions for its containment (even for a short time) without concomitantly causing a precipitous reduction in consumer demand followed by a steep rise in unemployment—a quagmire that could potentially trigger even further societal resentment and cynicism in an era of increasing income and wealth inequality? Second, and on a related note, how can this COVID-19 pandemic be sufficiently addressed in a market-based health care system that has left the public so ill-prepared to deal with the severity of this contagion crisis, especially when the impact exhibits all the characteristics of sharpening the societal divide between those who can afford to quarantine and those who cannot (Harvey, 2020)?

Assuming the validity of my central point here, one of the more troubling realities we may have to face, albeit under conditions of a prolonged pandemic, is the following conundrum: Can government and its institutions in today's market society competently govern during any major public health pandemic that most likely would lead to ubiquitous societal and market disruptions (and uncertainties) eroding not only the underpinnings of consumerism and economic growth, but perhaps calling into question the very efficacy and fairness of market-based correctives in this era of growing public distrust of government? Of course, medical advances in the search for vaccines, if developed in time, will temper the severity of any future pandemic. Yet, as the *Wall Street Journal* so succinctly put it, we should prepare ourselves for sweeping societal changes that will probably be long lasting: "As the [health] crisis deepens, it will transform the way we think about family and business, health care and high tech, politics and the arts [and how this pandemic] challenges and [offers] opportunities of our uncertain future" (*Wall Street Journal*, Review Section, March 28–29, 2020, p. C1).

How we respond to these transformative opportunities and challenges will undoubtedly shape many of the salient policy deliberations that lie ahead. But, equally important, it also offers the opportunity to ask new questions, to discuss new initiatives, and to ponder new ideas in these deeply challenging and uncertain times. Perhaps even to use this time of reflection to formulate a renewed sense of publicness, and, in the process, enrich democratic governance in the citizens' everyday lives.

In this book, besides the literature of public management/administration and public policy, my analysis draws from the fields of political and social theory, economic and urban geography, political science, sociology, economic history, and social ethics. These varied scholarly fields have helped me coalesce my thinking on a central theme with a deeper sense of conviction: that a renewed focus on publicness along with critical democratic thought can play a crucial role in expanding our intellectual and professional purpose against those corrosive forces that can undermine the democratic ethos in public affairs. This expanded role for both fields will require more than armchair theorizing or more studies to be conducted (as vital as both these endeavors are to our understanding of the administrative and policy process): it will instead require concrete action and a reordering of intellectual and professional priorities in these daunting times.

There are many friends and colleagues I would like to thank who directly or indirectly have influenced my thinking, even though I assume some of them would disagree with certain aspects of my major arguments: Guy Adams, Dan Balfour, Tina Nabatchi, Michelle Dennis, Terry Cooper, Jeff Chapman, Lou Weschler, Sandra Newman, Robert Bartlett, George Candler, Jim Perry, Jos Raadschelders, Lester Salamon, Michael Harmon, late Ralph Hummel, Camilla Stivers, Hugh Miller, Richard Box, Hendrick Wagenaar, Susan Gooden, and Mark Francis (my oldest and dearest friend). My sincere appreciation also goes to the anonymous reviewers who provided me with crucial feedback that helped me sharpen my arguments throughout this work. I have been influenced enormously on many subjects raised in this book with my graduate students and colleagues at the Institute of Policy Studies, Johns Hopkins University, University of Southern California, and the University of Oxford. I particularly extend my deepest thanks to my colleagues in Brazil who have tried to keep Guerreiro Ramos's thinking alive and relevant: Ariston Azevedo, Jose Francisco Salm, Sergio Luis Boeira, Genauto Caravalho de Franca Filho, and those scholars at the Federal University of Santa Catarina and the Fundacao Getulio Vargas (FGV) who have expanded on his theoretical insights. I also would like to thank Nancy Matthews, dean of The Rubenstein School of Environment and Natural Resources, University of Vermont, for partial financial support in completing this book.

My appreciation also goes to four research assistants from the department of political science at the University of Vermont who checked and rechecked my references: Natalie Lewis-Vass, Alexander Verret, Caleb Bogin, Lindsay Freed, and especially to Timothy Nyhus who went beyond the call of duty. Finally, many of the ideas I developed in this book came from my participation and discussions at the Minnowbrook Conferences, Syracuse University. It was at the 1988 Minnowbrook Conference that I first met Dwight Waldo, who has profoundly influenced so much of my thinking on certain key policy issues, which is not to say that he would concur with all of my conclusions here.

It goes without saying that my family provided much support and patience as I struggled at times to finish this work. My love and thanks to Donna Ventriss, Richard Ventriss, and Beverly Ventriss as well as my two stepsons Finn and Ian Davis. I hope one day my grandson, Grayson Davis, (who is two years old) will read this book and find something of value as he carves out his own path in trying to make this world a better place to live.

And my special thanks to Michael Rinella, senior acquisitions editor at the State University of New York Press, who nurtured and supported the value of this book from its very beginnings. I also would like to thank Eileen Nizer, senior production editor, and Anne Valentine, executive promotions manager, for all their help in moving this project forward. And finally, I was lucky to find a research associate for this project: Joshua Morse. Josh, a doctoral candidate in the Rubenstein School of Environment and Natural Resources, went line by line with me always questioning how I framed my arguments, how some of my evidence needed more clarity in support of my contentions, and how I needed to revise certain parts of this book. Simply put, he made this book possible and, I believe, a much better book.

Finally, I am grateful to the following for giving me permission to borrow certain themes and ideas from previous published materials that have been thoroughly revised and rethought for the purposes of this book:

1. "Two critical issues of American public administration" (1987), *Administration& Society, 9*(I), 25–47. doi.org/10.117710095 31978701900102.

2. (with W. Kuentzel) "Critical theory and the role of citizen involvement in environmental decision making: A re-examination" (2005), *International Journal of Organization Theory and Behavior, 8*(4), 520–540.doi.org/10.1108/IJ0TB-08-04-2005 B004.

3. "Public administration and the changing nature of space" (1994), *American Review of Public Administration, 24*(1), 1–23. doi 10.1177/027507409402400101.

4. "Radical democratic thought and contemporary public administration: A substantive perspective" (1998), *American Review of Public Administration, 28*(3), 227–245. doi.org11 0.11771027507409802800301.

5. (with E. Geczi) "Rationality, the public sphere, and the state: The relevance of Alberto Guerreiro Ramos that has largely forgotten him," (2006), *Administrative Theory & Praxis, 28*(4), 562–583; "The economic crisis of 2008 and its substantive implications for public affairs," (2013), *American Review of Public Administration, 43*(6), 627–655. doi.org/10.11771027507401349981 7.

1

Introduction

Our participatory model of politics, and the ethic of "publicness" that undergirds it, is at a crossroads. In *Strong Democracy*, Benjamin Barber calls for a revised understanding of citizenship in response to this crisis. His concept "rests on the idea of a self-governing community of citizens who are united less by homogeneous interests than by civic education and who are made capable of common purpose and mutual action by virtue of their civic attitudes and participatory institutions rather than their altruism or their good nature" (1984, p. 117). Three decades later, Barber's call retains its urgent relevance.

It is particularly interesting that Barber framed this bold assertion without the slightest hint of self-doubt concerning its intrinsic political validity. Barber's celebratory tone clashes with the tenor of much writing in contemporary public policy; yet, I find it both welcome and warranted. As Alexis de Tocqueville observed, there is an uneasy tension in America between the exaltation of the market ethos (or more broadly, the ideal of individualism, the more rugged the better), while, at the same time, a genuine yearning for a sense of community sustained by strong civic-minded instincts. In the context of twenty-first-century globalization, this tension has flourished and spread. Following on de Tocqueville's observations, I suspect that many, if not most social science scholars and practitioners would find Barber's assertion unrealistic in its political objectives, and utopian in its societal expectations, especially in the rough and ready world of global (and domestic) politics. These are legitimate reservations, but they ignore what Irving Howe (1984, p. 138) so eloquently articulated, in a manner both somber and optimistic, that still resonates with me:

> Today, in an age of curdled realism, it is necessary to assert the utopian image. But this can be done meaningfully only if it

> is an image of social striving, tension, conflict; an image of a problem-creating and problem-solving society.

Howe's 1984 statement identifies a worrying trend—the discouragement of meaningful critique of political powers and mores by our overarching structures of governance—prescient on both ends of the political spectrum. Recently, for example, some have argued that American conservatism itself has lost its way by focusing on only one overriding concern: "[s]eeking advantage over our opponents, [which has] poisoned the civic foundation from which we all drink, with predictable results" (Flake, 2017, p. 94). At the same time, American liberalism is increasingly criticized for its unwillingness to tolerate ideological tension within the institutions where it reigns supreme, particularly university campuses (Stephens, 2017). This trend is worth pondering in that it is fair to assume that we teach and conduct research in public affairs (and in the broader social sciences) with the main purpose to nurture the ideals of a democratic ethos in an effort to better understand and resolve the major societal issues of the day. This rationale is predicated on another assumption that often goes unspoken: that social conflict represents, to large degree, a fundamental failure in policy design, implementation, and management, rather than the broader political contradictions and economic tensions condensed in the existing societal arrangements of political power. Not surprisingly, there has been an ongoing debate on how best to achieve the goals of managerial effectiveness and policy efficacy given that it relates directly to the raison d'être of public policy and public management/administration. However, I argue that too many scholars of both fields writing since the 1980s, have been content to take primarily a managerial and analytical perspective, which has undoubtedly advanced our knowledge and practice of public affairs. Likewise, many others have emphasized the varying normative aspects of public affairs in teasing out the philosophical implications (and ideals) of policy objectives. Regardless of the different approaches pursued and their respective validity in providing crucial insights, the current culture of both fields prompts us to contend that scholars and practitioners have, for the most part, become increasingly cautious in choosing the questions we believe are important to explore. That is, the questions posed have become ever more narrow and pedestrian, leaving untouched the "domain assumptions," as Alvin Gouldner (1970) called them, that underlie the theoretical and pragmatic foundations of both public policy and public management/administration. This penchant can be seen in the paucity of recent scholarship exploring the relationship of public management and public policy with the modern state, and the inherent tensions of such a relationship. This tension, in part, is due to the theoretical uneasiness of the politics and administration dictotomy that continues to haunt both fields. After all, many in both fields would contend that we are at our best only when addressing primarily administrative questions central to the efficient functioning of the modern state. This book responds to these emergent norms by asking this crucial question: Are we as scholars of public management/administration and public policy willing to question the arrangements of modern power and governance under which we operate? By deemphasizing this question and its implications, we run the risk of both fields becoming nothing more than a legalistic, managerial, economic mode of inquiry with a procedural emphasis. To be sure, some might insist that this is precisely the role both fields should play in societal affairs. Generally speaking, I do not entirely disagree with this view. My contention is that we need to be something more in this time of political estrangement, polarization, and unequal democracy (Bartels, 2016).

To put this question in more provocative terms, does the relationship between public policy and public management/administration and the modern state inhibit the exploration of certain theoretical issues as politically infeasible and too controversial to pursue? To continue this same point but in a somewhat different direction, does the focus on professionalism—as critical as it is in an era of heightened politicized partisanship—carry with it potentially deleterious consequences that may erode democratic values considered pivotal in educating future policy analysts and public managers? Finally, and perhaps the most controversial point of all, have we in public policy and public management/administration—regardless of our empirical sophistication in analyzing complex social problems (and our confidence in doing this consistently in a rigorous manner)—become an intricate part of "a disguised normative dimension of the established power configuration" (Ramos, 1981, p. 4) and, knowingly or unknowingly, a managerial instrument of what some have referred to as a "good" techno-governance system (Mouffe, 2005; Dean, 2009; Swyngedouw, 2011; Purcell, 2008)? All of these questions are a reminder of Robert Lynd's polemic observation, in the classic work *Knowledge for What* (1939, pp. 125–126), that the social scientists should never be afraid "to be troublesome, to disconcert the habitual arrangements by which to live along, and to demonstrate the possibilities of change in more adequate directions."As cynical as these concerns may seem, and as understandably disconcerting, they nonetheless represent a cogent reminder of a point once made by John Dos Passos (1936), the novelist, who asserted that "the greatest enemy of intelligence is theoretical complacency."

These assertions (and questions) alone should give us pause to reconsider some fundamental issues that go to the heart of public policy and public management/administration. However, recent events throughout a good portion of the developed world have added another level of complexity to these questions. Some academic critics of modern public affairs have questioned both whether the focus on policy analysis has caused us to deemphasize normative questions and whether the incessant emphasize on empiricist/positivist approaches can lead to naive inductivism (Andreski, 1972). And, as this debate is taking place in academic circles, many societies face a populist backlash (Moffitt, 2016) with critics from primarily outside academia questioning whether the detached, professional public analyst/administrator works for the broader public interest.

These recent complications of the relationship between the social sciences and the public especially highlight that we call ourselves "public" policy and "public" management/administration. In fact, until recently the concept of publicness (and its changing meaning over time) did not attract much intellectual attention in our theoretical and professional discussions (Stivers, 2010; Natabachi, 2010; Ventriss, 1987). After all, as argued in the chapters that follow, those of us who study and practice public affairs put the word *public* first not merely for semantic reasons, but rather because it conveys, or should convey, some salient ethical and societal implications for what we seek to achieve in the broader social context.

When I first raised this point (Ventriss, 1987), my focus was on the development of a theory of the public—a reconceptualization of the meaning of publicness. Yet the notion of the public was—and remains—a concept fraught with inherent theoretical ambiguity (Ventriss, 1987; Pesch, 2008). I anchored the idea of publicness predominantly in John Dewey's terms; that is, as an integral aspect of the citizenry's capacity and maturity in understanding the interactive societal consequences of public actions on others. Since that time there has been an emerging debate on what might constitute the meaning of "publicness" and what it implies for both public policy, public management/administration, and public affairs in general (Pesch, 2005, 2008; Bozeman & Bretschneider, 1994; Haque, 2001; Frederickson, 1997; Barnes, Newman, Knops, & Sullivan, 2003; Low & Smith, 2005; Moulton, 2009; Williams & Shearer, 2011; Nabatchi, 2011). Irrespective of the varying theoretical perspectives taken on this concept, I maintain (as I will make clear in this book) that publicness denotes something more than a concept coterminous with the role of the modern state, or a term so amorphous that it lacks any viable guide to how we should proceed on important policy matters. Instead, publicness is fundamentally an adherence to democratic ideals and democratic aspirations epitomizing the following general characteristics: (1) publicness is inherently a process of civic responsibility, consistent with Richard Flathman's (1989) conception of high citizenship, that is, an inclusive critical learning process involving a network of different publics sharing crucial information in initiating and debating public action and, more important, critically examining the substantive impact of policy actions on others; (2) publicness also directly implies a responsibility for those in public policy and public management/administration in sorting out and exposing the misinformation and distortion of crucial data that can obscure the normative impact of certain policies on the citizenry (Stone, 2012); (3) publicness acknowledges the central validity of citizen dissent, or other venues of constructive public contestation, in publicly expressing concerns about unequal influence and societal impacts in the policy process, especially in this era of political and economic uncertainty; (4) publicness refers to the notion that, given there are so many "publics" in society, it is crucial to experiment with policies that are nonaggregate, that is, publicness requires the importance of including the unique and particularized knowledge of different publics into the policy process congruent to public service values; and finally, (5) in the face of the rise of pseudo-democratic populism often indifferent to factual information, a revigorated view of publicness is called for in confronting, among other things, the perils of interest-group liberalism and the growing distrust of governmental institutions.This later point will be discussed at length in subsequent chapters of this book.

This is hardly an exhaustive list of what could be considered as publicness and its relevance to those who practice and study public policy and public management/administration. However, I contend this approach to publicness can loosen, or at least weaken, the strong grip of an instrumental rationality and a market mentality that hovers over the theoretical landscape of public affairs. It is not claimed here that publicness would, or should, replace the value of other conceptual perspectives on public matters. Rather, a focus on publicness would demonstrate, and hopefully clarify, the *limitations* of these other perspectives. In short, it would have us refocus our role more attentively to the broader substantive obligations of those powerful residual political and economic conditions contributing to what David Harvey (1996) described as "parochialist politics" and "political passivity." To many, this may sound not only pretentious to our modern pragmatic ears, but as an invitation to a Sisyphean exercise in intellectual futility. No doubt, this intellectual endeavor will not be easy. Nevertheless, this new theoretical and pragmatic trajectory could be crucial in facilitating a "problem-solving" approach emphasized earlier by Irving Howe. This book is written to move us closer to reinvigorating publicness in this era of political and economic unceraintу with all the inevitable theoretical twists and turns that are bound to happen in this intellectual journey.

Some might argue that neglect of the theoretical underpinnings of publicness is hardly surprising given that public policy, and in particular public management/administration, have little theoretical coherency to speak of. As Iain Gow puts it, "The field has a hard time getting respect from academic colleagues in the social sciences" (2010, p. 31). This has especially been the case relative to political science, which has often criticized the field for being atheoretical; focused on applied empirical research meant to improve governance, rather than theory testing about governance. Gow has dismissed these discussions, accepted that "*[l]a science administrative est une science empirique par excellence*" (1993, p. 87), and has termed this "pragmatic institutionalism." The term nicely combines the emphasis on structure (institutionalism) and technique (pragmatism) in a single paradigm, and identifies this, for example, as "the default position in public affairs [and public policy] in Canada" (p. 10). He describes this paradigm as focused on being "comprehensive and accurate, to 'get it right' " (p. 5).

However, for many scholars in public affairs, this pragmatic, intellectual mosaic of different disciplines, while commendable in this age of specialization, has especially taken its scholarly toll on the reputation of public administration/management. But truth be told, both intellectual enterprises (with a few exceptions who argue for a more critical perspective) suffer from a conceptual parochialism and intellectual ambivalence that has left theoretically untouched the Hobbesian/Lockean mentality in modern politics and the consequential residue of possessive individualism which continues to run rampant through our political veins (Macpherson, 1973). Public policy and public management/ administration are, of course, historically and contextually specific to the country in which they are practiced and theorized. Even given this reality, a serious debate needs to emerge—a point I emphasize in many of these chapters—about the ideological, political, and economic forces that coalesce into a managerial consensual governing system that essentially undermines the consideration of different ways of incorporating democratic processes into community life (Ranciere, 1999). Peter Bachrach (1967, p. 99)correctly emphasized that what we face in modern politics is an uncomfortable Hobson's choice: "a theory which is normatively sound but unrealistic, or a theory which is realistic but heavily skewed toward elitism." While this theoretical dichotomy is admittedly overstated, this book echoes an approach that Foucault (in Simon, 1971, p. 201) emphasized:

> What I am trying to do is grasp the implicit systems of thought which determine our most familiar behavior without our knowing it. I am trying to find their origins, to show their formation, the constraint they impose upon us . . .

Inspirations and Areas of Inquiry

This book builds on the ideas of many preeminent scholars, and in this respect particular attention is owed to Alberto Guerreiro Ramos. At least three of his works, *The New Science of Organizations: A Reconceptualization of the Wealth of Nations* (1981), *A Reducao Sociologica* (1958), and the essay *Patologia Social do Branco Brasiseiro* (1955), serve as a springboard for my argument. Guerreiro Ramos was one of the earliest scholars to point to the risks of a social science that took *homo economicus* as its referent. A solution that he offered was to recognize the importance of nonmarket settings in which people could pursue other, nonmaterialist interests. As a result, Guerreiro Ramos criticized both mainstream public policy and public management/administration (and social science) as reluctant, or more accurately, intellectually unwilling to comprehend the irreconcilable conflict between instrumental rationality and substantive rationality, and the consequential implications of this tension on the body politic.

In light of the increasingly narrow scope of both fields that I have mentioned earlier in this introduction, it should come as no surprise that many have responded coldly to Guerreiro Ramos's thinking, with theoretical dismay or even "polite" neglect of his scholarship. This reception is primarily because, in Guerreiro Ramos's typical sharply edged polemic tone, he criticized the conventional scholarship in public affairs as indulging in a theoretical self-deception camouflaged by a ubiquitous market ideology which has shaped the manner in which we formulate, define, and design policy approaches, points also echoed by Crouch (2004, 2011). That these trends persist despite nearly a half-century of critique, and do not necessarily command the respect of public affair scholars and practitioners, illustrates the intellectual malaise that this book aims to address.

It is, to reemphasize, not my purpose in this book to elucidate all the various nuances of Guerreiro Ramos's thinking on political and administrative matters. Rather, it is to point out that Guerreiro Ramos tried, in his own way, to awaken us from our intellectual complacency and theoretical timidity—and, judging from where we are today, he has largely failed. This raises the question: What additional perspectives can we in public affairs bring to theory and practice to reinvigorate contemporary governance and participatory politics? Much like John Stuart Mill, Guerreiro Ramos reiterated the necessity of continuously scrutinizing the presuppositions of policy issues, thinking this intellectual posture could foster both a moral alertness and a more vibrant notion of "publicness." As an Afro-Brasileiro scholar and public official growing up in highly segregated Brazil, he was keenly aware of those forces of political domination, both subtle and explicit, that can emerge in society and, just as important, what can occur when such forces are ignored and/or unchallenged. While I disagree strongly with many aspects of Ramos's major arguments and his theoretical contentions (which will be explored later in the book), he did posit the need for theoretically unpacking, so to speak, the hegemony of deeply embedded belief systems that are often glossed over in our theoretical and pragmatic considerations of policy ends. The intellectual malaise, Ramos tells us, facing specifically public policy and public management/administration is not the result, as Udo Pesch (2008) has enumerated, of trying to reconcile various meanings of publicness or the inevitability of seeing publicness as an intrinsically ambiguous concept. The real issue, he emphasized, is how the notion of publicness itself has been eclipsed and distorted by "cognitive politics" (Guerreiro Ramos's term), which "consists in a conscious or unconsciousness use of distorted language, the intent of which is to induce people to interpret reality in terms that reward it direct and/or indirect agents of such distortion" (1981, p. 76).

In many respects, Ramos's conception of publicness is foundational to my own argument. Putting aside this awkward phrasing, Guerreiro Ramos illuminates a poignant issue missing in most of the literature in public affairs: that cognitive politics, in a chameleon-like fashion, has undercut the intellectual integrity of public policy and public management/administration—and much of the social sciences. This has resulted, in large part, in the legitimization of "the expansion of economizing organizations beyond their specific contextual boundaries by practicing a misplaced and mistaken humanism" (1981, p. 84). These fields, in other words, have become a mode of social inquiry peculiarly vulnerable to a utilitarian mind-set displacing social conflict and public dissent into new governance systems such as collaborative policy networks, participatory strategies, benchmarking for performance, or in new and revised managerial and policy strategies. Although these approaches are initiated for laudable reasons and are praised for their contributions to public affairs, little attention has gone into what this displacement means for our theoretical development and intellectual agenda. This neglect, Guerreiro Ramos would argue, has come, unfortunately, with a hefty intellectual and ethical price tag.

With that in mind, the first section of this book assesses the asymmetry of information and power among policy analysts, administrators, public officials, and the general public. This, again, is not new: writing in 1984, Eugene McGregor argued that "an extraordinary knowledge disparity exists between public service careerists . . . and a civitas that wants problems solved. The gap is not only large, it appears to be growing and the effects can only be worrisome. The knowledge gap may well contribute to mistrust of institutions by citizens to know when things are not working but not able to say what the possibilities for successful intervention are" (p. 127). Up until perhaps the last couple of years this claim would have been accepted by many: some citizens have lost faith with self-serving professionals and policy elites (an overwhelmingly elite class). McGregor continued, though: "The gap may explain some of the measured contempt public analysts have displayed toward an unknowing and disrespectful public" (ibid.). However, there is another question worth posing of professionalism: while policy experts can overlook the grounded information about policy provided by ordinary citizens, it is crucial to be cognizant of the current upsurge of anti-intellectualism, especially in the United States, that undercuts the specialized knowledge that professionals can bring to bear on important policy issues.

Both this imbalance of power and information, and the impact of anti-intellectualism, cannot be mitigated by merely appealing to the scientific method in exploring policy and administrative issues. While it is true this approach represents a significant aspect of what is usually done to achieve the goals of efficiency, expediency, and calculation of policy ends, one of the questions asked in this book is the following: Can this salient approach alone, for all its empirical acumen, expose the role of certain key powerful actors in the policy process without taking into consideration the broader historical and normative context of this issue, and how such power can marginalize political challenges to their continued influence on certain policy matters

(Lustig, 1982; Crouch, 2004; Mayer, 2016; Dean, 2009; Jessop, 2005; Swyngedouw, 2011)? The most common reaction to such claims is that in public policy and public management/administration we do not *make* policy; rather, we only analyze the viability of policies and appropriately implement (and manage) them congruent to the rules and regulations dictated by legitimate political institutions. This viewpoint, particularly by practitioners, is strongly held because of the danger of undermining the nonpartisan role of public management/administration and public policy. The reasoning here is explicit and direct: we do not need, nor should it ever be desired, to do anything that smacks, or is even suspected by others, of having any other purpose than what is specifically prescribed by the state. Furthermore, any other outlook, it is claimed, would expand the meaning of both fields perilously beyond their traditional role and appropriate societal purpose.

Although the rationale behind these concerns is certainly understandable, I emphasize the implications of publicness as a major challenge to both fields. This implies, I contend, a reexamination of neo-managerialism and the relationship of the state to both fields. I also focus in this section on critical democratic thought and the reinvigoration of publicness as a way of introducing the kind of questions we should be asking ourselves and the theoretical perspectives needed in these challenging times. I end this section with a critical analysis of some of the theoretical shortcomings of Guerreiro Ramos and others in assessing the substantive aspects of publicness. I argue that it is crucial in this era of political and economic uncertainty to take Guerreiro Ramos's project forward, albeit in a revised manner, when discussing the interrelationships of citizenship, the state, and the public sphere.

The second section focuses on those debates that have not received the appropriate attention in public management/administration, and to a lesser extent, public policy. For instance, the first chapter in this section examines the economic crisis of 2008 in reference to not only economic inequality and limited economic mobility, but to political inequality and unequal democracy and their enduring, corrosive influence on the policy and administrative process. On a related theme, the spatial aspects of the market economy will be discussed and why this warrants critical scrutiny in this era of capital mobility, economic interdependencies, and a ubiquitous social media, which have contributed to a growing breeding ground for economic and political uncertainty (and insecurity) among certain segments of society. And finally, I argue that for all the celebratory arguments in praise of public participation and deliberative democracy (which I largely applaud), I wonder whether such discussions are only tiptoeing around other key issues concerning the transformative goals these noble intentions hope to achieve. This is not to imply for a moment that these participatory goals are unrealistic, but rather that we have succumbed too readily to the rationale that by continuously tinkering with an endless variety of managerial approaches and theoretical perspectives, new and old, this somehow will better prepare us for implementing more effectively the incremental policies that so often emerge from the legislative process (Layzer, 2015). It is no wonder, given this view, that there has been minimal debate concerning the underlying conditions that caused the problem in the first place. This section is guided by one of Thomas Pynchon's central characters in *Gravity's Rainbow*, who evocatively declared the following: "If they can get you asking the wrong questions, they don't have to worry about the answers."

As the chapters in this section try to make clear, the time has come to put at the forefront of the intellectual agenda the glaring economic tensions and social conflicts emerging both domestically and internationally, and whether contemporary political discord can be successfully mediated by a managerial and empirical outlook without seriously questioning the prevailing societal and economic arrangements. Concomitantly, I also address the question of civic responsibility. The "inclusive learning process involving a network of different publics . . . critically examining the substantive impact of policy actions on others" that I identify as the first of the five general characteristics, is not something that can be implemented in a top-down fashion. McGregor emphasizes the need for public analysts/administrators to nurture "a potentially argumentative public . . . a dominant ethic of public service must be that careerists keep citizens fully informed about the possibilities for public service. . . . The democratic point is that the public need is for intelligently organized information presented so that informed decisions can be made" (1984, p. 128). Yet the provision of this intelligently organized information will only help if "citizens" can better understand those political and economic forces that call for more social division and simplistic solutions.

The final chapter of this book focuses on how those of us devoted to both fields might proceed in meeting these challenges. I do not claim that this is an exhaustive compilation of challenges before us or that any of my suggestions are a panacea to these respective issues. Undoubtedly, some will view this part of the book as a jeremiad that paints those of us who study or practice public affairs in an unfavorable light, or, as some of our colleagues might argue, in an overly pessimistic manner. My intention here is quite the opposite: it is a call for a renewed sense of what is referred to as "elenchic citizenship" (Ventriss, 2007). It is a citizenship of publicness, Dana Villa (2001, p. 20) explains, that is Socratic in nature in that

> it consists in the endless and seemingly circular questioning of the basic terms of our moral culture, those whose meaning seems self-evident and unarguable. Questioning is an end itself . . . [but it is also a questioning to] maintain a critical distance on all accepted definitions . . . and ridding the various false beliefs that promote injustice.

That said, I contend that no amount of empirical studies, nor normative theorizing, nor new managerial or participatory strategies will ever suffice in cultivating a democratic ethos if we do not fully comprehend the normative implications of an "unexamined citizenship" and how this lack of understanding might lead us down a path toward intellectual hubris and theoretical complacency. Montaigne's (1976) erudite insight is worth pondering here: "No wind helps him who does not know to what port he sails." This task will be neither easy nor, I suspect, very popular among some of my colleagues. But the recognition of this crucial task, and the need for it, is the real challenge that lies before us. This book, hopefully, will explain this imperative, and so nudge us into taking this intellectual plunge.

Theoretical Grounding

Like any other work of this sort, the themes discussed in this book have been strongly influenced by certain contemporary seminal thinkers. These thinkers include (besides Guerreiro Ramos) the following: Albert Camus, Donald A. Schon, Deborah Stone, Harold Lasswell, Nancy Fraser, Karl Polanyi, Hannah Arendt, Jeffrey Isaac, Dana Villa, Albert Hirschman, Sheldon Wolin, Michael Walzer, Robert Nisbet, Dwight Waldo, John K. Galbraith, Bonnie Honig, Fred Hirsch, Daniel Bell, Fernando Henrique Cardoso, and Alvin Gouldner. Each of these thinkers, in varying degrees, has argued that it is problematic whether democracy can come into full development if we do not first carefully analyze the concrete behavior, motives, desires, and ideals that make up moral life. Moreover, these thinkers, putting aside their different conceptual venues in addressing these issues, are united in their refusal to view public life solely in instrumental and utilitarian terms. A common purpose cannot exist in the interstices of a liberal culture, they indicate, if the existing moral instincts of society become increasingly antipublic, or contribute to "the retreat of the political." The intellectual thread that ties all these thinkers together is their emphasis on the quality of political relationships and public commitments, which can never be reduced to mere private acquisitive behavior; that any viable public purpose finds its meaning in a reflective citizenship, not in the thoughtless conformity of Arendt's (1973) "behaving citizens" or the related disenfranchisement of Margaret Somers's (2008) market-driven postcitizenship. In the end, the luminaries in this field identify that the civic ethos can be easily atrophied or overridden by the exultation of a market mentality and by what has been referred to as the "economization of politics" (Brown, 2015) that lacks a coherent public discourse adequate to the complexities of social and political life, trends we see playing out today.

These thinkers have also provided us in public affairs a rich theoretical tapestry of ideas that is both cautious and, surprisingly enough, optimistic in what can be accomplished in our modern polity. This optimism is founded on the premise that we who study and serve in public affairs can reverse our myopic underpinnings with a more concerted focus on civitas—a civitas that stresses publicness as a bulwark against the unrestrained pursuit of private interest and as a way to legitimize public spaces for displaying conflict and public struggle in the pursuit of public purposes. It is an optimism borne of the reality, as William Sullivan (1986, p. 158) avers, that "the citizen comes to know who he [or she] is by understanding the social relationships surrounding him [or her] . . . [an] awareness of the interdependency of citizens . . . [and that it is] basic to the civic vision because it enlightens and challenges . . . disparate parties about their mutual relations." This will require the formulation of a renewed emphasize on "public language," the ability to become a "public social science," and finally a renewed sense of publicness that puts human dignity, critical inquiry, public responsibility, public accessibility, and public learning at the center of what we aspire to be in societal affairs (Ventriss, 1987; Sullivan, 1986; Ku, 2000).

Yet, ironically, a degree of caution is called for in this endeavor. This caution is due primarily to the reality of a growing public disdain for politics, a fragmented public with a tenuous sense of social cohesion, a growing distrust for government in general (Will, 1983; Nye, Zelikow, & King, 1997; Thompson, 2010) and more recently, the full emergence of a heretofore underlying phenomenon that has contributed to these other realities: anti-intellectualism. No doubt, it is difficult to be persuasive in such a polarizing political environment when stereotypes of "faceless" administrators and policy analysts are continuously misrepresented in the minds of the citizenry (Goodsell, 2014). Indeed, Hannah Arendt's *The Origins of Totalitarianism* (1973) warns explicitly that the emergence of anti-intellectualism is one factor among others that can stifle productive dialogue and political critique. Thus, there is a need to walk cautiously, so to speak, knowing that we have intrinsic limitations of what can be actually achieved given the vicissitudes of public opinion, public attitudes, and public expectations about government itself.

This caution, moreover, also comes with a theoretical awkwardness and intellectual solicitude. It leaves us, who teach or practice in public affairs, essentially on an intellectual (and pragmatic) tightrope. This balancing act requires maintaining the intellectual conviction to present the world as it is, and then of asking critical (and probing) questions of political and institutional life. Furthermore, this balancing act further requires coming up with ideas to effectively manage and better understand the labyrinthine policies of the state, as well as certain political movements and powerful institutional actors that seek to present a self-serving perspective of the world, not least to obviate the need for the sort of critical (and probing) questions mentioned above. We operate, in effect, in a continuous state of in-betweenness among those competing forces of political and intellectual gravity that constantly tug at us and which subsequently makes our balancing act especially arduous, frustrating, exhausting, and, exasperating. It is important to note that these dynamic and powerful political movements are not just unique to the United States; they have been documented in such countries as Australia, Brazil, and to a lesser extent Canada, to name a few (Candler, 2014).

In sum, the questions I ask and the suggestions I offer in this book have been deeply influenced by these seminal thinkers, whose foundations give us much needed perspective on the depth and scope of the issues facing us in public affairs today. These thinkers are crucial because they understand just how unsettling it can be as we try to maintain our delicate balance between dedication to democratic progress and deference to convention, especially given the absence of any theoretical banisters to hold us steady. This terminal condition, one could argue, may be the new and stark reality of modern democratic policymaking. But, on the other hand, this state of affairs can be regarded as a long overdue opportunity to step back and "to retrace our cultural steps, and rethink what we think" (Will, 1983, p. 163).

The need for such rethinking comes at a time when, beginning in the 1970s, trust in key governmental institutions, public officials, professionals, and the media has plummeted, leading to a heightened political and economic uncertainty of how we can resolve in the future—with any sense of confidence—such key societal issues and daunting public challenges as income and wealth inequality, economic insecurity, climate change, wage stagnation, political polarization, and immigration. This book is in response to these formidable trends and the perception of many citizens in the United States and elsewhere that believe government can no longer effectively ameliorate or resolve the uncertainities by conventional administrative and policy approaches. The overall theme of this book is straightforward: those of us who do research in public management/administration and public policy (and who work in the public and nonprofit sector) need to reassess some fundamental assumptions of whether the questions we have been asking—and the intellectual and professional heritage we have taken as a given—are expanding or restricting the centrality of publicness. Such "rethinking what we think" and how we confront the exigency of the challenges before us has a lot to say about the direction of our intellectual future and the substantive purpose we aspire to in this time of policy complexity, social discord, and uncertainty.

Conclusion

In this introduction, I have focused on the two fundamental tensions in the study and practice of public affairs that this book undertakes to address. First, I outlined the conflict between normative and utilitarian influences on public management/administration and public policy. And second, I underscored the pressing need for a revitalized view of publicness to equip those dedicated to public affairs to engage with the political and economic uncertainties that will pose significant challenges in politics, economy, and public life in the twenty-first century.

In painting a picture of the conflict between normative and utilitarian forces in contemporary public affairs, I drew on thinkers including Guerreiro Ramos, Barber, and Gouldner, to highlight the crossroads at which we now find ourselves. These authors, in particular, identified the increasingly market-centered and quantitative nature of scholarship in both fields. More importantly, they collectively suggest that, unfortunately, scholarly inquiry in both fields has become increasingly narrow and pedestrian in nature. Given their theoretical insights, I argue that in both fields we seem reluctant to recognize and interrogate the domain assumptions (those underlying assumptions that are rarely questioned or examined) under which we operate.

Following on this argument, I suggested that a different conceptualization of publicness will be required if we want to realize both fields' potential—and mandate—that bridges civic life, professional practice, and academic scholarship. I outlined five crucial elements of such an approach, which are: (1) an emphasis on reflective civic responsibility and critical public learning; (2) a mandate for scholars and professionals alike to identify and clarify misinformation and distortion of data to enhance civic engagement; (3) improved capacity for debate and constructive citizen dissent; (4) recognition of the existence of plural publics, and the designing of policies congruent to their respective and distinct public needs; and (5) a clarified and strengthened relationship between the public and professionals. I grounded this theoretical sketch in the works of diverse seminal thinkers, especially Ramos, all of whom have in some way called for an expanded role for a fundamental rethinking of what we do in both public management/ administration and public policy.

In the coming sections of this book, I develop two related lines of inquiry. In the following four chapters (2–5, Section 1), I investigate the factors conditioning current tensions and theoretical needs in public affairs. Readers with a predominantly theoretical interest in the challenges facing public affairs today should focus their attention here. In the final three chapters (6–8, Section 2), I examine how these factors and theoretical needs play out in important contemporary issues/cases. Readers primarily interested in the more pragmatic aspects of contemporary public affairs may want to spend the bulk of their time with these chapters. Finally, in my closing chapter (9), I offer my personal reflections on steps to be taken at the individual and institutional levels to strengthen the normative dimensions of theory and practice in public affairs, based on insights developed over the course of my career. I hope that these insights will be especially relevant to graduate students and other professionals, who may be able to take advantage of them over their course of the study and practice of public affairs.

Section 1

The Importance of Publicness and Critical Democratic Thought

2

Conditioning Factors

Neo-Managerialism and the Modern State

Modern society is faced by myriad major economic and political issues, and mired in contentious debates concerning how best to resolve them (Arendt, 1958, 1961; Benn & Gaus, 1983; Warner, 2002; Calhoun, 2002, 2011; Sheller & Urry, 2003; Castoriadis, 1997). Given this state of affairs, why should there be any serious interest among social scientists—or the general public, for that matter—to address such subjects as the societal role of those who study and practice public affairs and the inherently ambiguous meaning of publicness in the contemporary human enterprise? Indeed, what purpose would this examination serve and who would really care beyond those directly engaged, or somewhat interested, in public affairs? The simple answer to this question is this: the study of public affairs is of importance because, perhaps more than any other mode of social inquiry, it is dedicated to analyzing and managing approaches that directly contribute to the resolution of the economic and political challenges facing society. However, the ability of public policy and public management/administration to fulfill this essential function is increasingly challenged by the conditioning factors under which they both operate.

Any field—professional or academic—exists in the context of an increasingly complex and changing society. Hence, in order to remain relevant in this context there is a penchant to develop a core identity that can inform and guide its direction and influence. In particular, scholars of public affairs face particular challenges in this respect not only because the work it undertakes is more intimately intertwined with the dynamic worlds of governance and public life, but especially because of its continued aspiration for theoretical and societal relevance.

The study of both public management/administration and public policy has often been described as mere amalgamations of the many different areas of inquiry that it represents. For example, Dwight Waldo (1968, p. 2) once somberly described public administration as "a subject in search of a discipline." Waldo reminds us that in public affairs there will always be a certain amount of conceptual uneasiness and confusion when any interdisciplinary field is conceptually scattered so widely over the theoretical and intellectual landscape. For this reason, it probably makes sense to acknowledge that such intellectual and professional enterprises are inherently, for better or worse, intellectually muddled; that as scholars of public affairs we are inexorably caught in the vexing pull between the different demands of the world of theory and the realities of practice; and, finally, that such modes of inquiry can become too often nothing more than a collection of contrapuntal theoretical voices that rarely combine into anything harmonic in conceptual terms. As one scholar so aptly put it, most of the professional and theoretical literature in the study of public management/administration and public policy resembles nothing more than a "hodgepodge of theoretical ramblings" (Ramos, 1981, p. 61).

This has led to a long and tortuous discussion in both fields about how this lack of theoretical consistency has conditioned the interaction of public affairs with the broader academic and professional environments in which it functions. For example, some would argue that in the absence of any organizing theory, public policy has wrapped itself comfortably in the conceptual garb of microeconomics, game theory, operations research, and an array of quantitative methods, while public management/administration has veered toward demonstrating its steadfast adherence to the merits of economy and efficiency in managing public affairs. Elaborating on this theme, Gerald Caiden pulled no punches in contending that the crisis of legitimacy, specifically confronting public administration, is inexorably related to its inability to formulate a viable and cogent theoretical base from which to defend itself. In the next breath, he concluded that public administration has consequently been unable to mount any effective reply against its critics who accuse it of being "parasitic, unproductive, inefficient, wasteful, incompetent, corrupt, and above all unnecessary" (1983, p. 1).

To understand how a field such as public management/administration concerned with public well-being has found itself vulnerable to such critique, this chapter investigates the context within which both fields of inquiry presently search for their respective theoretical foundations. In part, Swyngedouw (2010) writes, this situation is best understood within the context of a "post-politics" of neoliberalism that has largely eviscerated the publicness of social conflict, public contestation and civic dialogue. That is, social conflict, contestation, and dialogue are now comfortably ensconced in collaborative, polycentric networks and horizontal associations of private, public, and state actors. Such governing arrangements, he emphasizes, give the impression that they represent a major step forward in wedding progressive state power with policy innovations for the common good. Swyngedouw maintains that this proclivity for rechanneling and displacing conflict represents, in effect, the partitioning of publicness from its political nature in that any sense of publicness is legitimized only when it is predicated on reaching a cooperative arrangement among interested parties congruent to the political logic of neoliberal managerialism (Dahl & Soss, 2014; Wolin, 2008). I argue that this diagnosis is mainly accurate, and I will investigate its implications in the following sections: the rise of neo-managerialism norms and their impact on public affairs, and the role of the modern state within which both fields are practiced and intellectually engaged.

Neo-managerialism and the Economization of Political Inquiry

"From the late 19th century on," David Hart and William Scott (1982, p. 240) have observed, "public administration [specifically] has been challenged to emulate the presumed efficiencies of business administration." Hart and Scott go on to argue that "public administration responded to that challenge so enthusiastically that it lost its unique identity in the process. By now it has become nothing more than an undistinguished cousin of business administration [and economics]." Subsequently, public affairs, they lament, has become increasingly captive of a belief, albeit understandable in a market society, in the singular focus on efficiency and productivity as exemplified in the contemporary managerial, market approach to public affairs (Pollitt, 1993; Clarke, 2005; Dryzek, 2008). More broadly, this tendency represents the peril of stripping any resemblance of a democratic ethos from its political dimension grounded on the basis of public dissensus. Hart and Scott echo a similar concern that the theoretical residue of this perspective has resulted in an intellectual default whereby neo-managerialism becomes an ideological and empirical filter significantly biasing the direction of decision making congruent to instrumental rather than substantive ends (Adams & Balfour, 2012; Scott & Hart, 1979).[1]

This emphasis on neo-managerialism (Terry, 1998; Denhardt & Denhardt, 2015), as it is referred to in the literature, amounts to an epistemological and philosophical belief system. It specifies that because public management/administration and public policy are primarily utilitarian and pragmatic fields, their greatest contribution is in the application of managerial and empirically based strategies to solve public problems, thus underscoring what Ranciere (1995, 2010) referred to as a "managerial consensual governing." It is, moreover, a governing process that inevitably depoliticizes social conflict and dissent (Muller & Ventriss, 1985; Box, 2008, 2014; Mouffe, 2005; Wolin, 2008; Pateman, 2012; Peck & Tickell, 2002). Admittedly, this perspective is closely reminiscent of premises associated with the New Public Management movement and its focus on a technical and economic (read: market) rationality to public affairs (Barzelay, 2001; Lynn, 2006).

Of course, it can be argued that this managerial and economic predisposition is due to the growth of government in dealing with growing public expectations and public needs. For example, many public programs are run like businesses (for example, railroads, pension funds, power plants, and the like) that are almost indistinguishable from their entrepreneurial, private sector counterparts. The central premises of neo-managerialism, broadly speaking, incorporate these basic elements: (1) "a less than direct and conscious promotion of ethical values (Lynch, 2014); (2) inclusion of all even remotely relevant disciplines into the field due to an inability to define normative positions; (3) consideration of the needed social technology to achieve managerial and market efficiency; (4) a focus on an empirically minded policy orientation; and (5) the need for planning and managerial control absent a strong presumptive normative foundation" (Wald, 1973, 376; Latour, 2005; Fox, 1996; Clarke & Newman, 1997; Terry, 1998; Denhardt & Denhardt, 2015).

Assuming the validity of these characteristics, it is no wonder that many in public affairs have argued that those being educated for the public and nonprofit sectors need to master the requisite business, economic, and analytical skills because we are, after all, dealing more and more with classical problems of business and economic management (McCurdy, 1978; Osborne & Gaebler, 1992; Osborne & Plastrik, 1997). Understandably, many may find this characterization overdrawn and misleading, but there is no denying that for many scholars of public affairs this empirically grounded managerial and economic approach was generally greeted with enthusiasm as a long overdue and welcome development (Dubnick, 2000). However, if one follows this logic, the theoretical purpose of public management/

administration and public policy becomes on balance nothing more than the application of different managerial and technical approaches that can sustain both fields' pragmatic and nonpartisan appeal. According to Adams and Balfour (2012, p. 326), while there is nothing wrong per se with this view, this kind of reasoning leads "to a narrow concept of [the] public that limits public practices . . . [and] severely restricts what activities are available with regard to public values and ethics." A similar assumption made with this line of thinking also merits serious attention: that better government, for the most part, is synonymous with more efficient public organization. Within limits, this rationale is both understandable and commendable (Waldo, 1971; Lynn, 2006). However, the danger comes, John Schaar (1970, p. 306) cautions, when we believe "that finding the right solution is [always] a matter of finding the right technique." This is not to negate the crucial importance of obtaining and applying analytical and appropriate managerial strategies in order to increase efficiency in government. That point few would ever dispute. Alternatively, however, neo-managerialism may be no accident at all—it is part and parcel of the public organization's inclination to control how public problems are framed and defined, thus enhancing its own survival, growth, and power (Brown & Erie, 1979; Adams & Balfour, 2014; Hummel, 2007; Ramos, 1981; Perrow, 1986). Following on that same theme, Brown and Erie (1979) contend that a critical analysis of the original source of public problems could—and potentially would—call into question the very viability and direction of public organizations. Not surprisingly, some scholars have vehemently objected to the validity of such broad and sweeping generalizations (Goodsell, 2014; Neiman, 2000; Terry, 2003; Meier & O'Toole, 2006). Then again, as disparaging as this may sound, Richard Goodwin (1975, p. 330), who coined the term "The Great Society" while a policy aide to President Lyndon Johnson, interestingly made a compelling argument that government and its public agencies "cannot act effectively if the source of discontent is fundamental, residing in the design of society." Notwithstanding the troubling theoretical and practical implications of this argument, this contention has been rarely acknowledged, or even seriously debated, in the literature of public administration (Forester, 1993; Dunn & Miller, 2007; Denhardt, 1981; Hummel, 2007).

These polemic perspectives are hardly new. For, as Gary Wills (1969) explains, the managerial approach to social and political issues may be more serious than originally thought: we displace political problems into managerial and technical issues because we are an integral part of a "modern rationalist liberalism, an ideology of structures [that] has nothing to offer if structural or procedural reforms do not avail" (Ghelardi, 1976, p. 257; Mannheim, 1956; Polanyi, 1944). That is, we cling tenaciously to the strategy of revising administrative procedures, of arranging (and rearranging) various parts of the administrative state, of applying newer and more efficacious managerial and policy approaches, and of putting increasingly more of our faith in what economic reasoning (and markets) can offer. We do this without considering that political and economic inequalities, political discontent, and social conflicts within the modern polity might require a critical examination of the underlying assumptions of what we believe constitutes democratic accountability and substantive inclusion of citizens in the policy process. Bevir (2011, p. 17) argues that, in the long run, this will ultimately mean exploring new opportunities for a role that includes "more plural and participatory concepts of democracy" (Ventriss, 1985; Nabatchi & Leighninger, 2015; Pateman, 2012; Natatchi & Amsler, 2014; Dryzek, 2000; Fung & Wright,2003). Whether this actually happens, of course, remains to be seen.

But the intellectual influence of neo-managerialism is not just an issue of the economization of political inquiry; it also depicts a pragmatic outlook concerning the ubiquitous influence of the market mentality on modern society itself (Sandel, 2014; Polanyi, 1944). This marketplace mentality is an outlook that inevitably facilitates a ritualistic democracy on the shaky foundation of incessant political bargaining and competition (Sandel, 2014; Wolin, 1960, 2008; Kariel, 1977; Macpherson, 1962, 1973; Barber, 1984). Given that the political gamesmanship of constant bargaining and competition is here to stay as an integral part of how policy is made, it is not surprising that administrators and policy analysts find themselves too often acting, so to speak, like technocratic Hamlets trying to provide some managerial order to this messy, unruly process. We are to be forgiven, however. We are—like everyone else—just following the rules of the game. But following the rules of the game carries a certain intellectual price tag (Arendt, 1978). It is a cost reflected in a lack of diligence in addressing certain important and controversial subjects, namely: Does this propensity toward neo-managerialism of political inquiry not only result in taking a myopic perspective on social issues, but, equally important, in privatizing social conflict? For example, have neo-managerialism and the economization of political inquiry ignored the interdependency of political problems as inextricably interwoven within the economic and political fabric of society itself? And, in fact, do these approaches divert our intellectual scrutiny away from the issues concerning the structure of power (and the distribution of that power), who is attempting to control the policy agenda, and for what political or economic purposes? While the reaction is to be somewhat defensive (and dismissive) about even posing such inquiries, should we not ponder why "power represents a derivative rather than a primary category of analysis, defined by the value orientations reflected in the notions of *organization* and of *science*" rather than substantive meaning of "political" (Erie, 1978, p. 1; Wolin, 1960; Perrow, 1986)? This orientation, as Peter Nettl (1969, p. 2) warned, results in "the hard edges of power dissolving in a cloud of problems of choice, strategies, information channels, interests, and organizations—toothless neutral concepts all." The intellectual baggage that both these perspectives carry with them—particularly in the rough-and-ready world of the political marketplace—should make us wonder whether we need such an exclusive focus as we originally thought (Dryzek, 2012; Fischer, 2003; Wagenaar, 2011).

A related and significant aspect of this tendency also emerges in how best we prepare students for the challenges they will ultimately face in public affairs. Needless to say, the trend for MPAs and MPPs has always been to focus on how to make these degrees more marketable and professionally relevant. Presently, this implies underscoring skills such as policy analysis, systems analysis, computer science, operations research, accounting, management science, and budgeting, to name the most obvious examples. Undoubtedly, there are many pedagogical merits to this viewpoint inasmuch as students unquestionably need to master certain skills and the requisite technical knowledge to effectively address complex problems. Yet, this educational focus raises a critical issue that cannot be so easily brushed under the theoretical rug:

> Are we promoting an academic and professional field structured to put out socially acquiescent public managers [and policy analysts]? This question implies a tension which has always been present: is the purpose of public affairs to train students to be managerially competent professionals or to educate them as citizens able to recognize the multiplicity of social problems and their underlying causes? Most educators would argue that one approach should not negate the other. There is presently, however, a definite propensity toward amanagerial and economic approach to social affairs. Citizenship, once the key word in most public [affairs] schools, is being relegated to a secondary role. (Ventriss, 1982, p. 139; Piereson & Riley, 2013)

This educational focus is probably unavoidable as Max Weber (1946, 240) presciently warned: with the rise of bureaucracy, it is the "expert not the cultivated [individual] who is the educational ideal of the bureaucratic age." While this educational development is hardly unique to just public administration and public policy, it does pose a somber dilemma: again, as reiterated by Hart and Scott (1982) and others, if this trend is left unabated it could circumvent the broader normative purposes of a public affairs education, thus mirroring the instrumental goals of the "organizational imperative" (Ramos, 1981; Hummel, 2007). This organizational imperative, Hart and Scott (1982, p. 152) aver, serves as an ideological veil because "the most effective way to guarantee appropriate behavioral responses to organizational [and instrumental] needs is to build a [managerial] educational system that indoctrinates people in [these] requisite beliefs."

Recent research has suggested that while the public is without question concerned with increasing efficiency in government, the citizenry is equally interested in increasing public accountability in governmental, nonprofit, and private sectors (Denhardt & Denhardt, 2015; King & Stivers, 1998; Frederickson & Hart, 1985; Gawthrope, 1998; Harmon, 1995).Whereas, it is true, these issues are often discussed and debated at a variety of academic and professional venues, Perrow (1986, p. 6) offered an insight that, surprisingly, has not received the attention it quite rightfully deserves: "Organizations mobilize social resources for ends that are often essential and even desirable. But organizations also concentrate those resources in the hands of a few who are prone to use them for ends we do not approve of, for ends we may not even be aware of, and, more frightening still, for ends we are led to accept because we are not in a position to conceive alternative ones." Whether one can be taught to be responsible or ethical by merely taking certain classes is certainly debatable. On the other hand, even more questionable is whether more empirically oriented managerial and policy courses will appropriately prepare students to understand the responsibilities associated with the public purpose, irrespective of the recent emphasis by NASPAA (Network of School of Public Policy, Affairs, and Administration) (2009, p. 4) on "[demonstrating] that its students learn the tools and competencies to apply and take these [public service] values into consideration in their professional activities."

Another way of looking at this is to consider how we usually treat such policy issues as political and economic inequality. Assuming the literature on this subject is indicative of how it is taught, economic and social inequality is customary regarded as just another managerial problem of implementing certain tax reforms, of initiating better approaches to increase governmental efficiency, or of contending with what Martin Lipset and William Schneider (1983) once called the "confidence gap" (Ventriss, 2015; Oldfield, Candler, Johnson, 2006). These policy remedies are, of course, worth pursuing, but wealth and income inequality also involve the far more serious and contentious deliberation of the present distribution of wealth (goods and services) and how that distribution is legitimized to the public, particularly in containing any potential societal discord (Ventriss, 2015). Put simply, should it not puzzle us that we in the administrative and policy literature have remained, for the most part, relatively silent on the deleterious implications of the distribution of wealth and income in a society of unequal classes (Oldfield, 2001, 2003; Ventriss, 1991, 2015)? It is difficult to respond to this issue, and other related matters, when, in the literature of public management/administration in particular, such issues, if addressed at all, are regarded chiefly as administrative questions or best left to other disciplines

Unfortunately, relatively few who teach or conduct research, particularly in public management/administration, have spoken clearly about the meaning of social justice in an era of growing political and economic inequality and uncertainty (Box, Marshall, Reed, & Reed, 2001; Oldfield & Conant, 2001; Gooden, 2014; Ventriss. 2015). We obviously have the ability to do so, and a moral obligation as well, with respect not only to the social justice issues at stake but also to the intellectual relevance of both fields. The intellectual limitations of our present theoretical trajectory in public affairs have been conditioned by neo-managerialism and the economization of public affairs; how we mitigate this trend rests on the ability of scholars and teachers to make explicit the consequences of this trajectory and the institutional and professional impact that it will have on the next generation of public affairs scholars and practitioners.

Nurturing critical discourse that enables students to question the limits of neo-managerialism and the market mentality as their goal will be challenging. Even including those who see us moving more in the direction of a "new public service" (Denhardt & Denhardt, 2015), old habits may be hard to break (Piereson & Riley, 2013). Indeed, finding new ways to expand the conception of the role of the policy analyst/public manager, rather than affirming the boundaries imposed upon such roles by the increasingly market-driven, positivist nature of academia and government will be undoubtedly a vexing undertaking. Cynically, one might even argue that the majority of public affairs scholars do not see this issue as a problem at all or dismiss as mostly irrelevant.

If there is a path forward to a bolder perspective, I suggest that it exists through a fuller integration of our respective fields in public affairs confronting directly such topics as economic inequality, racial inequality, gender inequality, and unequal democracy (and other related macrosocial issues), which can only be addressed by researchers and practitioners who are unafraid of questioning domain assumption. Part of that unfettered critical inquiry will have to entail the questioning of the relationship of the state and the role and purpose concerning those who reside in and theorize about the governance process.

The Modern State and Public Affairs

The neo-managerialism so prevalent in public affairs has not occurred in isolation. The conditioning factors shaping the norms of academic inquiry and professional practice emerge from the evolution of that foremost institution of public life: the state. Many authors have described the emergence of a modern state characterized by supplanting tcommitment to public service with the union of bureaucratic means and corporate—which is to say, private—ends. Sheldon Wolin (2008, 135) captures this troubling condition this way:

> Politics and elections as well as the operation of governmental departments and agencies now are routinely considered a managerial rather than a political skill. Management is not a neutral notion, however. Its roots are in the business culture, its values shaped by the pressures of a competitive economy that persistently pushes the limits of legal and ethical norms . . . The consequences are registered in the decline of a public ethic.

To highlight Wolin's provocative observation, I will focus on Poulantzas's analysis of the modern state, because he shows us, albeit within a polemic perspective drawn from Marx, Gramsci, and Althusser, how a hegemony of beliefs can be disseminated throughout society and how powerful forces come together to forge what he referred to as a power bloc. And while I disagree with the Marxist overtones of his analysis on many key points, he is important in drawing our attention to such issues as what he called authoritarian statism and the recent emergence of authoritarian populism. Concomitantly, the French Regulation School is also worth discussing in that it shows us how the modern state must be understood within the context of a post-Fordist economy. Although these theoretical vantage points are hardly representative of the varied theories of the state, jointly they do provide a better understanding of the issues Wolin describes, and offer a perspective rarely discussed in the policy and administrative literature.

The changing role of the state in the modern era, especially with respect to globalization, is best characterized in terms of its relationship with two forces: the public/private nexus and the primacy of the market (Fraser, 2014; Block & Somers, 2014). Given these realities, I will briefly discuss first some of the ideas articulated by Poulantzas followed by the French Regulation School. Poulantzas (1975, 1978), in his provocative discussions dealing with the role of the state, posits that the modern state is not some monolithic bloc or group that serves as an instrument for the domination of society, nor is it the relationship of a particular class and its influence over powerful institutions. Rather, the state is best understood as an arena for political and social conflict (what he has called the "condensation of a balance of forces")[2] and as a social relation between citizens mediated through their relation to state apparatuses and capacities. Poulantzas further contends that bureaucratic power is the exercise of the state's function and is "relatively autonomous" from the different interests and factions in society. This relative autonomy, insists Poulantzas, is how the state can protect (and enhance) the market economy, "even if it means severe conflict with some segments of society" (Held, 1989, p. 69). Yet, the state also plays an active role in "creating, transforming, and making reality" (Poulantzas, 1978, p. 30). Part of the effectiveness of the state is in how knowledge and information is used within the governmental apparatus.[3] In other words, "[T]he state helps define expertise by financing and employing intellectuals, then uses this expertise in particular ways . . . legitimizing its role as the center of power and decision-making" (Carnoy, 1984, pp. 113–114).

For Poulantzas, the salient aspects of this situation are obvious. The pivotal problem confronting democratic public affairs in the modern state is how citizens can engage the state without being co-opted and how to deepen the political institutions of democracy "in the name of current liberties and those yet to be won" (Isaac, 1992, p. 247). He also alerted us to how a market society might exist with relative stability and gain needed public consent by appealing to nationalism, making it difficult for various publics to organize themselves. And, perhaps more critically, he contended that the state provides the institutional space for different powerful factions in society to form alliances in what he called a power-bloc, while at the same time, seeing the state more as a social relation in a contested struggle between different interests in society (1978). According to Poulantzas, the state therefore is always more or less in flux and contestation. Granted this is only a brief and selective overview of Poulantzas's thinking on the nature of the state, he does chronicle certain tendencies that are difficult to ignore on many contentious themes involving the modern market economy, civil society, and the distribution of power—themes developed in dialogue with the works of Louis Althusser and Antonio Gramsci. To be sure, this conceptualization differs in fundamental (and radical) ways from the conventional view of liberals and conservatives alike who see problems of the state as due to inadequate procedures of democratic accountability, mismanagement, and/or unrealistic citizen expectations (Jessop, 1985; 1990). While Poulantzas has been correctly criticized, among other reasons, for ignoring such issues as the separation of "public" and "private" and problems associated with representative democracy, he does focus needed attention—putting aside his critical view of the state—that a market society based on possessive individualism and skewed political influence will be inherently riddled with uncertainties, contradictions, and dilemmas.

The French Regulation School, despite criticisms with respect to its conception of the state (Boyer, 1990; Lipietz, 1985; Swyngedouw, 1996; Jessop, 1994, 2014),[4] calls attention to the development of the modern state in tandem with the emergence of a post-Fordist economy. The French Regulation school, while controversial in its implications, adheres to the perspective that a new form of production largely replaced the Fordist system (a system characterized by Tayloristic management practices and state intervention to maintain a balance between consumption and production to secure economic growth), which started to break down in the 1970s. A new era emerged, post-Fordism, that emphasized flexible production, specialization, and accumulation. This post-Fordist strategy is characterized by a fragmented mode of production that has led to a spatial reconcentration of production in the form of clusters of small firms in new industrial districts. That is, under the weight of vertical disintegration a new flexible specialization occurred that created agglomeration tendencies at the regional level. Equally important, this school of thought has provided insights into the integration of what is referred to as the mode of regulation (state action, political practices, and behavioral norms) to what is termed a regime of accumulation. In particular, the Regulation School spells out these modes in terms of social relations that are reproduced through different historical periods irrespective of their contradictory and conflicting character (Swyngedouw, 1996). Moreover, according to Jessop (2014) this school of thought provides us a deeper conceptual understanding of the economic linkages between the international and local levels, whereby the nation-state's discretionary powers become somewhat eroded. What is actually occurring is what Swyngedouw (1996, p. 1503) called the re-scaling of the state:

> The re-scaling of the state, therefore, does not suggest a diminishing role of the state apparatus. In fact, these new global/local institutions, in close cooperation with private capital, launch the development largely on the basis of public capital and state capital. In short, the production of post-Fordist [economic] spaces is paralleled by disturbing political transformations and a redefined citizenship.

All that said, what the regulation theory has us explore is the position of the nation-state in a global economy and how localities within those nation-states must attempt to produce globally competitive spaces in competition with other localities. This new post-Fordist reality, in turn, intensifies the struggle for capital, thus reinforcing political and economic fragmentation in civil society (Cox & Mair, 1991; Jessop, 1993, 1994, 2002, 2007). The deleterious trajectory of this trend is that the concept of citizenship itself is transformed into a redefined "citizen entrepreneur" who now advocates only for the creation of competitive market regions to maximize jobs and economic growth (Swyngedouw, 1996; Ventriss, 2000; Terry, 1998). In sum, citizenship is stripped (both theoretically and pragmatically) of its normative character to conform to the cognitive patterns inherent in a market-centered society (Polanyi, 1944; Somers, 2008; Block and Somers, 2014). To a large degree, this is the present context in which the neo-managerialization of public affairs has occurred in this neoliberal milieu. I contend that it is crucial to challenge this situation with reinvigorated theory and practice of publicness. A better understanding of the nature of the modern state will be foundational to this task.

As Max Weber indicated, the modern state could not exist without an elaborate administrative system. Because public management/administration is usually regarded primarily as a state function and because the state does possess "a legal monopoly of coercive power," (Weber, 1948),[5] we are confronted with some interesting questions that strike at the very core of this relationship. Interestingly, the issues addressed by these questions have generated only a modicum of, if any, significant reflection by either practitioners or public affairs scholars. And what are some of these questions?

First, are the respective fields of public management/administration and public policy particularly vulnerable to being intellectually hobbled by what the state defines as legitimate policy considerations and alternatives, thereby undermining any attempt to develop an independent and critical intellectual foundation upon which to raise certain controversial issues (Offe, 1972; Mills, 1951; Harvey, 2007; Carnoy, 1984)? Second, does the analytical and managerial acumen we employ, even though it may take place within a constitutional/democratic framework, inevitably sanction "the legitimation of the state through the application of its technical expertise" (Beauregard, 1978, p. 236; Block, 1980; Carnoy, 1984)? Or, to put it in slightly different terms, do both disciplines inadvertently displace issues from the political and economic fabric of society, thus elevating an administrative process over substantive purpose? Finally, are there other societal roles for public affairs beyond the parameters of what the state delegates or expects both disciplines to do, especially public management/administration? Are the customary public roles and purposes for both fields too restrictive (in relationship to the state) or do we have broader responsibilities for leadership in the community?

These questions at first glance seem rather disconcerting in their implications (Ventriss, 2015). Many will claim, and rightly so, that the role of those in public management/administration and public policy—at least involving democratically elected governments—is fundamentally both managerial and normative: to serve the public interest in the most efficient and equitable manner, and perhaps, most important of all, in a nonpartisan manner (Goodsell, 2014). Yet, as Luther Gulick (1983) has pointed out, the instinctive drive for group action under the "banner of the state" (as he called it) is one of the greatest shortfalls concerning our approach to public affairs—a poignant observation that has largely fallen on deaf ears. At heart, the questions posed above raise not only the perennial issue of the politics/administration dichotomy, but the more troubling issue of the relationship of our intellectual role and purpose to modern power and how we define both fields primarily in governmental or quasi-governmental terms.

From a different theoretical angle, Robert Nisbet (1953) has claimed that the modern state has tried to fill a social vacuum created by the decline of local associative groups; that is, kinship, religious, and other locality groups.

The state has tried to create, Nisbet concludes, what is essentially a "pseudo community" that is unable to meet the psychological and social needs of the community. Emile Durkheim (1964, p. 28), who deeply influenced Nisbet's thinking on this issue, wrote that

> the state is too remote from the individuals; its relations with them too external and intermittent to penetrate deeply into individual consciences and socialize them within where the state is the only environment in which we can live communal lives, they inevitably lose contact, become detached.

Nisbet (1953, p. 7), extending Durkheim's idea, reiterated that the decline of "community has made ours an age of frustration, anxiety, disintegration, instability, breakdown, and collapse." Even if this postulation is dismissed as merely hyperbole, Nisbet raises a point seldom discussed in public management/administration and public policy. As conceptually and pragmatically aligned with the modern state as both fields tend to be, when stripped of their normative and pragmatic clothing, do they ultimately find themselves embedded in a politically awkward position inasmuch as they must always act more or less in concert with the powers of an authoritative political structure? In other words, does this state of affairs come at the cost of managing a potentially unsatisfying social harmony in a market society of contradictory social interests, varied public needs/expectations, and vast differences in the exercise of political power? Asking this particular question, I suspect, will prompt an immediate negative reaction by most in the fields of public policy and public management/administration. Still, it is a question that will not go so easily away and will eventually require a response (Rosenbloom, 1986, 2005; Box, 2014, Hummel, 2007; Poulantzas, 1978; Carnoy, 1984; Harvey, 2007). Carole Pateman (2012) was correct when she pointed out that our various ideas in attempting to achieve a democratic ethos in public affairs will have little effect if we do not first question the "conventional institutional structures" (her term) and their relationship in promoting democratic public purposes.

Assuming the validity of both Gulick's and Nisbet's theoretical views, their usage of the term *state* demands some clarification. However, according to David Easton (1953, p. 108), "the word [state] should be abandoned entirely." The reason for Easton's uneasiness is that the concept of the state is difficult to separate empirically from such notions as society, political organizations, and government. We tend to trip over political definitions such as the meaning of the state that become, according to Almond and Coleman (1960), nothing more than philosophical quibbles. Even John Dewey (1927, p. 241) admitted that "the moment we utter the words 'the State' a score of intellectual ghosts rise to obscure our vision." While any definition will assuredly arouse quibbles of what the state is (Weber, 1948; Jessop, 1983; Poggi, 2012; Amenta, Nash, & Scott, 2012; Vincent, 1991; Panitch, 1980; Skocpol, 1979), Morton Fried (1967, p. 229) has provided a good general working definition: "A state is not simply a legislature, an executive body, a judiciary system, an administrative bureaucracy, or even a government . . . a state is better viewed as the complex of institutions by means of which the power of the society is organized."

If this definition is correct, or even partially so, does this imply—as some theorists assert—that in both fields we are a critical part of a dominant complex of institutions and technical processes that, in turn, legitimize a particular arrangement of political power (Box, 2014; Offe, 1973; Evans, 1995; Wolfe, 1977; Harvey, 1982, 2007; Miliband, 1969; Ramos, 1981)? As one prominent sociologist has argued, "Science, rationality, bureaucracy, and power are not just random concepts but stand in a tight causal chain" (Nettl, 1969, p. 22).

That said, what is crucial for those of us in public affairs is the recognition of an intellectual tension between what the state requires in managerial expertise and accountability and the alternative possibilities and responsibilities that both public management/administration and public policy may pose in impacting public affairs. This discussion has ranged from analyzing the implications concerning the "hollowing out" of the state to exploring policy networks nested in modes of coordination and collaborative partnerships among nonstate actors. Guerreiro Ramos (1981) tried to articulate a much different alternative possibility. He elucidates that social science in general, and administrative theory in particular, must shed their Hobbesian assumptions and instrumental view of political reality and help design different social systems or enclaves (as he called them) that are congruent with a variety of individual and community substantive ends sensitive to the factors of technology, size, cognition, space, and time (which will be discussed in more detail in later chapters). The relationship of the state in this regard would be as "an authoritative convenor of social systems, whose assignment is to guarantee their functional complementarity" (Ramos, 1981, p. 169). For Guerreiro Ramos, those who practice in public affairs should play an important role in revitalizing the public sphere, as illustrated by such contemporary thinkers as Mannheim (1948), Habermas (1962), Wolin

(1960), Barber (1984), Fraser (1992), Polanyi (1944), and Arendt (1958), a point that will be discussed in a later chapter.

Whether Guerreiro Ramos is theoretically correct or realistic in articulating this new role for the state in relationship to public affairs is open to serious debate. He does, however, make an implicit argument that both fields have fallen into a precarious Hegelian trap, that the "real is the rational"; that we believe that to critically question and examine the "real" is tantamount to circumventing the goals and purposes of public management/administration and public policy. The crux of our difficulty, John Dyckman (1978, p. 293) writes, is that unfortunately, "we lack a vision of what kind of state and what kind of politics we want. . . . We indulge in this ignorance," he somberly tells us, "at our own peril, both as [administrators and analysts] and as citizens." Yet, raising such concerns is like opening Pandora's box. Given the inherent plurality of thought about these issues, it could run the risk of polarizing the field into antagonistic intellectual camps and encouraging academic skirmishes that will seem to others as needlessly idiosyncratic and foolish. Additionally, it might politicize the field, making it even more vulnerable to attacks from all partisan angles (Danzinger & Gottschalk, 1995; Lowi, 1979; Fischer, 2003). Alan Wolfe (1977, pp. 262–263) articulated this point in these vivid terms: "Caught between its politicized tasks and its depoliticized tasks, public administration [and public policy] . . . searches for answers to [their] intractable tasks wherever it can find them, only to discover that each possible option causes as many problems as it solves." Perhaps. But as practitioners and theorists struggle with these concerns, it might also, ironically, serve as a catalyst to redefine the respective public roles of both fields and consequently change their praxis in public affairs and community life. Hopefully, such an exercise and its implications for the public may not be seen as an act of reckless behavior, but a long-overdue act of civic duty in this era of political and economic uncertainty. The influence of neo-managerialism, the economization of public inquiry, and the role of both in relationship to the modern state, have come dangerously close to supplying—piecemeal and unreflexively—an epistemological and normative orientation that erodes the notion of publicness. If public affairs is to curb the trends toward those values and methods determined by these influences that presently grip it, I suggest a renewed emphasis will be necessary that allows scholars and practitioners to consciously evaluate their work against normative, rather than utilitarian measures. In the following chapters, I propose that such an approach can be derived from a revitalization of the concept of publicness and a commitment to democratic critical thought.

Some interesting research questions warrant further examination given some of the issues I have raised in this chapter. For example, what role can both fields play in impacting societal affairs if they are not honest about their inherent limitations in what they can realistically achieve in a political culture that is largely suspicious of their influence in first place? Second, given the declining trust of certain public institutions in the United States and elsewhere, some have argued that this sentiment coupled with economic and societal uncertainty has contributed to the rise of pseudo-democratic populism. What specific role can we play in creating a dialogue with those who are attracted to this kind of populism, if any? And finally, how can we bring back into our discussions the nature of the state as an important research focus in understanding such issues as the changing relationship of the state to civil society, the role of the state in meeting competing political interests, societal pressures, and differing economic claims while still maintaining its neutral role in the allocation of public resources? Although this only a small sampling of research questions, it nevertheless, I hope, should prompt us to shift some of our agenda in a different direction.

Conclusion

In this chapter, I have examined the conditioning factors pivotal in understanding the present theoretical and pragmatic tensions that are critical to understanding the role of both fields. I drew on authors including Waldo, Ramos, and Caiden, to outline this tension and underscore its importance. Moreover, I elaborated on the works of Swyngedouw and others to suggest that a powerful new orientation is tipping public affairs away from the critical and normative and toward a more technocratic perspective: neo-managerialism.

Generally speaking, neo-managerialism has the following five elements: (1) its proclivity to avoid ethical issues; (2) its diverse inclusion of all relevant fields due to an inability to define normative positions; (3) its technocratic approach to achieving market efficiency; (4) its deep entanglement with empiricism; and (5) its emphasis on expert planning and managerial control. I drew on Wills's arguments, along with others, to argue that these elements are drivers of a trend deemphasizing both fields' critical and normative inquiries of economic and political problems and to view them as merely technical and managerial issues to be resolved.

After outlining the nature and rise of neo-managerialism, I turned my attention to tracing its consequences in academia and in practice. I observed that the present neo-managerial turn causes public affairs scholars to emphasize education that prepares students primarily to fulfill analytic and managerial functions even when it is clothed in normative garments. Likewise, I identified that in the world of practice, the neo-managerial turn encourages public affairs professionals to heavily privilege expert judgment over public judgment. I suggested that these trends might threaten the underpinnings of democratic governance, and I suggested that educators and practitioners should instill a critical dimension to their work through engaging public affairs scholarship and methods with the pressing issues of contemporary societal importance.

I concluded the chapter with two historical critiques. Drawing on Poulantzas, I argued that he gives crucial insights, albeit within a controversial framework, that characterize the state as an arena for conflict and as a function of political, economic, and ideological factors. Drawing on the French Regulation School, I argued that the ever-tighter entanglement of state and market in the modern global economy is at the root of some of the challenges we presently face. I offered that Weber's insight is correct that our increasingly complex modern state requires a complex administrative system, but warned—developing on Ramos, Gulick, and Nisbet—that we may need to rethink the administrative state in how we meet the needs of the public. In the service of this goal, I devote the following chapter to an ambitious project: developing a revitalized view of publicness. This approach seeks to offer normative and substantive grounding for thinkers committed to challenging the trends of neo-mangerialism and recommitting public management/administration and public policy to substantive public well-being.

3

A Conceptual Foundation

Reinvigorated Publicness

As evidenced in chapter 1, one of the greatest intellectual challenges facing us in public affairs today stems from our struggle to frame a strong theoretical foundation for the importance of the public in our scholarship and practice. This struggle to develop a viable theoretical foundation for publicness, however, does not result from any lack of empirical work. Nor is it the result of hostility to new ideas (evident by the many who are interested in ideas developed by postpositivist or critical theorists). The primary reason, in large part, for not having a strong conceptual foundation for publicness is that we have been unable to formulate any meaningful theoretical linkages to the meaning of "the public" that goes beyond a shareholder view of governance and citizens as an "occupant of a managerial authorizing environment" (Dahl & Ross, 2014, p. 502).

Notwithstanding the varied theoretical angles taken on what constitutes publicness, the meaning of "the public" still eludes us (Pesch, 2005, 2008; Barnett, 2008; Keane, 2000; Habermas, 1962; Fraser, 1990; Warner, 2002; Calhoun, 1993). When attempting to ascertain its meaning, or meanings, we usually couch it in discussions about public participation (although to a point this is important to do), or a congeries of many different publics, or associated with public institutions, public goods, the public interest, and/or as public values (Bozeman & Bretschneider, 1994;Gause, 1983; Pesch, 2008; Wamsely & Zald, 1973). All things considered, these responses are understandable. After all, the public is not a monolithic concept with one overarching, universal meaning (Moulton, 2009; Pesch, 2005, 2008; Haque, 2001). However, even given the theoretical difficulties of defining "the public," one wonders if we have perhaps, too often, reduced the notion of the public to a mere abstraction—an amorphous statistical configuration that becomes real, or acknowledged, only when voices are raised.

The need for a more viable conceptual foundation for public is apparent. Such a foundation would provide the meaning and purpose for whom and for what we are administering and analyzing. Put candidly, the need for such a substantive view of the public is that we cannot—as many are beginning to understand—separate our view of social problems from our view of the public. They are inextricably linked. This is precisely why we call issues that we confront *public* problems and the actions we take *public* policies. Lingering behind every policy action is some conception of the public, regardless of how broad or pedantic that view may be. Is it not worth pondering, for a moment, just how many public policies have failed due not only to an inadequate theoretical understanding of the problem we are defining, but also to an inadequate understanding of the public's multidimensional substantive needs?

Faulty or ill-conceived assumptions generally have a way of returning, keeping both public management/administration and public policy in a state of ambivalence and theoretical confusion. One can see this, for example, in the often-held belief that because both largely serve the needs of the state (or government), they concomitantly serve the needs of the public, as if the state and the public are one and the same (they are not). Among others, David Mathews (1985) has exposed, as it were, the fallacy of this perception quite effectively. He reminds us that "the root words for public are not the same as the root words for the polity, the state, the government. The public [instead] consists of those people who act together with an understanding of their relationship to each other" (p. 123). He concludes that in fact "the concept of government [or the state] is a very distant cousin of the public" (ibid.). His message is clear: maintaining that the public and the state are synonymous is done at our own theoretical peril (Ringeling, 2013). The tendency to confuse them stems from our belief that by becoming more managerially and analytically sophisticated, we will ultimately make public organizations more responsible, as if efficiency (and professional managerialism) will promote the public's support for our efforts (it will not). This does not imply that "efficiency" is not a critical part of what we in public affairs need to facilitate, but that it cannot serve as a substitute alone for fostering a stronger sense of public purpose and democratic public governance (Ventriss, 1991; Nabatchi, 2010; Denhardt & Denhardt, 2000; Love & Stout, 2015; Hummel, 2007). Yet, publicness is perceived by most scholars in public affairs primarily in terms of how "the organization is affected by political authority" (Bozeman, 1987, p. xi), even though the emphasis has shifted to the centrality to both public value and public values (Moore, 1995, 2013; Moore & Fung, 2012; Bozeman, 2007; Moulton, 2009; Stoker, 2006; Williams & Shearer, 2011).

It is worth noting that "public value" is a managerial philosophy associated with Mark Moore's (1995) formulation of this term. Public value, he declares, refers to how policies are managerially feasible and sustainable and of substantive importance to the public (Moore, 1995). Briefly stated, it is a framework, or what he calls a strategic triangle, in which public managers operate: the authorizing environment; the operational capability; and the public value (strategic goal). Moore succiently put this approach in the following terms: "The aim of managerial work in the public sector is to create public value just as the aim of managerial work in the private sector is to create private value" (p. 28). On the other hand, "public values" refers to those values that "provide normative consensus about (a) the rights, benefits, and prerogatives to which citizens should (and should not) be entitled; (b) the obligations of citizens to society, the state, and one another; (c) the principles on which governments and policies should be based" (Bozeman, 2007, p. 13). Bozeman goes on to articulate what he calls public value failure that "occurs when neither the market nor public sector provides goods and services required to achieve publc values" (ibid., p. 144). In the next breath, Bozeman contends that public value failure is exacerbated when "there are insufficient means of ensuring articulation and effective communication of core values, or if processes for aggregating values lead to distortions" (p. 145). Overall, the public values literature chiefly focuses on what values are crucial at various times in the governance process. Moore and Bozeman both tend to link their respective views as integrally associated with public institutions, even though the public values literature (or at least some of it) raises serious concerns about the encroachment of a neoliberal ideology in governmental institutions. Moreover, Bozeman has proposed a normative linkage of public values to the public sphere as they apply to public administration (Bozeman & Johnson, 2014). That said, while Moore and Bozeman have made important contributions to our discussion on this subject, they have both deemphasized attention to conflict and the asymmetrical exercise of power in the prevailing political system (Jacobs, 2014). Although Bozeman's analysis is much closer to what I see as pivotal to publicness, it is a publicness that is reluctant to question the legitimacy of managed democracy or to confront the dominant economic actors that can influence the policy agenda (Dahl & Soss, 2014). A reinvigorated view of publicness would see the necessity of confronting both realities.

The ability (and willingness) to confront the enduring implications of what publicness implies is one of the paramount challenges we face today. We need, therefore, to begin with the notion of the public itself. At this juncture, it is worth quoting David Mathews's (1985, p. 124) thoughts on this matter:

> Absent public awareness and spirit, absent the ability to translate individual concerns into larger common concerns, absent the people's ability to understand not just the particulars, but the relationship of the whole, there is no capacity "to public." And with relations of the sort that we have in a country as diverse as ours, with issues as intertwined as they are, the task of "publicking"—of understanding both consequences and potential in relationships, over time—is no small task. Educating for public life the civic self takes on new meaning when the public is recognized for what it really is. Civic literacy, the capacity of people to think about the whole of things, of consequences and potential, becomes education of the most critical kind. Public policy education becomes imperative in light of what the public can and must do; indeed what it can alone do.

One can object to this romanticized notion of the public as articulated by Mathews. That is, in a society that many view as filled with privatism and distrust of public institutions run rampant (in the United States, anyway), it is highly unlikely that such a notion can serve as any working model in confronting critical problems facing society. In other words, can we, as some scholars have argued, be so naive as to expect people to express true "publicness" whose lifestyle and behavior indicate the most passive and disinterested definition of citizenship? Such objections are difficult to ignore (Lippmann, 1955; Roberts, 2008; Ventriss, 1985). However, Mathews (1985, p. 122) does have a point: a proper understanding of the public denotes a *capacity*, not an abstraction; it moreover denotes a *maturity*, "implying the ability to understand the consequences of individual actions on others, the ability to see beyond ourselves." Although Mathews's conceptualization may be a bit sketchy, he does raise the crucial point that not every group is a "public," which is to distinguish it from the interest-group liberalism that presently dominates modern politics or as a manifestation of a crude form of urban populism (Lowi, 1979; Wilson & Swyngedouw, 2014). That is to say, the public is a condition in search of actualization, not a static conceptualization predicated on a certain definition of human nature. In a similar manner, Barber (1984) and others have argued this exact point as well (Ventriss, 2016, 1985; Leighninger, 2006, 2012; Nabatchi, 2010; Nabatchi, Gastil, Leighninger, & Weiksner, 2012).

Publicness, then, involves more than a capacity and maturity; it also involves relationships that are interactive, which, John Dewey maintained (1927, pp. 80–81), must "include the give and take of participation, of a sharing that increases, that expands and deepens, the *capacity* and significance of the interacting factors." The public, consequently, involves "all those who are affected by the indirect consequences of transactions to such an extent that is deemed necessary to have those consequences systematically cared for" (p. 245). Dewey's phrasing should not obscure his central idea: that because public actions are by definition interactive, and can have a variety of public consequences or impacts, the public must act in a public learning capacity in the formulation and deliberation of policy actions—a deliberation that takes place in the context of political and social formations that are constituted in endless civic questioning, contestatory debate, and political struggles in modern political life. At the heart of any substantive perspective of the public, then, is the conception of citizen inquiry and public action, which implies, as Tocqueville (1956, pp. 207–220) recognized, "the transformation of commitments, the cultivation of the public virtue." One can only cultivate public virtues, Tocqueville believed, by participating in public life. This is precisely why he saw the jury system, town meetings, and other citizen-based institutions as educative vehicles to engage the public in its responsibilities as citizens. What is hinted at here should now be more directly stated: the capacity, the maturity, and the learning process of the public must be inexorably linked with the publicness of a civic process: an asymptotic—to use Alfred Whitehead's (1929) term—exercise in deliberative public learning, a public learning that enhances the citizens' capacity, maturity, and knowledge in civic matters by "exploring the vicissitudes, inequalities, and conflicts associated with the old formations of publicness" in order to create new possibilities for public action" (Newman & Clarke, 2009, p. 16). In this regard, publicness is a process that is inherently conflictual, dialectic, open to new possibilities, and continuously searching for novelty, which concomitantly encourages democratic discourse and public action in furthering both human dignity and political and economic rights. Public discourse, therefore, is an ongoing process whereby consensus on public matters is only partial and ephemeral. Accordingly, publicness is not to subdue conflicts and disagreements regarding how power is distributed, but rather to make such conflicts and disagreements visible and transparent for all to see. Dewey (1930, p. 67) was right when he wrote that "conflict is the gadfly of thought. It stirs us to observation and memory. It instigates invention. It shocks us out of sheep-like passivity . . . conflict is the 'sine qua non' of reflection and ingenuity."

But, in concrete terms, what does it mean for public management/administration and public policy? How do we even begin to link this conceptualization of the public to both disciplines? The ramifications of this approach are numerous, but for purposes of discussion here, I will highlight only three important implications this perspective holds for public administration and public policy.

Toward a Public Social Science

Public policy and public management/administration, as fields intellectually linked to the social sciences, can play an even more crucial role bridging the gap between theory, practice, and civic life by becoming explicitly a "public" social science. This statement might sound perplexing, if not confusing. What is meant here is that it is problematic whether the study of public management/administration and public policy is understood as merely a collection of different approaches borrowed from a variety of social sciences. It really does not matter whether these disciplines are a subfield of political science, or economics, or any other branch of social science for that matter. What distinguishes public policy and public management/administration from other social sciences is that it should be committed to becoming a *public social science*; that is, applying a critical intellect to those social science approaches so that the public can better understand, debate, discuss, and question important policy issues in a manner that fosters careful deliberation. This critical inquiry, for example, would attempt to sort out the misinformation and distortion of data (and the underlying domain assumptions of empirical information), to clarify the differing sources of potential and real conflict over policy choices, to analyze the various policy tradeoffs and distributive effects implied for each policy choice, and to carefully examine the impact of past policy decisions. The dissemination of this information, although hardly enough to engage the public in civic concerns, does provide an important role for public affairs as a public social science: it challenges both fields to take an interest in knowledge that can have liberating public relevance. C. Wright Mills (1963, p. 613) articulated a similar point when he argued that "only when publics and leaders are responsive and responsible, are human affairs in democratic order, and only when knowledge has public relevance is this order possible."

But what does a public social science mean for the intellectual growth for us who study public affairs? Certainly, we cannot derive the important theoretical insights described above. This is, of course, true, but a public social science does have important theoretical implications for the study and practice of public affairs. First, and most evident, it implies that public affairs cannot become captive of a modus operandi that regards theory as only a functionalization of knowledge that masks the importance of normative and philosophical concerns as they relate to the foundations of democracy. That is, if we try to transpose all public questions into a methodistic framework, we will nudge ever closer to what has been referred to as "rigorous irrelevance" (Majone, 1989; Wagenaar, 2011). It is worth noting that economics has been criticized by some scholars within its own ranks on this precise point (Krugman, 2012). This should not be regarded as a dismissal of empirical analysis (quite the contrary); rather, a reminder that public affairs should embrace the intellectual and theoretical posture *of methodological pluralism:* the adoption of a variety of methodologies that are appropriate to the level of abstraction one is trying to research (Ramos, 1981; Kaplan, 1964). For instance, a historical, comparative, and philosophical analysis is more amenable in examining the bureaucratic experience in modern industrial societies than a strictly quantitative approach. This is not to imply that it always is a question of either/or, but rather a mixture of different methodological perspectives that can, it is hoped, accentuate a critical, interpretive, and empirical inquiry into public affairs at all levels of analysis (Morse & Ventriss, 2018; Bernstein, 1976; Muller & Ventriss, 1985; Ramos,1981).

A public social science can further enhance the intellectual growth of both fields by combating the growing mechanization of theory (a philosophical view that dates back to Hobbes, Bacon, and Descartes) to avoid the theoretical pitfalls of reductionism. The methodological flexibility that a public social science would promote might awaken other social sciences, not only to the advantages of such a theoretical posture, but also to the advantages of restoring the supremacy of theory over method (thus dispelling the fallacious notion that the application of empirical methodology alone can advance theory). Only when we are not empirically frozen to one methodological perspective are we in the position to understand the complexities of issues pertinent to the public. This theoretical approach of methodological pluralism may even help us extend the field's knowledge to address Max Weber's probing and haunting question: "What shall we do and how shall we live?"

But becoming a public social science implies more than applying the appropriate methodology. It also connotes the discovery and analysis of new possibilities for public debate and exploration in understanding the sources of injustices and antinomies that can undemine the democratic ethos. It is, furthermore, to address those institutional, historical, and cultural processes that inevitably change over time, and their interplay in shaping the attitudes and norms of the modern polity. This directly implies the historical and empirical examination of how problems started in the first place, and subsequently making such an examination an intellectual priority in addressing societal issues of critical public relevance—and their impact on publicness—in an age of complexity, volatility, and widespread uncertainty.

Intermediary between Citizen and State

It has been pointed out that we in public affairs must deliberately expand activities to those civic and voluntary associations that mediate between individuals and the state, encouraging public spaces for critical deliberative debates, contestation, and for empowered publics to emerge. To be sure, the saliency of this idea is hardly new. Durkheim and Tocqueville, for example, both emphasized the importance of intermediary associations. Peter Berger and Richard Neuhaus (1977), moreover, have argued that such associations serve not only the crucial purpose of providing a link between individuals and the state, but also of protecting individuals from the impersonal dictates of the state. Also, the vast literature on public participation and co-production can be added to this chorus. But it is important to keep in mind that, as Sam Warner (1968) posits, such voluntary associations in themselves do not necessarily inspire involvement of the citizenry in public life. For example, Philadelphia had a vast network of associations (from 1930 to 1960), but they were mainly private social cells that were indifferent to the common life of the city. To overcome this tendency, public administrators/policy analysts must directly engage citizens so that civic associations can become lively democratic laboratories to enhance further civic engagement and responsibility. Louis Gawthrop (1985, p. 104) has made this provocative argument that is as relevant to us today as when he first wrote these words:

> [T]o make government interesting, the values of an actively engaged citizenry in the essential characteristics of citizenship becomes a primary—if not the primary—responsibility of professional public servants. Specifically, this is to suggest that a basic responsibility and ethical obligation of public administrators and managers is to infuse the individual citizen with the character of citizenship and to provide the citizen with an ethical sense of purpose in the system of democratic governance.

Understandably, suspicions are immediately aroused that even subtly hint that administrators/analysts should be playing the role of knowing what is best for the public (Lawson, 1994; Gottfried, 1999; Lasch, 1995). This notion smacks of elitism or as an enlightened form of policy entrepreneurship that would be viewed by many as "impractical, presumptuous, humorous, and outrageous" (Waldo, 1985, p. 108). These suspicions ignore, however, the broader issue that public institutions and the prevailing neoliberal notion of governance already teach a form of citizenship. Too often it is a citizenship that tells the public that information and policy issues are more than likely too complex for their meaningful input, that inclusion of too many participants will only lead to needless delays in the administrative and policy process, and finally, that public input can sometimes lead to unintended consequences that can undermine the public interest. Following on this latter point, one can also argue that the counterpublics of populism also engage in a mode of public education that cultivates interest and skill, albeit often in a distortive way, in what some would contend is a form of participatory politics. Although these contentions contain validity, this is the negative side of citizenship that further separates public administrators/policy analysts from the public. What is needed is an affirmative role that accentuates the positive side of citizenship—citizenship whereby the public builds its confidence and knowledge in associations that prepare the citizenry for meaningful, effective participation in public affairs and perhaps a democratic revitalization of the meaning of involvement in the public realm (Benhabib, Cameron, Dolidze, Halmai, Hellman, Pishchikova, & Youngs, 2013). This approach is not a panacea, but rather it is a bridge—as Charles Levine (1984) once put it—that connects the citizen and the administrator/analyst in the spirit of loyalty, innovation, and policy experimentation (Ventriss, 2016). But how would one even begin to develop a participative learning infrastructure, as Nabatchi and Leighninger (2015) so eloquently argued, when much of the public is politically acquiescent and/or distrustful of government and its institutions? This will, undoubtedly, require some new approaches and thinking from both fields beyond what has been usually advocated. In this regard, let us turn to our final point.

Encouraging Self-Governance and Accountability

More than ever, we in public affairs should begin experimenting with various public learning models that encourage both a social knowledge transfer and a disaggregate approach in forging new forms of public governance and public/civic accountability. This premise builds upon the two points mentioned previously. Specifically, in order for public affairs to actualize its role more efficaciously as a critical public social science and as a facilitator of citizenship, we must be aware that the "citizen is in possession of a world of his own, and that nobody can interpret this world (more expertly) than he himself" (Berger, 1976, p. 60). This point is raised because there are, contended Thomas Dewar (1978, p. 4), "tensions between freedom and control, independence and dependence, and competence and incompetence [that] are built into helping relationships from the beginning." This inherent tension can be partially mitigated by implementing a social knowledge transfer and a disaggregate approach to policymaking. Put simply, disaggregate policymaking is a client-oriented approach to policy—a perspective that acknowledges the unique needs of different publics and the necessity of defining those specific needs in the policy process (Biller, 1979; Ventriss, 2016; Ventriss & Luke, 1988; Muller & Ventriss, 1985). A disaggregate approach recognizes that clients' interests and needs cannot be treated uniformly, or as one homogeneous social unit, by policymakers. The public in this regard is composed of *persons* who cannot be regarded as part of some analytical category of some aggregate grouping. Robert Biller (1979, p. 162) correctly emphasized that public servants must deal with "person[s] [who] bring questions that are uniquely contextuated in a lifetimes' increasingly particularized experiences." Biller's assertion is predicated on the idea that we must begin experimenting with policies that are tailored in a "nonaggregate" and "person-specific" manner. Unfortunately, Biller never addresses the logistical issues of how this can be achieved. Still, if we are to take this perspective seriously, a social knowledge transfer becomes evident. Social knowledge transfer refers to the direct exposure of public servants to the unique experiential knowledge of clients, and the provision of a forum for critical dialogue and open exchange of information of relevance to the community. This transfer of knowledge presupposes a "fit" between the beneficiaries and the assisting organization:

> Between beneficiaries and the assisting organization, the critical fit is between the means by which the beneficiaries are able to define and communicate their needs and the program by which the organization makes decisions. This may require changes both at the community level—developing a way for the poor to express their needs—and the assisting organization level—developing ways for the organization to respond to such information. (Korten, 1980, p. 496)

In the forefront of initiating various approaches along these lines, which are still very much in a theoretical, embryonic stage, are the ideas being developed by certain scholars (Ventriss, 2016; Korten, 1981; Korten & Klass, 1984; Donald Michael, 1983; Friedmann, 1973; Friedmann & Abonyi, 1976; Muller & Ventriss, 1985; Schon, 1971; Ventriss & Luke, 1988). The implementation of these ideas, even for those sympathetic to this perspective, is no doubt ambitious to achieve. For instance, how do public servants and the public participate in this process given the stark realities of scarce resources and time constraints? And, more important, although most critics would admit that *persons* are different from *categories,* public servants must still grope with the daunting strategic problem that there are too many people and communities "out there," hence the troubling reality that could result in policy discontinuity and the lack of any cohesion in the delivery of public services

These legitimate concerns deal almost exclusively with the related issues of *size, scale,* and *complexity* of governmental operations, not to mention the vast information necessary to implement these approaches successfully. The issues of size and scale, however, are becoming increasingly elastic. This elasticity is due primarily to the growth of communication technology, as Benjamin Barber (1984) and others have argued (Gordon, Schirra, & Hollander, 2011; Milakovich, 2010; Coglianese, 2005; Polat, 2005; Zavaestoski, Shulman, & Schlosberg, 2006). In fact, it was Ithiel de Sola Poole (1973), who was one of the first to argue that citizens might have access, if properly instituted, to critical organizational information through a nationwide computerized system. Furthermore, citizen surveys and citizen juries might be more widely utilized, particularly surveys that employ Del-la-Fave's "value stretch model" methodology. This model has been found to be effective in defining the specific needs of clients in a large community on a cross-cultural basis (Kipnis & Ventriss, 1984). Notwithstanding the fact that no one approach will be entirely effective, the growing sophistication of communications technology (along with citizen surveys, citizen juries, value stretch methodology, and other related approaches) can provide a fertile ground for new public learning not thought possible that long ago (Nabatchi & Leighninger, 2015).

Surely, not every public service or good can be disaggregated. And the challenge of complexity and scale will continue to be a difficult problem to overcome. The importance that a disaggregated approach and a social knowledge transfer poses—leaving aside some of the logistical problems of implementing these approaches—is that it forces us in public affairs to be experimental and constantly reestablish concrete links with the public that are not merely procedural in nature, but experientially substantive in content (Ventriss, 2016). If nothing else, it is a noble calling in this time of growing citizen distrust of public institutions, public officials, and the mass media.

I have attempted in this chapter to clarify one overarching theme: that fundamental issues of publicness facing public affairs require more attention from scholars and practitioners beyond strictly limited and instrumental managerial/organizational approaches, whether analytical or behavioral. And claims for legitimacy based upon "dedication," "competence," "technical acumen," and "intellectual commitment to democratic principles"—as well-intentioned as these notions are—will probably never be sufficient to sustain needed credibility. Furthermore, I have argued that because the public is not entirely synonymous with the state, neither should public management/administration and public policy be viewed so narrowly. Obviously, this idea has controversial implications, but it is an issue that is pivotal in any endeavor to redefine our civic purpose, both as an intellectual and a pragmatic enterprise, in doing and thinking about public affairs.

The suggestions offered here are not intended as any final statement, or resolution. These suggestions are presented as one way of provoking more debate and discussion, and are thus open to serious criticism and further refinement. What might surface in such a debate is the view that as our conceptualization of the public changes, so must our understanding of both fields' purpose change to reflect a more dynamic relationship with the public. This recognition may just nudge us to explore what Iris Young (2000, p. 13) called an "emancipatory politics of difference" whereby we engage in an ongoing project of discussing with the respective publics questions of group difference and multiple policy perspectives. Perhaps, as some have claimed, both disciplines have already reached a point in their intellectual development that is more or less irreversible. If this is indeed the case (which I hope it is not) we should take heed of the warning that the late historian Arnold Toynbee emphasized: a civilization that does not directly meet its challenges is a civilization on the brink of moral decline. We need only substitute the words "public affairs" for "civilization" to understand the crucial importance of the task before us. Yet that said, a paradox hovers over public affairs: How can we successfully reconcile a pragmatic idealism promoting a democratic ethos and, concommitantly, deal with such a pervasive and ingrained distrust of professional elites by the American public (and in other countries), which is not likely to end anytime soon? And, finally how is it possible to challenge the stark reality that both disciplines function in a constant state of American ambivalence and false caricatures without falling prey to a misplaced cynicism or denial? Or put another way, "how to achieve idealism without illusions and realism without cynicism" (Kammen, 1990, p. 276). How successfully we respond to these contradictory forces will mark the days ahead.

Conclusion

In this chapter, I have formulated what I contend are the foundations of a revitalized publicness, and discussed the barriers to their formulation and implementation. Too often, publicness is viewed as chiefly atomized, self-interested, and consumeristic, or as the tendency to render the public in abstract statistical terms. To overcome these barriers, I have called on scholars of public affairs to reflect on *what* they seek to accomplish, and *whom* they seek to ultimately influence.

In this line of inquiry, I drew on Matthews to suggest that, contrary to common perception, the needs of the state and the government are not necessarily interchangeable with those of the public. I identify the public as a body characterized by relationships both internal (within itself) and external (with collaborative relations with various associations), with the maturity and normative capacity to engage in these endeavors. I called for a publicness to recognize these substantive qualities and to commit both fields to their stewardship.

In the service of this vision of the public, I suggested that public affairs must become a public social science. That is, public management/administration and public policy should commit itself to critically and analytically addressing the challenges of public life and should embrace the plural methods needed to do so effectively. I cautioned against the temptations of overly mechanistic approaches, or adherence to rigor at the expense of relevance, in this vision.

I concluded the chapter by outlining a series (though, not an exhaustive one) of steps that public affairs practitioners and scholars might take to realize both public management/administration and public policy's potential as a public social science in the service of a mature, capable, and civically literate public. I called for a retreat from the perspective of privileged and isolated expertise and advocated for direct engagement by professionals in the field in public life. This engagement—and the disaggregated policy-making it would entail—I argued could help facilitate the social transfer of knowledge necessary to engage meaningfully with the realities of individual experiences within the broader public. Such engagement will be crucial in enabling scholar and practitioner alike to operate at the scales and complexities needed for efficacy across entire states, but also substantively at the level of individual experience. But, achieving this standard of public affairs research and practice will not be easy. In the following chapter, I introduce a line of thinking, critical democratic thought, to help guide us toward implementing a revitalized notion of publicness in the context of the many obstacles posed by the modern polity.

4

A Substantive Approach

Critical Democratic Thought

> Better it is for [us in public affairs] to err in active participation in the living struggles and issues of [our] own age and times than to maintain an immune monastic impeccability, without relevancy and bearing in the generating ideas of [our] contemporary present.
>
> —John Dewey

> The critical ontology of ourselves must be considered not, as a theory or a doctrine; rather it must be conceived as an attitude, an ethos . . . in which the critique of what we are is at one at the same time the historical analysis of the limits imposed on us and an experiment with the possibility of going beyond them.
>
> —Michel Foucault

> We need a past from which we spring rather than from which we seem to be derived.
>
> —Frederick Nietzsche

Not surprisingly, those of us who study the practical aspects of public management/administration and public policy rarely address broad philosophical issues other than by an occasional reference to such seminal thinkers as Habermas, Rawls, Weber, Mannheim, and Dewey. Of course, given the applied focus of public policy and public administration/management this intellectual omission is hardly unexpected. Yet, this lack of interest remains evident in the scarcity of responses from contemporary scholars from both fields to the great thinkers—Aristotle, Hobbes, Kant, and Marx, to name a few—whose works are regarded as classics in public affairs. The issue here is less about the relevance of these thinkers to public affairs, and more about the broader factors underlying the general reluctance, or intellectual indifference, in public management/administration and public policy to engage with their works in the first place (Bowles & Gintis, 1986; Box, 2014; Hummel, 2007; Ramos, 1981; Forester, 1989; Waldo, 1981). Is this merely an accidental oversight? Or do some of these thinkers—putting aside their various theoretical perspectives—make us in both fields, as Louis Weschler[1] once articulated, intellectually uncomfortable, given that many of the perspectives they raise may question some of the cherished underlying intellectual presuppositions in these disciplines? Or, is this because, as indicated in chapter 1, that in public policy and public management/administration we have adopted largely a penchant toward a managerial and instrumental approach to public affairs (Fox & Cochran, 1990; Adams et al., 1990; Adams & Balfour, 2007; Box, 2009)?

There is probably some element of truth to all of these possibilities. Of course, there are a few thinkers tolerated for their theoretical hymnals to critical thought and the relevance of political theory, but these scholars are, for the most part, ignored when their approaches skirmish in any serious manner with the conventional wisdom of public management/administration and public policy (Bowles & Gintis, 1986; Hummel & Stivers, 1998; Hummel, 2007; McSwite, 1997; Box, Marshall, Reed, & Reed, 2001; Dryzek, 1990; Fischer, 2003; Ramos, 1981). The more troubling implication of this trend is that we might be neglecting certain essential theoretical perspectives outright. This point is best articulated by Mills (1959), whose observation (and warning) merits the serious attention of public policy and public administration/management:

> Their positions change—from the academic to the bureaucratic; their publics change—from movements of reformers to the circle of decision-makers; and their problems change—from those of their own choice to those of their new clients. The scholars themselves tend to become less intellectually insurgent and more administratively practical. Generally accepting the status quo, they tend to formulate problems out of the problems and issues that administrators believe they face . . . in so far as social science consists of bureaucratic work, it tends to lose its social and political autonomy. (pp. 106–107)

If Mills's point is valid (and I think it does have merit), should it really surprise us that there is overall a diminution of critical thought in public management/administration and public policy? Some scholars have gone so far as to conclude that we seem to have little to contribute, or are reluctant to contribute, when confronted with major political and economic dislocations of the global economy, the growing wealth and income gap between the rich and the rest of society, and issues of societal injustices (Adams & Balfour, 2010; Bowles & Gintis, 1986; Harvey, 2010; Ventriss, 2015). These critiques require a substantive response, which I contend must take the form of a return to the principles of critical thought that undergird some of the Western humanistic cannon.

In the following chapter, I will argue that critical thought in particular, and political theory in general, can make salient contributions to the theory and practice of public management/administration and public policy. At heart, as it has been previously pointed out, all policy and administrative issues are related in one way or another to political theory (Waldo, 1948). In this respect, I propose an exploration of such thinkers as Antonio Gramsci, Nicos Poulantzas, Jürgen Habermas, Karl Polanyi, Fred Hirsch, Hannah Arendt, and others,[2] as well as what I referred to earlier as the French Regulation School.[3] Some of these thinkers have been already mentioned or will be discussed in subsequent chapters. These thinkers, although representing different theoretical leanings, attempt to restore the purpose of rationality as a normative category and as a way to develop a more critical perspective for understanding society. Not all these names mentioned will (I suspect) be familiar to scholars in the many disciplines concerned with the administrative and policy process. Nevertheless, these thinkers provide crucial insights on such issues as the role of the state (and the bureaucracy) in relationship to civil society, the emergence of new social movements, and the changing political economy in a post-Fordist economic era.[4] Collectively, these perspectives provide a framework from which to approach critical democratic thought as a reinvigorating standard for the practice of public affairs in the complex context of neo-managerialism, the modern state, and the urgent need for reengagement by scholars and practitioners with macrosocietal issues.

The Relevance of Critical Democratic Thought to Public Affairs

It has been more than forty years since Guerreiro Ramos argued that organization theory, and modern social science in general, is naive "because it is predicated on the instrumental rationality inherent in extant Western social science" (1981, p. 3). He went on to contend that this instrumental view, when taken to its logical conclusion, promotes an uncritical approach to societal matters (p. 4). Ramos's more prosaic (and perhaps more controversial) point is that contemporary social inquiry is primarily acquiescent to those political forces that sustain and reinforce the totalization of a market mentality over human associated life (Polanyi, 1944; Hirsch, 1976; Sandel, 2013). That, in turn, leads Ramos to his most salient question: Does the efficacy of conventional theoretical approaches to public affairs—regardless of how they are couched in terms consonant to public service values—reinforce an intellectual quietism?

Undoubtedly, there will be those who argue that these claims are more appropriately (and better) addressed by economic geographers, sociologists, historians, and political scientists. Yet, it was Charles Lindblom who argued, somewhat to the amazement of his fellow political scientists, that the "issue is not that [critical thought] is superior, but only that the mainstream . . . ought to bring it in from the cold" (1982, p. 20). Keeping Lindblom's suggestion in mind, I refer to critical democratic thought as a historical and normative analysis of those political, economic, and social leitmotifs that distort or reify the role of substantive rationality and publicness in democratizing political and economic systems.

But what relevance would critical democratic thought have for a practitioner-oriented field such as public management and an empirically grounded public policy? Louis Gawthrop (1984, p. 103) posed an argument many years ago on a related point:

> The basic question to be examined is how the craft of public management [and public policy] can be directed to revitalize the character of citizenship and the meaning of the concept of citizen. One beginning step that is certainly suggested is the need to revitalize the . . . mission of public service and public management . . . if the craft of management [and policy] can be seen as amplifying the art of government for the individual citizen, then the citizen may become the energizing force for a new focus on democracy.

Conversely, Dennis Thompson (1983) provides a slightly different viewpoint on this issue by pointing out that the problem for public management/administration is that "democracy does not suffer bureaucracy gladly. Many of the values we associate with democracy—equality, participation, and individuality—stand sharply opposed to hierarchy, specialization, and impersonality we ascribe to modern bureaucracy" (p. 235). In fact, some question the compatibility of democracy in an era of neoliberalism that incessantly focuses on "deregulation, privatization, and withdrawal of the state from many areas of social provisions" (Harvey, 2007, p. 3).

What makes the political and intellectual landscape characterized by Gawthrop, Thompson, and Harvey even more salient for public management/administration and public policy is the realization that we live in a time of what Robert Pranger (1980) has described as "the eclipse of citizenship." Modern liberalism, William Sullivan (1986) has alleged, offers little help in resolving this issue because, fundamentally, it "is deeply anti-public in its fundamental premises" (p. xii). Echoing a similar line of logic, Sheldon Wolin (1960), C. B. Macpherson (1962), Benjamin Barber (1984), Michael Sandel (1996), and William Connolly (2013) have asserted through the decades that modern liberalism has contributed to the atomization of citizenship itself—an atomization that has left citizens escaping into privatism and consumerism.[5] Notwithstanding other views that extol the positive merits of modern liberalism (Macedo, 1990; Berkowitz, 1999), Niebuhr (1944, p. xii) might have been right all along in taking a middle ground on this issue: "Democracy has a more compelling justification and requires a more realistic vindication than is given by the liberal culture with which it has been associated in modern history."

This need for a new vindication and justification for democracy other than modern liberalism (particularly its present economic variant, neoliberalism), is where critical democratic thought can play a central role in revitalizing public management/administration and public policy—both pragmatically and theoretically—by a renewed emphasis on what I have referred earlier to as "a critical learning process." Although hardly a thorough list, this process stresses the following factors:

- involvement of citizens in determining the conditions of their association (involving an assumption of respect for the authentic and reasoned nature of individual judgments) (Held, 1987, p. 270; Roberts, 2004; Leighninger, 2010; Pateman, 2012);

- initiation of policy experiments (and the policy learning obtained from such experimentation) in the expansion of economic opportunities to maximize the availability of public resources for democratic projects (Held, 1987, p. 270; Fung & Fagotto, 2009);

- an emphasis on public spaces that the citizenry can critically deliberate, act, judge, and choose—an activity absent the denaturation of language that can distort communication and the role of substantive rationality in community life (Evans & Boyte, 1986; Arendt, 1958; Habermas, 1962; Ramos, 1981); and

- finally, an affirmative role of an educated citizenship in which the citizenry builds its knowledge, maturity, and confidence in civic affairs and as a venue for constructive public contestation and civic dignity (Muller & Ventriss, 1985; Pateman, 1970; Putnam, 2000; Nabatchi & Munno 2014; Denhardt & Denhardt, 2015).

The relationship of critical democratic thought to critical learning process, then, is that it provides a way of enhancing and expanding the debate on the relationship between democratic rights and economic and political life. Let me elaborate further in what I mean here. First, as a pragmatic concern, critical democratic thought directly questions the ubiquitous intrusion of the market system into our political and social existence and tries to delimit this influence by calling for the creation of "new public or civic spaces" for meaningful public deliberations. Specifically, as I briefly mentioned in chapter 1, some scholars have raised concerns about the normative implications of the incessant focus on the market on both democracy and citizenship (Sandel 2013, 2005, 1996, 1992; Walzer 1965, 1983; Taylor, 2011, 2007). Though not the most current of these, Tussman (1960, p. 108), summarizes the condition best:

> Added to our prevailing style of communication the familiar emphasis on individualism, private interest, and private enterprise, and the story of our education is almost complete. We teach men to compete and bargain. Are we surprised, then, at the corruption of the tribunal into its marketplace parody? Democratic political life turns upon the office of the citizen and upon the demands of that office. The citizen is, in his political capacity, a public agent with all that implies. He is asked public, not private questions: "Do we need more public schools?" not "Would I like to pay more taxes?" He must, in this capacity, be concerned with the public interest, not with private goods. His

> communication must be collegial, not manipulative. He must deliberate, not bargain. This is the program. And it is simply the application of tribunal manners to the electoral tribunal. Nothing is more certain than the abandonment of this conception spells the doom of a meaningful democracy.

The ramification of this point will be elaborated on in more detail in another chapter; here, I am concerned only with the proposal that in the absence of a tradition of critical thought, democratic participative governance can be undermined and lose its importance. Salman Silvert puts his finger on the consequences of such a state of affairs when he argues that what we suffer most from is a lack of democracy. "The problem of democracy," he concludes, "concerns how to permit intelligence and effectiveness to be brought to bear in the reestablishment of self-governance, self-adjustment, and self-definition" (1977, p. 31).

But regardless of the merits of this notion, how does this insight really help public administrators or policy analysts working, metaphorically speaking, in the belly of the organization and in the hallways of major political institutions? Arendt contends that the risk of of ignoring critical thought in public affairs is far-reaching: at its very worst, an individual devoid of any notion of citizenship and critical reflection is in reality the perfect administrative cog; the risk is higher still when that individual is entrusted with making decisions on behalf of a wider community. Arendt's reasoning was crafted in response to administrators of the Holocaust—a response that still has a disturbing message for us:

> He has driven the dichotomy of private and public functions of family and occupation, so far that he can no longer find in his own person any connection between the two. When his occupation forces him to murder people he does not regard himself as a murderer because he has done it not out of inclination but in his professional capacity. Out of sheer passion he would never do harm to a fly. (1978, p. 234)

Although some might contend that Arendt's point is overdrawn, the ethical and pragmatic implications of what can happen to citizenship and critical reflection "doing one's professional capacity" speaks for itself.

Critical democratic thought—especially the intellectual tradition I will tease out later—forces us to confront the fact that in both fields we are inevitably caught between the Scylla of what the state perceives as their primary function and role in shaping societal affairs and the Charybdis of trying to defend (and promote) democratic principles without being in direct opposition to the prevailing interstices of institutional power that legitimizes their purpose and role in the modern polity. Indeed, as mentioned earlier, this is an awkward position, regardless of how we try to theoretically maneuver around the conceptual and professional ambivalence and its implications. Moreover, to confront the implications of this issue raises a thorny point concerning the potential politicization of both public management/administration and public policy. In short, does any critical democratic approach presuppose, for example, a partisan slant in the political issues it addresses? Chantal Mouffe (1993) elucidates an interesting response to this legitimate claim: critical democratic thinking (and learning) is an attempt to extend and deepen democracy commensurate with the pluralism of modern democracy, which further implies a new view of citizenship adequate for multiethnic and multicultural societies. According to Mouffe, what is needed "is a hegemony of democratic values and this requires a multiplication of democratic practices" (1993, p. 18). Such democratic practices, among other approaches, imply not only widespread citizen involvement and critical thought, but also suggest how public administrators or analysts can play a role by opening up new avenues for meaningful participation, not as way to contain contradictions and antagonisms, but by expanding the field's mission to enrich those civic associations, as mentioned previously, that mediate between individuals and the government. That is, to mitigate against the pervasive lifestyle and behavior that often foster passive and disinterested expressions of citizenship, public administrators/policy analysts need to—and should—engage the citizenry by playing a role in making these civic associations lively "venues of publicness and critical learning" to enhance and encourage public engagement and civic responsibility. No doubt, this is a tall order. But eventually we need to move more in this direction, even if we take small incremental steps at first.

To echo Laclau & Mouffe's (1985) point, a critical democratic perspective implies a different view of the governance process itself. Here, Mary Parker Follett (1965) gives support to this view in her insistence that one of the most important challenges facing the modern polity is how we can rediscover the methods of self-government. To Follett, this meant nothing less than a citizenship firmly anchored in neighborhood organizations (or other civic associations) and an educative/learning perspective that stresses the interdependency of people in modern society—an interdependency that is achieved through group relationships (p. 335). Yet, here is the rub: according to Rohr (1984), public management/administration and public policy in comparison to citizenship are rooted in two very different traditions. "One tradition centers on management [and analysis] and the other centers on personal initiative" (Rohr, 1984, p. 190). John Rohr's (1984) astute observation requires more of a response than it has received so far. What is hinted at can now be stated: critical democratic thought requires a redefinition (or wider conception) of both fields as more than the delivery and analysis of public services and policies (as important as that is), but also as facilitator in the deliberation of policy actions—a civic deliberation that promotes a participative infrastructure necessary in encouraging critical policy learning as well as an explicit democratic ethos rooted in achieving and promoting policy innovation (Ventriss & Luke, 1988; Ventriss, 2016; Nabatchi & Leighninger, 2015). The practical questions that this point raises—chiefly, how practitioners in particular can navigate governmental structures that enable a reinvigorated citizenry and publicness and participating as a peer rather than an architect in that civic life—will be developed in subsequent chapters.

It becomes imperative given this inherent tension to recognize the importance of both the contingent nature of politics and the plurality of society that emphasizes there is a common human condition, a human condition that stresses the normative values of economic justice, human dignity, political freedom, participatory democracy, and human rights "as historically produced values that are invaluable discursive weapons in the struggle for emancipation" (Best & Kellner, 1991, p. 242). These historically produced values represent, in turn, an effort to democratize power in society by, ironically, "forcing liberal societies to be accountable for their professed ideals" (Mouffe, 1992, p. 2). This accountability for professed democratic ideals is becoming particularly acute given the reality of capital mobility and the global economy. Consider how citizens and their communities are now confronted more and more with new international economic processes that are increasingly altering their economic and social spaces (Johnston & Taylor, 1992; Harvey, 2005; Swyngedouw, 1996; Stiglitz, 2012), and are left with little means to influence these processes through representation or direct action. As I emphasize in chapter 7, what we are seeing is the restructuring of space and its impact on communities, which, inevitably raises the sensitive issue of whether the citizenry can be empowered to organize democratic control over their "place" in the face of fierce competition for capital and the dominant role of the market over their lives (Harvey, 1990, 2005, 2010;

Smith, 1984, 1996; Soja, 1989). As bolstered by critical democratic thought, this requires that we bring a democratic notion of publicness directly into the sphere of economic life. William Sullivan (1986, p. 210) strongly voiced this issue in these candid terms:

> Democratizing and realigning economic relationships at national as well as regional levels according to a civic conception of justice means aggressively developing alternatives to the dominance of private capital over public life. Such a transformation, requiring nothing less than a renegotiation of the public covenant against powerful particular interests, will be the long-term test of the viability of the republic. Yet, though immensely difficult, this project also opens the heartening possibility of transforming the nation's international stance toward a more republican sense of equity.

It is on this point that the contribution of Guerreiro Ramos's (1981) thinking is so important. He believed that we need to reformulate a theory and practice that "delimits" (his word) the influence of the market system and, more importantly, for us to assume the new (and more relevant) role of *social system designers* in creating a variety of social spaces commensurate to the different needs and activities of the individual. Guerreiro Ramos tried to link the plurality of society (and how we should design enclaves that are reflective of those differences) to a common human condition of ethical concerns that transcend issues of administrative expediency and efficiency. It is a democratic calling that has gone, unfortunately, unheeded in most of the public management/administration and public policy literature.

Admittedly, the question remains how administrators and/or analysts can realistically balance their adherence to this process and, at the same time, implement the mandates of elected and appointed policymakers. After all, how can they serve two masters whose goals and purposes at times may inevitably conflict with one another? This conflict, in varying degrees, goes to the heart of the most important normative issues confronting those in public service. One simple answer to this conflict is that administrators and/or analysts cannot serve two masters—at least with any sense of integrity and honesty. This raises a new point worth thinking about: whether there is an alternative role for administrators and analysts outside their official positions in formal organizations that involves trying to foster a citizenship in their immediate communities or neighborhoods by creating "civic spaces" for citizen involvement and for lively debates. The mandate here is not, of course, to implement any approach as one would in their professional role, but rather to play the role of a citizen whose broader responsibility is to engage in a mutual learning relationship with his or her fellow citizens in examining the normative implications of governmental policies on public life. Whether this can be realistically achieved as citizen-administrators and citizen-analysts in their respective communities is understandably a vexing question. That said, if we are to fully grasp the normative implications of critical democratic thought, it must be linked to other challenges facing public affairs. Let us now turn our attention to what theoretical possibilities it may offer to public management/administration and public policy.

The Challenges and Opportunities of Critical Democratic Thought

Robert Behn (1995) has argued that the "big questions" facing specifically public management/administration involve basically three major conceptual areas: (1) How can public managers break the micromanagement cycle? (2) How can public managers motivate people? And finally, (3) How can public managers measure achievement? What is especially intriguing about these so-called big questions as voiced by Behn, which, I suspect, most practitioners and academicians would probably agree with, is the lack of any interest in "the issues of public administration in a democracy" (Kirlin, 1996, p. 416). In a thoughtful response to Behn's assertions, John Kirlin (1996), on the other hand, contended that any big question(s) of public administration need to satisfy at least four criteria: "(1) achieving a democratic polity; (2) rising to the societal level, even in terms of values also important at the level of individual public organizations; (3) confronting the complexities of instruments of collective action; and (4) encouraging more effective societal learning" (p. 417). As laudatory as Kirlin's analysis seems to be, particularly engaging the field in broader substantive issues than those of just managing agencies (which is a welcome relief), he does not push the logic of his own argument to raise those equally salient concerns.Or, as James O'Connor (1987) has so aptly put it, involving "economic, social, and other problems [that have risen] not because of the personal failings of leaders [but because] of social contradictions of a late [market] economy, society, and the state" (p. 93). Almost astonishingly, Kirlin gives little, if any, consideration to the issue that public management/administration and public policy often find themselves merely "managing" the implications of these social contradictions. O'Connor believes that these social contradictions, and the state's need to manage them successfully given their volatile political nature, involve such contemporary issues as the growing polarization of income and wealth distribution, stagnant wages, and the devastating impact that plant closures can have on local communities. What is important for our purposes is that O'Connor contends that addressing these societal concerns and their underlying causes would require a new approach capable of analyzing the economy, society, and state not as separate spheres of social action, rules, and values but rather as interrelated in a concrete totality.

O'Connor is correct in his call for a reinvigorated theory and practice of how we approach policy issues, but his proposal does not take into account the major obstacle of our time: the impact of a utilitarian culture (both politically and socially) on theory itself, and the resulting implications for practice. As many of the proponents of critical democratic thinking have articulated, a utilitarian culture, when left unchecked, can undermine theory's critical and confrontive aspects. Alvin Gouldner (1971), in an eloquently stated argument on exactly this point explained it this way:

> Insofar as theory is regarded as the least practicable aspect of social science . . . the social science of a utilitarian culture always tends toward a theoryless empiricism, in which the conceptualization of problems is secondary and energies given over to questions of measurement. . . . A conceptual vacuum is thus created, ready to be filled in by the common sense concerns and practical interest of clients, sponsors, and research finders; in this way [any applied discipline] is made useful to their interests. (p. 82)

These two factors—the conceptual interrelationship among economy, society, and the state, and the need for a redefinition independent of a utilitarian approach to theory—have been addressed already in chapter 2, primarily because we tend to be reluctant to raise macrosocietal issues. Here, I delve more deeply into the theory of the modern state and the response that it demands from both fields.

The primary consequences of utilitarian culture on theory and practice in public affairs—political quiescence and nonconfrontativeness—are addressed in their attendant economic, cultural, and political incarnations in the works of Gramsci and Luxemburg. Gramsci's (1971) thinking, while for the most part ignored in the administrative and policy literature due to his Marxist perspective, presents nevertheless two critical issues: (1) the influence of ideology over the economic structure of society, and (2) the saliency of civil society over political society (Bobbi, 1979; Carnoy, 1984; Jessop, 2009). Gramsci's approach would have us concentrate our theoretical enterprise upon those political, moral, and intellectual concepts that shape the interests and needs of the broader culture of society. Hegemony, Gramsci tells us, is a ubiquitous process that is manifested in such things as political parties, the educational system, the cultural apparatus, and the state. More important, Gramsci introduces the concept of "passive revolution," which conveys how governmental institutions undergo constant reorganization and how this reorganization of power merely preserves the dominant hegemony, diverting attention away from the prevailing political and economic institutions and the power they exert.

Gramsci (1971) and Luxemburg (1971) both raise the issue of self-governance and participation in the political process as remedies for the conditions of the modern state, and offer the beginnings of a map toward their realization. For Luxemburg, self-governance would take the form of a council government, where citizens would define and articulate their common interests. These councils, Luxemburg notes, could serve as educational vehicles for what she has referred to as "the enormous productivity of action." These council organizations provide citizens the opportunity to actually practice democracy—a pragmatic undertaking to build a revitalized democracy in every aspect of society. Although Luxemburg (1961), unfortunately, tended to put too much emphasis on the progressive march of history and the primacy of social class, she strongly believed in the creativity of citizens independent of governmental institutions and applauded their spontaneity in action and their right to make mistakes and to learn from them. Both Gramsci and Luxemburg have argued, in their different ways, that democracy itself—in all its complexity and fragility—cannot be separated from the willingness to combat the hegemonic forces that can reify the potential antagonisms in society. Democracy, in short, cannot be divorced from the broader struggle for social justice and equality—a struggle that does not take place among the cobwebs of rules and procedures in the bureaucracy, but rather in the associational public spaces "where freedom can appear . . . and [where] men [and women] act together in concert" (Arendt, 1961, p. 4).

Additionally, Habermas's and Arendt's theoretical works provide a valuable contribution toward the rethinking of the public sphere and the role of new social movements. For example, in Habermas's *The Structural Transformation of the Public Sphere* (1962),he tries to historically analyze the decline of the public in bourgeois society, a decline he aptly has called the "refeudalization of society." In a particularly interesting analysis of Habermas's approach to the public sphere, Seyla Benhabib (1992) offers this astute observation of his thinking:

> [Habermas believes] that the public sphere comes into existence whenever and wherever all affected by general social and political norms of action engage in a practical discourse, evaluating their validity. In effect, there may be as many public as there are controversial general debates about the validity of norms. Democratization in contemporary societies can be viewed as the increase and growth of autonomous public spheres among participants. (p. 87)

What Habermas (1984, 1962), in particular, and critical thought, in general, brings to our attention—admittedly with various degrees of theoretical insight—is the fate of "publicness" in a market society and the importance of social movements (environmental groups, women's rights organizations, etc.) in reasserting the substantive role of participatory decision making outside the direct influence of formal economizing organizations. Notwithstanding Habermas's (1984) acknowledgment that contemporary advanced societies cannot do without large formal organizations and markets, this does not mean that democratic politics can be achieved through the organized political channels of political parties, interest groups, and the like (McCarthy, 1992). Although Habermas does not explicitly admit it, they both seem to be trying to link a democratic political critique of society to a procedural form of radicalism that has some practical intent—an intent that locates points of resistance and political struggle among citizens of color, women, and human rights groups; that can recreate a sense of publicness and that has no resemblance to the public as essentially passive, individualized consumers. Both Arendt and Habermas have argued that the public sphere has deteriorated into an incessant pursuit of private and acquisitive interests. It is interesting to note that Nancy Fraser (1990, p. 77) in her classical article on the public sphere has argued that Habermas tends to deemphasize the elimination of social inequality and how it can "taint deliberations within publics in late capitalist societies." Yet, Habermas and Arendt are also quick to note that with the growth of new social movements this could serve as a way to resurrect public spaces for public discourse and discursive politics in facilitating communicative discourse (Dryzek, 1987).

This intellectual perspective raises some interesting and provocative questions in regard to the relationship between the restructuring of economic life and the restructuring of civic life. A relationship not as just another management or procedural legal issue, but rather as an attempt to ascertain those political and economic forces that can undermine the role of a revitalized citizenship in the modern polity.

Alternatively, critical democratic thought presents the following challenges to public management/administration and public policy: Is it possible to have a view of both fields that can also accommodate a nonutilitarian outlook; that examines the limits (and poses critical questions) of state power (and social power) and analyzes the limits of the market on human associated life; that examines the displacement of social and value conflicts into issues of administration and social analysis; and that theoretically recognizes the contingency of politics and plurality of public life while acknowledging that "to give up the search for [foundational principles] is to resign ourselves to a destiny against which everything that makes us human should compel us to resist" (Jay,1984, p. 537)?

As we contemplate these questions (and the different responses that might emerge) it is worth pondering why so many in both fields have, to a large extent, been reluctant to pose such issues. The specific reasons for this reluctance are open to debate, but for those who want to take up such big questions, Peter Berger (1963, p. 176) offers this comforting thought:

> We locate ourselves in society and thus recognize our own position as we hang from its subtle strings. For a moment we see ourselves as puppets indeed. But then we grasp a decisive difference between the puppet theater and our own drama. Unlike the puppets, we have the possibility of stopping in our movements, looking up and perceiving the machinery by which we have been moved. In this act lies the first step toward freedom.

Admittedly, many of the issues I have raised here run contrary to the conventional thought in both public management/administration and public policy. Many, I know, will conclude that this is an endeavor to romanticize some unrealistic or radical goal for both fields. And, more pointedly, others will see this as a veiled attempt to politicize the activities of the respective disciplines that would only in the end undermine the efficacy of their central role in society. Still, even after saying this, the attraction of critical democratic thought and critical learning process is that it nudges us who "think" about and "do" public management and public policy to realize that the most crucial problems facing us not only involve finding the correct managerial and policy strategy or the proper leadership style; they also involve our partaking in a search for the underlying causes of major social and economic problems (wherever that may take us) and in the process being open—to use Lindblom's (1982) prescient words—"to bring [critical] thought in from the cold." I am not claiming in public policy and public management/administration that administrative issues are not critical in what we do and the role we play in regard to understanding and resolving these issues. Rather, we also need to recognize that central to our intellectual enterprise is an obligation to partake in studying and understanding the critical struggles of our era and not as just another administrative problem to be solved. These struggles are both institutional and normative. They are manifested in the conflicts of politics, economics, and community life and the competing ideals about the individual and society that interplay with them (Hansen, 1976). I think Eric Posner and Glen Weyl (2018, p. B18) got it exactly right: "In an era threatened by rising inequality and authoritarian populism, we hope that boldness rather than caution will be the new watchword."

I know many will strongly disagree with the tone and arguments in this chapter. I hope that, at a minimum, this discussion gets us to think that if we have a past to spring from—as flawed and feeble at times as it may appear—it is beholden on us to take the ethical responsibility of putting that past within a new (and critical) context that now directly addresses the substantive necessities of the citizenry and its active involvement in political life. C. Wright Mills (1963, p. 195) succinctly argued a point that is hard to dismiss:

> [We live in a world where] the seat of rationality is no longer ambiguously the individual; [where] the centers of power are as often hidden as explicit. And so the question becomes whether the ideals [of democracy] themselves must be given up or drastically revised, or whether there are ways of re-articulating them that retain their moral force in a world that moral liberals never made.

This reformulation of the ideals of a democratic public, and the modes of thought needed to nurture it, might just encourage us to redefine our civic purpose, with the help of critical democratic thought and learning, in promoting publicness in a way that does credit to the best in the traditions and ideals of citizenship we value.

Conclusion

Public affairs scholars and practitioners, for the most part, have tended in recent decades to increasingly shy away from the "big questions" facing modern society. For example, those big questions of unequal democracy, political polarization, economic insecurity, and other issues related to political and economic uncertainties that should have subsequently a direct bearing on the theory and practice of public management/administration and public policy. The harmful consequences of this reticence for the public in civic practice, and for conceptions of the public in theory, have been considerable, as outlined in chapter 3. In this chapter, I introduced a framework to combat this trend: critical democratic thought. Drawing from Mills and Ramos, I characterized critical democratic thought in terms of two essential characteristics and four aims. Characteristically, critical democratic thought is both normatively (1) historical and (2) contextual. That is, it grounds empirical and critical analysis in ethical considerations and awareness of historical trends. Functionally, critical democratic thought aims to: (1) prompt citizen-practitioners to take action in determining the terms of their involvement in public life; (2) encourage political experimentation (public learning) to develop methods that advance material and nonmaterial aspects of human dignity; (3) demand that public administrators/policy analysts foster spaces for dissent and debate at all levels of public life; and (4) affirm the importance of an educated citizenry.

Subsequently, I argued that critical democratic thought will be particularly important in challenging the implied norms of our market-driven approach to government in Western democracies today. Following on Arendt and others, I contend that approaches to executing such a challenge are especially important for public leaders in contemporary bureaucracies. Without such approaches, we run the risk of becoming mere cogs in an administrative machine that discourages reflexivity and reform at every turn. However, I draw on Ramos to suggest that practitioners and scholars capable of critical democratic thought and committed to a revitalized theory of publicness might help public affairs by developing fields of inquiry able to design and maintain new social systems that broadly advance the multidimensional needs of the citizenry.

To be effective in this endeavor, I brought Kirlin and O'Connor into dialogue to consider the kinds of questions that critical democratic thought will be most useful in addressing. Although Kirlin offers useful criteria for guiding public affairs away from the technical and narrowly applicable questions commonly fielded today, his standards are lacking in a key regard: their failure to consider what kinds of questions might guide public affairs toward more substantive endeavors. O'Connor highlights this shortcoming, reminding us that the "big questions" in public affairs must approach issues of public relevance: not merely managerial relevance, but issues such as rising economic inequality and social injustice. These issues go beyond the traditional view that we in both fields should mainly confine our attention to administrative questions. Yet, neither thinker sketches the challenge facing public affairs fully. In keeping with the historical attention demanded by critical democratic thought, I returned to Ramos to remind the reader that decades of entanglement between market and state stand in the way of a public affairs practice capable of addressing these sorts of issues.

In closing, I reflected on how critical democratic thought might equip us in public affairs today to challenge what Gramsci identifies as the hegemonic inertia that plagues modern Western democracy. I drew on Luxemburg to argue for active self-government as a logical outcome of applied critical democratic thought. But, I tempered this call by returning to Habermas and Arendt for evidence that self-government flies in the face of the market-centric society. In this context, I asked the reader to consider whether it is possible for public affairs to be committed to both analyzing quantifiable elements of public life that are in demand by contemporary public agencies and government leaders, and, at the same time honor and elevate the quality that makes civic life worthwhile. Looking ahead to the closing chapter of this section of the book, I challenge readers to conceive of what kind of changes may be necessary if critical democratic thought is to be taken seriously.

5

Rationality, the Public Sphere, and the State

> Human dignity needs a new guarantee which can be found only in a new political principle, in a new law on earth, whose validity this time must comprehend the whole of humanity while its power must remain strictly limited, rooted in and controlled by newly defined territorial entities.
>
> —Hannah Arendt

Some of the trends and conditions—and their theoretical consequences—that I have described thus far are not entirely new to scholars of public affairs. The rise of neo-managerialism and the changing role of the state have been of interest to philosophers since Hobbes, although its continuous evolution and, some might say, metastacization, makes it a subject of perennial critical interest. Likewise, the emergence of professionalism in public affairs and the academy more broadly has elicited a vast body of critique both harsh (as in the case of Sheldon Wolin) and hopeful (as in the works of Donald Schon). Guerreiro Ramos eloquently called for a new normative project to streamline and redirect the efforts of public management/administration and public policy as both a discipline and a practice. And in reply (in spirit if not direct intention), Michel Foucault brilliantly deconstructed the notion that any objective normative theory could persist in a field as crisscrossed with fault lines of power and relative significance as public affairs. Guerreiro Ramos and Foucault address in their different ways how publicness must be viewed as part of a substantive rationality approach (Ramos) and within the context of local and specific struggles (Foucault). Both approaches have salient implications for publicness in this era of political and economic uncertainty.

With that said, the larger work of revealing openings for the pragmatic insertion of a reinvigorated theory of publicness into the practice of public affairs can properly begin.

☙

It is particularly ironic that it was none other than Hannah Arendt, who in her own lucid and deliberative analysis of the historical and political forces that would define much of what we regard as the darkest moment of the twentieth century, would also exclaim that "even in the darkest times we have a right to expect some illumination" (1968, pp. ix–x). Alberto Guerreiro Ramos also echoed that same concern in the context of our own dark times, which inevitably strip the individual of human dignity and instead put in place a "behaving" individual, devoid of any notion of a substantive associated life.

Guerreiro Ramos would nod with approval of Jeffrey Isaac's (1998, pp. 198–199) percipient observation of "democracy in dark times"—an observation that merits serious consideration:

> The pathos of modern freedom is the fact that we are subject to the forces of our own creation, expressions of our freedom, and yet the resources available to mitigate these forces are literally pathetic—limited, fragile, destined to be incomplete, frustrating, and unsatisfying. The political world is increasingly like a wasteland, subject to processes of encroaching and intensifying desertification. . . . Even in the most flourishing of the gardens we create the desert encroaches. For this reason it is equally important . . . to cultivate and to preserve those oases in the desert where freedom still thrives, those small and marginal spaces that strive to keep the desert at bay.

However, Guerreiro Ramos, for all his noble theoretical and practical intentions to awaken scholars of public affairs to the importance of these "oases in the desert," seemed to neglect the saliency of powerful economic forces and the complexity of the relationship between the state and civil society—forces that isolate these oases from one another and divert the paths of travelers seeking them.[1] Given these lacunae, it will be argued that, while Guerreiro Ramos draws our attention elsewhere, we need to remain cognizant that the individual and rationality are concomitantly crisscrossed by multiple relations of power. And, we must remain aware that these, in turn, are contingent on the discursive regimes circulating in given places and times, and which can prevent the kinds of public spaces where substantive goals can be pursued.

In the end, Guerreiro Ramos left us not only a mordant critique of contemporary public affairs—a critique overlooked by many—but also a framework that, while somewhat sketchy and underdeveloped, might just help us to escape from the theoretical parochialism that plagues the practice of public affairs in the twenty-first century. Such an escape will imply building upon and going beyond his insights as well as refining some of his theoretical shortcomings. Guerreiro Ramos's *The New Science of Organizations* (1981) serves as our beachhead in this effort.

As I have done in the preceding chapters of this book, *The New Science of Organizations* also challenges us to reevaluate the epistemological underpinnings of public management/administration and public policy. In fact, the very first pages of the book make it clear that Guerreiro Ramos is seeking nothing less than a redefinition of the normative premises of social science. Guerreiro Ramos contends that public administrators, policy analysts, and social scientists in general have become lax in their thinking about the core assumptions of their respective disciplines. That is, both fields' blindness to certain domain assumptions under which they operate. Guerreiro Ramos argues that this intellectual "permissiveness," feeds into supporting the institutional and political status quo, a conclusion that has only continued to be borne out through the end of the twentieth century and into the start of the twenty-first.

Especially for these times, this is a wide-ranging assertion, and Guerreiro Ramos defends it by reviewing the development of rationality in the modern West. He notes that Hobbes's *Leviathan* marked a watershed moment in the West's conceptualization of reason. In Hobbes's work, functional imperatives and an "a-ethical" orientation to the world systematically replaced normative considerations—such as the nature of the good society and the good citizen. This "transvaluation of reason" has stayed with us, continues Guerreiro Ramos, as "mainstream social science in both its academic and popularized versions is largely a footnote to Hobbes" (1981, p. 5).

Guerreiro Ramos's analysis relies to a large extent on the distinction Max Weber made between instrumental rational and value-rational types of social action. The former designates the pursuit of rationally calculated ends, while the latter depends on "a conscious belief in the value for its own sake of some ethical, aesthetic, religious, or other form of behavior, independently of its prospects for success" (Weber, 1968, pp. 24–25). Weber noted that modernity was associated with an increase in the reach and effectiveness of instrumental rationality. This process could be observed in several institutional domains: scientific and technological developments led to an increased understanding of the processes of nature and thus to an "intellectualized" view of the world; liberation of production and exchange from "sentimental obstacles" empowered pursuit of personal gain by an ascendant market economy; juridical formalism enabled individuals to calculate and predict the legal consequences of social actions; and formal and bureaucratic organization allowed for the exercise of a calculable, systematic, and efficient administrative authority (Murphy, 1994, pp. 28–29).

Weber argued that, from "a purely technical [instrumental] point of view," bureaucratic organization is superior to any other form of exercising authority thanks to its "intensive efficiency" and broad scope of operations (Weber, 1968, p. 223). However, Gerth and Mills (1946) point out that Weber also saw bureaucratic organization as "adverse to personal freedom." Weber felt regret for the human being "that the mechanization and the routine of bureaucracy selects and forms . . . a petty routine creature, lacking in heroism, human spontaneity, and inventiveness" (p. 50). But Guerreiro Ramos argues that Weber ultimately resigned himself to the advance of instrumental rationality and indeed referred mostly to this type of social action when developing his theories. In fact, according to Guerreiro Ramos, modern social science in general (and this includes for him the field of public management/administration and public policy) is built on "precarious" assumptions "that the human being is nothing but a reckoning creature and the market the paradigm according to which his associated life should be organized" (1981, p. 22).

Guerreiro Ramos criticizes both fields field for superimposing the premises and requirements of instrumental rationality on the entire scope of human behavior, a thesis which has in various forms been reiterated and developed by the likes of Sheldon Wolin (2008) and Chris Hedges (2011) some thirty years later. Organization theory, for example, argues Ramos, has internalized so much the criteria of efficiency, expediency, and calculation of ends and, therefore is now judged to be the entire range of social conduct. Guerreiro Ramos condemns this trend and argues that not all conduct follows the imperatives of the market; rather, some conduct expresses "concern for the enhancement of the good character of the whole" (1981, p. 28). This "ethical" type of conduct is driven by each person's exercise of his or her substantive reason. The encounter and deliberations of these bearers of substantive rationality are the proper means of designing a good society, argues Guerreiro Ramos.

While it might be argued that his distinction between instrumental rationality and substantive rationality is overstated, we are now in a better position to understand Guerreiro Ramos's critique of both fields and modern social science. The following quote nicely summarizes his concerns:

> Current . . . theory does not systematically distinguish between the substantive and the formal meaning of organizations. This confusion obscures the fact that the formal economizing organization is a recent institutional innovation required by the imperative of capital accumulation and the enhancement of processing capabilities characteristic of the market system. (1981, p. 105)

Guerreiro Ramos urges us to recognize the historical character of economizing considerations and to envision a more substantive approach to public affairs. He does not call for an elimination of market-oriented criteria from our public decisions. In fact, he is quite open to the possibility that a market economy may be the most appropriate and effective approach to producing and delivering goods and services. But he does argue that the market system should be politically regulated. Guerreiro Ramos declares that production "must be managed ethically" (1981, p. 171) and that the criteria of reciprocity, redistribution, and exchange should figure equally in our decisions. In short, both instrumental and substantive rationality have their own crucial and specific roles to play in public affairs.

But Guerreiro Ramos's use of substantive rationality as the guiding principle of public affairs is not unproblematic. Andrews (2000) argues that Weber never awarded substantive rationality the same benevolence that Guerreiro Ramos did. The very fact that substantive rationality is grounded in specific value-sets makes groups espousing regressive values just as likely to invoke it as progressive groups. Indeed, since the time of Andrews's writing, this perspective has come into sharp focus in the context of the increasingly well-documented social agenda of the so-called Radical Right in American politics and elsewhere. The ideological aegis that market-like efficiency is its own normative ends and thus capable of self-regulation, is a view foreshadowed in the writings of Ayn Rand and F. A. Hayek. Conservative elements of the twenty-first-century American political and corporate interests have carried out a similarly political campaign to safeguard their respective interests in the policy process (Mayer, 2016; MacLean, 2017). As such, Andrews's call to amend Ramos's model with a provision for establishing the legitimacy of public decisions is both intellectually astute and urgent.

However, Andrews leaves much to be desired in her prescriptions. She concludes that only a process approaching Habermas's ideal speech situation can ensure that policy goals—be they the outcome of instrumental or substantive decision processes—will gain the endorsement of those affected. She notes that communication allows people to present and critique validity claims irrespective of context or historical period. This "universal pragmatics . . . is ingrained in language itself. Consequently, meaning cannot be disconnected from validity claims of truth, rightness and sincerity" (Andrews, 2000, p. 266). Andrews rightly criticizes Guerreiro Ramos for grounding his analysis in the individual psyche. But her argument for shifting the locus of meaning and validity from the individual to intersubjective communication dismisses too summarily the challenge posed by some critics: that language is not a transparent means of conveying meaning. Further, a call for the application of theory, absent a clear pathway for this process to play out, such as the vast influence of well-established political/corporate networks, is largely ignored outside of the academy. It is this conundrum which the remainder of this chapter better prepares us to address.

In the following section, I criticize Guerreiro Ramos's conceptualization of substantive reason from the perspective of Michel Foucault's writings. I argue that, instead of grounding a critique of instrumental rationality in an individual's conscience, we ought to allow normative standards to emerge from the voices of those who are affected by public decisions and in whose names we often speak. While, as we shall see, Foucault does not offer a panacea to the shortcomings of Ramos's conception, or a solution to its potential for flawed or malicious application, his critique offers the foundation necessary for the modern theorist to make an honest attempt at bridging the gap between social theory and the practice of public affairs.

A View of Substantive Rationality

We have seen that the cornerstone of Guerreiro Ramos's critique of public management/administration and public policy is the distinction he draws between instrumental (or formal) rationality and substantive (or value) rationality. But while Guerreiro Ramos describes the object of his critique—instrumental rationality—carefully and teases out its main characteristics, he leaves substantive rationality somewhat poorly defined and gives few examples of this type of rationality at work. One thing is certain, however: the starting point for his reconceptualization of reason is the individual consciousness. As we shall see, this move makes Guerreiro Ramos's theoretical edifice a prime target of postmodern critique and forces us to think carefully about the political ramifications of grounding an analysis in subject-centered rationality.

Very early in *The New Science of Organizations*, Guerreiro Ramos lays down the groundwork for his critical project. He declares that he will attempt to recover "an age-old sense" of reason that, before Hobbes, was anchored in the individual psyche. This form of reason

> was understood to be a force active in the human psyche which enables the individual to distinguish between good and evil, false and genuine knowledge, and, accordingly, to order his personal and social life. Moreover, the life of reason in the human psyche was envisioned as a reality which resists being reduced to a historical or social phenomenon. (Guerreiro Ramos, 1981, pp. 4–5)

Throughout *The New Science*, Guerreiro Ramos insists on the mind's capacity to function as a moral compass and to discern between true and false knowledge—no doubt, a controversial assertion. There is always a tension for Guerreiro Ramos between an individual's capacity to reason and the demands made by society upon that same individual. For instance, Guerreiro Ramos contended that "rationality in the substantive sense can never be a definitive attribute of society. It is directly apprehended in the human consciousness, not by social mediation" (1981, p. 17). Guerreiro Ramos declares that the human psyche is "the proper site of reason" and "the referent for ordering social life" (1981, p. 23), and proceeds to build a theory of public affairs on these presumptions.

With substantive reasoning firmly positioned in the individual mind, Guerreiro Ramos's model of human life needs two further conditions to allow for the possibility of emancipation from a market-oriented, formal rationality. First, the individual mind needs to perceive reality in an "undistorted" manner. And second, all individuals need to participate in this reality in common. What Guerreiro Ramos's substantive theory ultimately depends on is "the exercise of a sense of reality common to all individuals at all times and everywhere" (1981, p. 43). For Guerreiro Ramos, history is an "intelligible symposium in which all generations and societies understand each other. . . . It is reason, in the substantive sense, which enables human beings to understand the historical varieties of the human predicament." In the next breath, he contends that substantive reasoning, which is part and parcel of the "basic structure of human nature," can provide us with the only viable high ground for evaluating our institutional arrangements and for building a truly critical social theory (p. 43).

But Guerreiro Ramos's conceptualization of substantive reasoning remains somewhat ambiguous.[2] In short, it is unclear how this type of rationality operates and what kinds of judgments it pronounces. Guerreiro Ramos does write that substantive rationality "moves the individual towards a continuous, responsible, and arduous effort to subdue his passions and inferior inclinations" (1981, p. 17), but does not elaborate on what these passions and inclinations might be or why reason should be repelled by them. We get a better sense of Guerreiro Ramos's understanding of substantive rationality in his later discussion of the lack of ethical imperatives in Machiavelli's and Hobbes's political theory. In that context, Guerreiro Ramos declares that wars, mass killings, deceit, and cruelty are "deplorable to common sense" and that only instrumental theories of social action could ever sanction such deeds (1981, p. 52). This is certainly a debatable point. But apart from examples of such black-and-white ethical situations, all that Guerreiro Ramos leaves us with for visualizing substantive rationality at work is his affirmation that values and aims are "inherent in things themselves" (1981, p. 49) and that consciousness of the "intrinsic ends" of things is a precondition for proper ethical conduct (1981, p. 45).

Guerreiro Ramos cites Max Horkheimer in *The New Science*, and the two authors' conceptualization of reason is strikingly similar. Horkheimer, like Guerreiro Ramos, distinguishes between a type of reason concerned with utilitarian calculations of means and ends, and a type that finds its sustenance in "the objective world" and which focuses on the notion of the greatest good and the "realization of ultimate goals" (Horkheimer, 1947, p. 4). Horkheimer makes it clear that the "objective" form of reasoning is rooted in "the nature of things, and that the right human attitude springs from such insight." He allows for differences of age, sex, or status, among others, in perceiving such objective truths, but he is committed to the idea that an objective "insight is universal in so far as its logical connection with the attitude is theoretically self-evident for each imaginable subject endowed with intelligence" (1947, pp. 10–11). Guerreiro Ramos credits Horkheimer with diagnosing the pernicious shift of reason from the human psyche to society, even if he ultimately criticizes him for failing to offer an adequate remedy for our present condition. Both authors agree that only by affirming the truth inherent in things themselves can one's identity fully unfold and confront critically the social and economic demands made by modern political life.

The theoretical seductiveness of this stance is immediately apparent. But, its shortcomings are far more consequential. As a narrative, the notion that a normative basis for rationality resides in each of us is powerful. It appeals to our desire for both normative certainty and simplicity, two commodities in increasingly short supply in the modern practice of public affairs. However, Michel Foucault offers an alternative narrative that articulates some of the potential theoretical shortcomings of Ramos's thinking, which merits attention. This is an issue to which I will now turn.

The Foucauldian Challenge

If Guerreiro Ramos's substantive rationality does not quite offer adequate guidance to practitioners of public affairs seeking to slow the onslaught of neo-mangerialism and a distortive conception of rationality, where then ought we to turn? Some point to the relevance of the postmodern tradition as a likely answer. Guerreiro Ramos's terms and categories of thought—the discerning human psyche, its rational access to reality, and a common participation in this reality—are problematized by authors working within this framework. These authors are frequently criticized for not providing systematic political theories to replace the grand narratives of the past that make up their favorite targets of criticism. But it can be argued that an author such as Michel Foucault not only provides important critiques of notions such as reason and subjectivity, but also points us in the direction of a responsible and practical basis for a critique of instrumental rationality in both public management/administration, public policy, and social science in general.[3]

One of Foucault's key theoretical contributions, and one of the most pertinent to this discussion, concerns the role of the individual in history and human affairs. In a series of studies of human experiences such as madness, discipline, and sexuality, Foucault attempts to remove the individual subject from the central role that humanist histories usually reserve for it. Instead, Foucault's analyses focus on discursive practices—systems that make knowledge possible. These practices arise at the intersection of "institutions, economic and social processes, behavioral patterns, systems of norms, techniques, types of classification, modes of characterization" (Foucault, 1972, p. 45). For example, in his analysis of the emergence of the modern disciplinary complex, Foucault uncovers "elements of discourse and architecture, coercive regulations, and scientific presuppositions in a single functional apparatus for the correction of delinquency" (Patton, 1987, p. 232).

Foucault tries to show that statements and preoccupations typically seen as originating in the individual mind are in fact determined by discursive rules and regularities. One of Foucault's central questions is "Who speaks?" or better yet, "Who is allowed to speak?" on specific subjects and topics. Not every individual is allowed to utter authoritative statements on, say, madness or social well-being. Discourses not only give rise to the objects and concepts of various sciences and disciplines (disciplines such as psychiatry or clinical medicine), but also endow specific sites (such as the hospital, laboratory, or research library) and positions (such as that of the medical examiner or lab technician) with the right to speak to and extend our knowledge. Foucault declares that he is not interested in seeing "discourse as a phenomenon of expression—the verbal translation of a previously established synthesis; instead I shall look for a field of regularity for various positions of subjectivity" (1972, p. 55). Rather than assuming the presence of a consciousness with access to a pure and synthesizing form of rationality that simply needs to be expressed in words, Foucault documents the systematic "dispersion" of the speaking subject to the various sites and positions sanctioned by discourse.

Furthermore, Foucault argues that our criteria for differentiating between true and false knowledge are also effects of discourse. His studies tend to focus on the breaks or discontinuities in discursive practices and the subsequent impact on our characterization of knowledge and truth. The notion of unmediated access to reality has no room in Foucault's analyses. Our perception of reality is always a function of the historical and contingent discursive "regime" in which we operate. Speaking on the development of medicine, Foucault states that,

> [u]p to the end of the eighteenth century one has a certain type of discourse whose gradual transformation, within a period of twenty-five or thirty years, broke not only with the "true" propositions which it had hitherto been possible to formulate, but also, more profoundly, with the ways of speaking and seeing, the whole ensemble of practices which served as supports for medical knowledge. These are not simply new discoveries, there is a whole new "regime" in discourse and forms of knowledge. (1980a, p. 112)

It is important to note that Foucault does not conceive of discursive regimes—that is, the practices that produce truth and knowledge—as bearing down on the individual human being as so many other social forces. Rather, Foucault proposes that discourses have a *productive* nature. The individual is *created,* rather than constrained, by discursive practices. In *Discipline and Punish*, Foucault (1977) argues that the increased accumulation and centralization of knowledge on the individual (through practices such as record keeping and surveillance) goes hand in hand with the emergence of disciplined and "docile" bodies. In Foucault's words, "It is not that the beautiful totality of the individual is amputated, repressed, altered by our social order, it is rather that the individual is carefully fabricated in it, according to a whole technique of forces and bodies" (1977, p. 217). Ultimately, for Foucault, the production of truth and the exercise of power presuppose each other. We institutionalize, professionalize, and reward the pursuit of knowledge of humans as psychological, biological, moral, or other kind of beings (Foucault, 1980a, p. 93). In turn, we employ this knowledge to classify individuals (as mad, ill, delinquent, etc.) and to judge them against such distinct norms as appropriate age-group attainment scales, cholesterol levels, income, etc. (Rouse, 2005). It is noteworthly at this point to briefly mention his concept of biopolitics. While it is not my purpose here to give an extensive analysis of biopolitics, this concept is crucial to note because it focuses attention on understanding governance as an integral part of the rise of the technologies of governance—technologies that govern both human social and biological processes. Foucault put it this way:

> To say that power took possession of life in the nineteenth century . . . is to say it has, thanks to the play of technologies of discipline on the one hand and technologies of regulations on the other, succeeded in covering the whole surface that lies between the organic and the biological, between body and population. We are, then, in a power that has taken control of both the body and life or that has . . . taken control of life in general—with the body as one pole and the population as the other. (1976, p. 252–253)

Putting aside his awkward wording, biopolitics is in essence a social field of power, struggle, and conflict and as a political rationality that perceives population as a political and scientific problem (Foucault, 2008). Accordingly, government through its regulative function serves as political power over life, or, as he so candidly argued, the management of the population. Hence, from a Foucauldian perspective, Guerreiro Ramos's reliance on individual insight alone into the reality of things as the basis for a critical theory is highly problematic. Guerreiro Ramos assumes the existence of a discerning individual whose inner "basic structure" can evaluate and put forward the right ethical response to our present condition. One objection that a Foucauldian critic would raise to Guerreiro Ramos's conceptualization is that it fails to account for the effects of discursive practices on the notion of the individual. Flax (1993, p. 96) summarizes the critique of the individual subject leveled by an author such as Foucault, and merits to be quoted at some length:

> Postmodernists insist that subjectivity is a discursive effect, not a transcendental, ahistoric, and unchanging, objective status, entity, or state. These theorists have begun to delineate the political genealogies of subjectivity and how its "nature" is constituted and transformed over time. They also insist concepts of subjectivity operate as regulative ideals within historically delimited contexts. . . . Such ideals are the product of complex knowledge/power networks. These networks generate interdependent categories of subjective experience such as health/pathology that underwrite and legitimate therapeutic and punitive social interventions.

Flax argues that the Cartesian ideal of an independent rational subject—and the theories built on this ideal—enforce normative hierarchies such as mind/body, reason/affection, male/female. She declares that "the unitary self is an effect of many kinds of relations of domination. It can only sustain its unity by splitting off or repressing other parts of its own and others' subjectivity" (1993, p. 109).

In contrast to Guerreiro Ramos's Aristotelian categories of analysis—intrinsic ends, final causes, full actualizations—Foucault's analyses seek neither the "true" origins of things nor their "true" purposes. Foucault submits that "there is 'something altogether different' behind things: not a timeless and essential secret, but the secret that they have no essence or that their essence was fabricated in a piecemeal fashion from alien forms" (1980b, p. 142). Friedrich Nietzsche, for example, argued that something's "purpose" and "meaning" are constantly "reinterpreted to new ends, taken over, transformed, and redirected by some power superior to [them]" (1967, p. 77). Foucault subscribes to Nietzsche's approach and declares that his own aim is not to recover the eternal origins of things, but to render visible the "discontinuities" that cross them (Foucault, 1980b). While Foucault never claims to offer a universal theory of our condition (he insists that his conceptual and methodological tools are suggested by the particular human experiences he studies) it is important to ask what site he himself occupies when he criticizes institutions such as psychiatry, medicine, and the penal system. If power relations determine all knowledge, how can anyone engage discourses critically?

Foucault offers an interesting, if not altogether satisfying, answer to these questions. He states that criticisms are always local and contingent. The critical dimension of his studies lies precisely in the meticulous and careful "rediscovery of struggles" beneath seemingly unitary, scientific, and universal discourses. He attempts to follow the traces of "low-ranking knowledges, these unqualified, even directly disqualified knowledges (such as that of the psychiatric patient, of the ill person, of the nurse, of the doctor—parallel and marginal as they are to the knowledge of medicine—that of the delinquent, etc.)" (Foucault, 1980a, p. 82). His critical endeavor consists in using these local, marginal, and unofficial knowledges to counter the universalizing claims of organized, powerful, scientific discourses.

Best and Kellner (1991) state that "a Foucauldian postmodern politics . . . attempts to break with unifying and totalizing strategies, to cultivate multiple forms of resistance, to destroy the prisons of received identities and discourses of exclusion, and to encourage the proliferation of differences of all kinds" (pp. 56–57). But the authors rightly criticize Foucault for failing to fully develop a theory of resistance. Terms such as *struggle, power relations,* and *resistance* remain woefully undertheorized in Foucault's writings. Despite Foucault's emphasis on local and specific struggles, he does not put forward a theory of how oppositional political movements might develop or how publicness can express itself (Best & Kellner, 1991, pp. 69–71).

As has been intimated in chapters 2 and 3, a conceptual foundation for the reinvigoration of publicness in the social sciences remains the necessary gap between critical thought and practice (in every sense of the word) that must be closed. And yet, the presence of this disconnect is disturbingly evident in contemporary global politics, specifically in the rise of populism fueled by a dangerous and novel "post-truth" approach to creating governing narratives. Nowhere is this trend toward post-truth politics more evident than in the forty-fifth presidency of the United States, whose willingness to deny the validity of information that in a previous political climate would be considered reliable fact (Leonhardt & Thompson, 2017) and to label politically inconvenient reporting as "Fake News" (Barbash, 2018), in order to bolster the appeal of his populist narrative. Interestingly, one could argue that the theoretical routes of post-truth politics are alarmingly evident in the very resistance ideology established by Foucault.

In the claim that "there is 'something altogether different' behind things: not a timeless and essential secret, but the secret that they have no essence or that their essence was fabricated in a piecemeal fashion from alien forms" (1980b, p. 142), Foucault might very well be putting words to the normative assumptions that appear to undergird Trump's post-truth politics. To Trump and his media machine, the truth of things appears strictly to be delimited by what they can be fashioned into. The Trump administration's recent response to evidence that President Trump sought to fire the special counsel appointed to investigate allegations of his collusion with Russia in the 2016 presidential election, makes an exceptional case point. In political climate more strictly governed by multiple claims to what is or is not valid information in deciphering "truth," the preponderance of evidence would pose a serious obstacle for the accused party. However, in the present climate, the allegation appears much more significant for its potential to be refashioned in support of Trump's populist, antiestablishment narrative. His response to the accusations as "Fake news," (Barbash, 2018) appear to have gained sufficient traction, at least with his political base, to further discredit the once-respected mainstream news media, and to insulate Trump from their critiques. To make reality by simply claiming it to be so, is nothing short, albeit in its worst manifestations, of a masterful performance of Foucauldian postmodernism.

Performance, as it happens, is a crucial consideration in our investigation of the cooption of postmodern resistance theory by political demagogues. Although postmodern theory has without question been empowering and liberating in the life of social theory writ large, we must acknowledge that it can also be coopted by potential antidemocratic forces. To understand this development, *performance* is the operant term. Politics has, arguably, always been a matter of performance. However, the current political moment is characterized by a novel style and media context, which jointly constitute fertile ground for the dangerous applications of postmodern meaning making evidenced by the Trump administration.

In his masterful debut *The Global Rise of Populism: Performance, Political Style, and Representation* (2016), Benjamin Moffitt makes the case that the modern incarnation of populism (of which we consider Trump to be exemplary) is a political style characterized by opportunistic presentations of a crisis. He writes: "The leader is the figure that performs and renders-present 'the people' within populism" (2016, p. 52), going on to articulate the ways in which the leader's performance gives form to a previously inchoate collective whose values are reflected and crystalized in the leader's (preexisting) platform (p. 53). Likewise, he observes that: "populist actors actively 'perform' and perpetuate a sense of crisis, *rather than simply reacting to existing crisis.* Moreover, this performance of crisis allows populists an effective way to divide 'the people' and 'the elite', and to legitimate strong leadership by presenting themselves as voices of the sovereign people" (2016, p. 118; my emphasis). Again, we see the populist leader as a shaper or creator of truth, whose formulations of crisis—like their formulations of "the people"—have more to do with expediency and narrative power than any empirical or normative reality.

In suggesting twenty-first-century populism as a key factor in the subversion of postmodern resistance theory to the service of political demagoguery, we must—as Moffitt does—acknowledge that populism itself is not a new political style. As such, we must seek an explanation for its new relationship to social theory. Here also, Moffitt offers valuable insights. In his estimation, contemporary populism is very much a part (that is, both product and co-producer) of the media landscape of the twenty-first century. He observes that modern populists have demonstrated a remarkable canniness in their use of novel media forms (e.g., social media and an increasingly corporate print media), and goes on to suggest that "the wider trend of mediatisation [of politics] has come to affect the shape of the political in these 'spectacular' time" (2016, p. 73). Crucially, these media are ideally suited to performance, and also demand it: "[A] growing number of political actors who wish to enter and succeed in the political arena seem increasingly compelled to adopt *some* version of the populist style in order to gain media coverage and obtain political success" (2016, p. 77). He follows with the observation that "some of the most successful cases of populism in recent years have come from leaders who literally *own or control* parts of the mass media" (2016, p. 81). The relationship is bilateral and catalyzed by the ever-tightening hold of corporate powers and values upon public institutions and their private adjacents. And it is a relationship positioning the modern populist demagogue ideally to engage in the sort of radical acts of anti-empirical interpretation that have enabled, in part, Trump's rise to power. Let us now turn to a discussion of other thinkers who offer a different conceptualization of these critical issues.

The Nature of the Public Sphere: Leonard's Reconciliation and Arendtian Influences

Guerreiro Ramos's critique of instrumental rationality in public affairs theorizing is compelling, although his reliance on subject-centered reasoning as the normative grounds of criticism remains highly problematic. And while Foucault urges us to pay attention to the discontinuities in our knowledge of the self and of the social order, as well as to the political effects of totalizing knowledge claims, he does not offer a compelling normative grounding for a critical approach to public affairs needed to safeguard his postmodern stance from being coopted for antidemocratic purposes. In light of this, I ask the following: Is there a path forward from the theoretical insights of Ramos and Foucault that can serve the liberating and democratic ideals to which both theorists aspired?

Stephen Leonard (1990) suggests an interesting perspective on this predicament, and I conclude this section with a brief discussion of his ideas. Leonard's project is to provide a sound base for a critique of dominant "disciplinary orthodoxies" and their universalizing claims of truth and objectivity. He shares with Guerreiro Ramos a commitment to balancing instrumental forms of rationality with normative considerations. Leonard attempts to build a critical theory that "undermines the all-too-common tendency today to treat practical, political issues as if they could be answered in purely technocratic, instrumental terms. [Critical theory] provides good reasons for seeing that it is moral and political argument that should guide our instrumental interests, and not the reverse" (1990, p. 267). Leonard notes, however, that the modernist theories of Marx, the Frankfurt School, and Habermas share a normative universalism that closes them off to "the plurality of ways in which emancipation might be realized" (1990, p. 258). Furthermore, Leonard contends that Foucault's critique appears to be unable to nourish a collective form of resistance to dominating discourses. Instead of seeking a normative grounding for critical theory within theory itself, Leonard proposes that we verify our knowledge claims in actual struggles for empowerment of what publicness should denote. He provides examples of "critical theory in practice" such as feminist theory and Paulo Freire's critical pedagogy. Leonard believes that these theories' expression of concrete political struggles makes them capable of projecting ways of life "in which particular forms of domination have been overcome" (1990, p. 266). While not providing us with universal standards of right and wrong, of the "good" citizen and the "good" polity, these politically committed forms of theorizing allow us to envision better selves and better lives in the confrontation with the globalizing tendencies of instrumental forms of reasoning and the resurgence of antidemocratic governments.

The normative basis of this critique ought not to be attached to an ahistorical insight into the true nature of things. Rather, it must emerge from solidarity with the victims of history. Leonard concludes that "when we take the perspective of those whole lives are most damaged, most distorted, most deformed, we are in a better position to understand what is required for us to act responsibly and rationally" (1990, p. 269). Empathy and openness to difference—not transcendental forms of rationality—are among the prerequisites of a responsible engagement of achieving publicness in comparison with the increasingly broader reach of the utilitarian criteria of efficiency and expediency.

Premonitions of this insight can be glimpsed in the work of past theorists. Having argued that instrumental forms of rationality and economizing considerations provide the principal bearings of contemporary public management/administration and public policy theory, Guerreiro Ramos proceeds to discuss a model of social organization that addresses utilitarian human needs *along with* substantive ones. A key aspect of Guerreiro Ramos's proposed model is the correspondence between various types of human concerns and the sites (or "enclaves") in which these concerns can be expressed. Guerreiro Ramos emphasizes that the marketplace cannot, and should not, provide the sole context for human actualization: "The sites where human beings are to come to grips with issues of their actualization, properly understood, have system requirements other than those of economizing settings" (1981, p. 117). Guerreiro Ramos's call for a "para-economic paradigm" for ordering human affairs attempts to limit the reach of utilitarian concerns to well-defined enclaves and allow for the pursuit of substantive goals outside of market-dominated settings.

Such a multidimensional model of human organization not only has practical consequences, but also forces public administration and policy theorists to think about the normative implications of their own analytical tools and categories. Guerreiro Ramos's charge is that conventional administrative theory and policy theory "is predicated on a unidimensional model of the individual which envisions social space as horizontal and flat: wherever the individual goes, he never leaves the market" (1981, p. 123). This is an important criticism of human affairs theorizing, and it is useful to trace some of the finer points of Guerreiro Ramos's analysis back to one of his main sources of inspiration: the writings of Hannah Arendt.

In *The Human Condition*, Arendt (1958) distinguishes between three fundamental human activities: labor, work, and action. Labor is concerned with the satisfaction of biological needs and with things necessary for subsistence. Work creates lasting objects and is marked by a strongly utilitarian ethos; its products—tools, furniture, buildings, works of art, etc.—are meant for use rather than consumption. But Arendt argues that neither labor nor work allows a person to reveal his or her individuality. That enabling capacity belongs only to action, an activity that is carried out in the public realm, "directly between men." Action, on the other hand, is concerned neither with necessary things nor with useful ones. Its function is to allow individuals to come together ("neither for nor against" each other) and reveal their unique distinctiveness. Action is thus sharply opposed to conformity and habit. It expresses itself in words and deeds unconstrained by external forces and free of biological and economic imperatives.

Arendt's significance for Guerreiro Ramos is twofold. First, she argues that each of the activities she describes—labor, work, and action—denotes a proper location associated with it in the world. The proper locus of action, for example, is "the organization of the people as it arises out of acting and speaking together. . . . It is the space of appearance in the widest sense of the word, namely, the space where I appear to others as others appear to me, where men . . . make their appearance explicitly" (1958, pp. 198–199).

Arendt's influence is unmistakable in Guerreiro Ramos's first guideline for a new theory of organizations: "Man has different kinds of needs, the satisfaction of which demands multiple types of social settings. It is possible not only to categorize such types of social systems but also to formulate the operational conditions peculiar to each of them" (Guerreiro Ramos, 1981, p. 118). Guerreiro Ramos devotes a substantial portion of *The New Science* to a description of six such social settings and the relationships between them. Two of these social spaces merit closer scrutiny, for they point to the crux of Guerreiro Ramos's argument and they show the importance of his thinking to public affairs scholarship and the differing conceptualizations of publicness.

But first we should note that Guerreiro Ramos does not reject rent-seeking behavior in itself. He simply insists that the space of the economy should not encircle the entire range of human activities. Thus, in an *isonomy*, profit and revenue are merely incidental to the participants' concerns. What matters instead is freedom from coercion and superimposed organizational constraints. In this enclave, people seek consensus on public issues; they come together as equals, in order to "enhance the good life of the whole"

(Guerreiro Ramos, 1981, p. 131). The classic example of an isonomy is the Greek *polis,* but Guerreiro Ramos believes that modern arrangements such as parent-teacher associations and neighborhood organizations point to the same human need for engagement in substantive decisions.

A second enclave discussed by Guerreiro Ramos, the *phenonomy,* is similarly characterized by a lack of subordination to the demands of the market. This setting is "necessary for people to release their creativity in autonomously selected forms and ways and is part of the expressive endeavor . . . which mobilizes the creative efforts of a small group or a single individual" (Guerreiro Ramos, 1981, p. 133). Guerreiro Ramos lists freelance artists, writers, and craftsmen as examples of persons engaged in phenonomies. These individuals are expressing their unique distinctiveness at the same time as they are adding something substantive to the life of the community.

Guerreiro Ramos's multidimensional model of human organization is an important resource for any public management/administration or public policy theory that aims to account for both instrumental *and* substantive concerns. Its conceptualization of the human person goes beyond the notion of the rational, calculating individual and allows for an original and critical engagement with society's demands. But it is Guerreiro Ramos's reading of a second claim made by Hannah Arendt that gives his model its real punch.

Arendt asserts that the ancient Greeks regarded labor—that is, activities geared solely toward the maintenance of life—with contempt: "[W] hat men share with all other forms of animal life was not considered to be human" (Arendt, 1958, p. 84). In modern times, however, labor has risen through the ranks of human activities until it has come to occupy the highest position. Arendt's indictment of modern society is quite pointed:

> We have almost succeeded in leveling all human activities to the common denominator of securing the necessities of life and providing for their abundance. Whatever we do, we are supposed to do for the sake of "making a living"; such is the verdict of society, and the number of people, especially in the professions who might challenge it, has decreased rapidly. (1958, pp. 126–127)

Arendt argues that, as long as activities concerned with consumption and accumulation dominate the public realm, only the market can dictate our behavior. There is no room left for action—the encounter between individuals who are more than just economic actors. Guerreiro Ramos picks up this line of thinking when he makes the case that isonomies and phenonomies—settings where economic considerations are only incidental to quality of life concerns—are in decline. In contemporary society, argues Guerreiro Ramos, "the market tends to become an all-inclusive category for ordering individual and social life" (1981, p. 129). To counter the propensity of the market to colonize other enclaves, Guerreiro Ramos's multidimensional model of organization calls for a restriction of the economy to its own space. Unless we recognize the limits of the economy (as well as of the other enclaves) we obstruct the unfolding of certain fundamental human activities.

The practical and contentious consequence of this multidimensional model is that the market needs to be delimited and regulated politically. Guerreiro Ramos believes that we should not employ the criteria of efficiency, expediency, and calculation of ends to judge each and every human endeavor. Different activities have different procedural, cognitive, spatial, and temporal requirements. Guerreiro Ramos declares that

> [t]he multicentric society is a deliberate undertaking. It implies design and implementation of a new kind of state empowered to formulate and enforce allocative policies supportive not only of market-oriented pursuits, but of social settings suited for personal actualization, convivial relationships, and community activities of citizens as well. (1981, p. 135)

While Guerreiro Ramos emphasizes that his model does not imply socialism, he admits that the state must exercise some level of control over the economy, lest market goals and priorities dominate all of the other social enclaves.

Guerreiro Ramos does not flesh out the role of the state in nurturing a model of organization that allows for both economic and quality-of-life pursuits. But his brief discussion of how a "para-economic," multidimensional society might be brought into effect clearly hints at the state's crucial responsibility for ensuring that the market does not usurp the entire range of human activities, thus leading to a one-dimensional view of publicness. No doubt, the relationship between the state and the public sphere needs to be better articulated. Guerreiro Ramos assumes that the state can implement policies that strike a balance between instrumental and substantive imperatives. However, before such an assumption becomes tenable, we need to find that the state is indeed capable of protecting the public sphere, and that it can continue to do so even in the wake of globalization with its attendant challenges of political and economic uncertainty.

The State, Citizenship, and Globalization: Taking Guerreiro Ramos's Project Forward

In Guerreiro Ramos's formulation, the state appears to operate quite autonomously of the public sphere (made up of social enclaves such as isonomies, phenonomies, and economies) and is potentially the main source of policies that combine a classic economic calculus with normative concerns. But Poggi's (1978) classic study of the development of the modern state suggests that the line between civil society and the state has become blurred in the twentieth century. According to Poggi, one needs to be careful when calling for a political regulation of the economy, for the political system and the economy, both public pursuits and private, are no longer clearly differentiated. Poggi's argument is straightforward: "The institutional differentiation between sociocultural and economic processes on the one hand and political processes on the other, which was characteristic of the West in the nineteenth century, has largely ceased to operate in our own" (Poggi, 1978, p. 121).

Poggi cites several causes for the "compenetration" of state and society. Some of the main factors that undermine the state/society separation originate in the desire of certain economic actors to maximize their economic advantage. (Poggi lists as examples the pressures of trade unions and employers' associations impacting the formulation of public policies.) Other factors are introduced by the dominating presence of large (often multinational) corporations in the West's economies. Poggi declares that "the control that the large firms exercise over the economic process and hence over the whole societal realm allows them to influence the state itself, to persuade the state at the very least not to 'interfere' with their activities, and at best to place some of its faculties of rule at their disposal" (1978, 129).

But another reason for the increased overlap between state and societal concerns, according to Poggi, is found in the state's need for new sources of legitimacy, following the faltering significance of procedural rules (Weber's "legal rationality") and international conflict. Beginning in the 1950s and 1960s, nation-states in the West began to promote "economic growth" or "affluence" as their principal goals. Since that time, the business of government has been performed "through acts of rule that assist the economic system in producing an ever-increasing flow of goods and services for the consumer" (Poggi, 1978, p. 134). This has enormous consequences for the relationship between the state and the public sphere. Given that one of the state's principal concerns is to increase the national gross domestic product—a technical, rather than a political, goal—what the state seeks is professional expertise, not substantive debate. Increasingly, Poggi argues, administrative decisions are "articulated in a language that effectively screens them from parliamentary criticism and public debate" (1978, p. 142). Once expert opinion drives policy formulation, the citizen is shut out of the decision-making process. Poggi's account seems to suggest that the relationship between the state and civil society is thornier than Guerreiro Ramos allows.

But what exactly do we understand by the category of *citizen*? In a remarkable essay, David Held (1989) argues that, historically, citizenship has entailed membership in a community. Membership, in turn, has involved "degrees of participation in the community" (p. 199). That is to say, it is about the "involvement of people in the community in which they live; and people have been barred from citizenship on grounds of gender, race, and age among many other factors" (ibid.). Held submits that various social movements (he lists feminism, reproductive rights, and animal rights activism as examples) have attempted to enlarge, in various ways, the boundaries that define citizenship. The struggle over the meaning of citizenship has been "a, if not the, central medium of social conflict—the medium through which various classes, groups and movements strive to enhance and protect their rights and opportunities" (1989, p. 200). Margaret Somers (2008), in her brilliant analysis of a social theory of citizenship, has forcefully argued that citizenship has been largely privatized in political arguments, being "reduced to a cluster of prepolitical, antipublic, and naturalized attributes of the market, mechanism of global commerce, and a political culture of antistatism" (p. 287).

Both Held's and Somers's conceptualizations of citizenship compel us to think about the many political battles that have been, and continue to be, fought by different social groups to gain recognition in the community. It is imperative that our social designs allow for spaces in which a diversity of political and civil rights can be pursued. The affirmation of diverse citizenship rights strengthens civil society, even as it reveals the complexity of social relations that influence who is and who is not allowed to participate in the life of the community.

Guerreiro Ramos never intended *The New Science of Organizations* to be more than a theoretical prolegomenon to a model of social organization that allows humans to appear as full, dignified beings as they deliberate on the issues facing them. Future scholarship on multidimensional models of civil society would benefit from employing a definition of citizenship that highlights the many struggles for affirmation that go on in our midst. The importance of critical democratic thought and a revigorated publicness can play a central role in this process. An analysis grounded in these types of action not only broadens our vision of the public sphere, but also counters the depoliticizing thrust of what Beck (2000, p. 9) calls "globalism": the notion "that the world market eliminates or supplants political action—that is, the ideology of rule by the world market, the ideology of neoliberalism." Only by maintaining an inclusive perspective in our analyses—a pluralist social science that can scrutinize ecological, cultural, and political processes, along with economic ones—can the globalist ideology be explored in terms of its impact on publicness.

Beck contends that social science has been subscribing to a "methodological nationalism": the assumption that society and the nation-state are coextensive. According to Beck, the intensification of globalization means that we can no longer presuppose that space is defined and controlled by the state:

> This architecture of thinking, acting and living within state-cum-social spaces and identities *collapses* in the course of economic, political, ecological, cultural and biographical globalization. World society means the emergence of new power opportunities and new social spaces for action, living and perception, which break up and muddle the nation-state orthodoxy of politics and society. (2000, pp. 64–65)

A substantive theory of human organization must take these "new social spaces for action" into account. Following a cue from Robertson (1995), theories that attempt to build on Guerreiro Ramos's project need to pay attention to the increasingly "glocal" character of the public sphere, that is, to the notion that "what is called local is in large degree constructed on a trans- or super-local basis" (Robertson, 1995, p. 26). An inclusive conception of citizenship and a "glocal" view of society ought to be among the principal features of a critique of public affairs that uses and refines Guerreiro Ramos's ideas while broadening our view of publicness, a point that will be raised in a subsequent chapter dealing with the forces of globalization on social spaces.

Conclusion

With this chapter, I close the first section of this book by examining how the two core theoretical perspectives I proposed—a revitalized concept of the public, and the application of critical democratic thought to public affairs—have interfaced, and may continue to interface, with the realities of modern political and administrative affairs. And, in the absence of a tradition and method to shape their application, I revealed the risk that these theories can be, ironically, sometimes co-opted by powerful political forces, by which a public social science should stand.

To this point, I explore how the metastasis of neo-managerial and market influences has advanced, and how both Foucauldian discursive rationality and Ramos's substantive rationality are subverted. The question facing those of us who teach and practice in public affairs, then, is whether these trends can be reversed through the application of different ways of approaching these issues. Obviously, this project is no different in its fundamentals than the projects undertaken by Ramos, Foucault, Arendt, or countless others; it is the goal of the public affairs theorist to observe what warrants correcting and, by proposing a better way forward, affect its remedy. So, I asked whether the present undertaking—guided by critical democratic thought in the service of a revitalized view of publicness—has any greater chance of success than those efforts whose shortcomings are discussed in this chapter.

In response, I paraphrased Foucault's notion of the contextuality of meaning, and Ramos's implication that communities and institutions should also be viewed a project of social system design. At this particular political moment, there is a growing awareness—among both scholars and the public—that things are not right. The populist resurgence described by Moffitt is built on the expression of discontent and desire for a sea change in the nature of public life evident in the United States, and the across the globe. Movements such as Me Too, Black Lives Matter, and student outcries against political inaction on gun violence are also forms of resistance to the economizing and atomizing forces bearing down on the public oases where Arendt's notion of "action" continues to thrive. In the context of such resistance, I suggest that the moment may be ripe for a new sense of publicness, and a new mode of critical democratic thought to reshape civic practice.

With examples of civic-minded social movements, Leonard offers a perspective that supports this claim. In other words, it is a perspective that positions itself to be accessible to those who are politically and economically least well off and is formulated as a means of empowering them to reshape our public life. The question before us is whether we can redefine the professionalization of what we do, and assert a new set of critical and confrontive norms in place of the domain assumptions of neo-managerialism and the market presuppositions that have tended to dominate our thinking. If this can be achieved, the next generation of scholars and practitioners may be able to work from a foundation that honors both substantive reason and the significance of context and relativity as contributors to the stewardship of publicness in this era of political and economic uncertainty. In the second section of this book, I investigatethree contemporary challenges confronting public affairs scholars and practitioners today.

Section 2

Contemporary Challenges

6

The Enduring Implications of the Economic Crisis of 2008

> The charm of history and its enigmatic lesson consist in the fact that, from age to age, nothing changes and yet everything is completely different.
>
> —Aldous Huxley

On an overcast morning on October 23, 2008, Alan Greenspan, the chair of the Federal Reserve from 1987–2006, looked particularly uncomfortable as he gazed at the members of the U.S. House Committee on Oversight and Government Reform. He suspected that many members of this committee were eager to ask some rather difficult questions concerning his specific role in the policies that might have contributed to the economic meltdown that started in 2008. As one of the leading advocates of deregulating the financial markets and an ardent supporter of a free-market ideology, Greenspan admitted—with almost a monotone pitch to his voice—that he indeed found a flaw in his ideology. "I made a mistake," he conceded, with his head lowered as he spoke. In the next breath, he acknowledged that he was, in fact, shocked "because [he] had been going for 40 years, or more, with very considerable evidence that [the market] was working exceptionally well" (cited in Cassidy, 2009, p. 6).

Since that time, the disturbing ripple effects of this economic crisis have continued to reverberate throughout citizens' lives here and abroad, leaving, among other things, a troubling set of questions for those of us in public affairs. This chapter will not attempt to explain how this crisis started, a topic that is, after all this time, still part of an ongoing debate.

Notwithstanding the myriad of competing explanations of the economic crisis, there is nevertheless a growing consensus among economists regarding the salient factors that played a definitive role.[1] Putting aside for the moment the nature of this debate, I am more interested in exploring what specific lessons can be learned from this cataclysmic event, which rattled the economic foundations of many countries across the globe. For example, what questions do we need to ask ourselves concerning the substantive implications of the economic crisis of 2008 on community life? What challenges does this economic crisis pose for public policy and public administration/management's relevance in this time of political and economic uncertainty? What public implications will the crisis have on both the practice and intellectual agenda in public affairs scholarship for decades to come? And finally, what questions have not garnered the attention they should have, particularly those pertaining to social equity and the changing economic and political landscape of public decision making? And has the very idea of publicness itself become so market centered that it has contributed—at least to some degree—to the emergence of a populism accelerated by the forces of globalization, economic insecurity, and distrust of public institutions?

No attempt is made here to be comprehensive; rather, I want to raise a sampling of the kinds of issues and questions that should not, and cannot, be easily swept under the theoretical rug. To date there has been a lack of discourse (and concrete policy responses) to these tough questions, rooted in the trends identified in the first section of this book, namely, the operating political environment of neo-managerialism, the changing role of the state in which policy prescriptions are forged, and the lack of an overarching substantive view of the public that plagues those of us who participate in and study public affairs. In this chapter, it is my aim to explore the consequence of these factors in public affairs, and to propose some paths of inquiry that might free us from their influence.

To wit, I contend that we in public affairs face four major challenges in light of the economic crisis of 2008 and its aftermath: (1) the troubling trend of limited social mobility, income and wealth inequality, and underemployment that could exacerbate the potential for social discord and further fuel the public's estrangement and distrust of political institutions; (2) the need for, and recognition of, the delimitation of the market and the importance for strong public accountability; (3) the formidable challenge of managing what I refer to as political/economic involution in the policy process; and (4) the failure (to date) to instill a stronger emphasis on a historical inquiry by scholars and practitioners of public affairs in the aftermath of this economic and political crisis. I do not claim that each of these issues was brought about as a result of this economic crisis of 2008, but rather that they have become even more important *because* of what has occurred.

Undoubtedly, there are other issues that could, of course, be raised. Hopefully, these four concerns will invite a robust debate concerning the normative, theoretical, and pragmatic ramifications of what we in public affairs have become, regardless of how we try to constantly clothe the discipline in normative garments or sometimes shield ourselves from exploring certain timely issues under the pretenses of the politics/administration dichotomy.[2] This inquiry will raise some difficult questions. Yet, in the end, we will ultimately benefit from such debate and, if we are thorough, unflinching, and fortunate, elevate and enrich the intellectual enterprise to which we are party.

Social Inequality, Social Mobility, and the Potential for Rising Social Discord

> You have to be blind not to see that we are headed in the wrong direction, and we've been heading that way for too long. . . . The worst thing we could do with [the] Great Divergence [in income equality] is get used to it.
>
> —Timothy Noah

It was in December 2012, during the waning of the crisis, that McKinsey & Company released the highly anticipated report "Education to Employment: Designing a System that Works." This study surveyed more than 8,500 educators, employees, and young adults in nine different countries. What made this research report interesting and salient reading is not only the sober reality that seventy-five million individuals from fifteen to twenty-four years old in countries across the globe (Brazil, Britain, Germany, India, Mexico, Morocco, Turkey, Saudi Arabia, and the United States) are presently unemployed, but that half of the young adults surveyed in nine countries believed that their college education did not necessarily improve their chances of getting a job commensurate with their educational background. The report concluded that this ominous trend might have enormous social consequences, and is relevant even today, particularly in light of the economic fallout of the COVID-19 pandemic:

> If young people who have worked hard to graduate from school and university cannot secure decent jobs and the sense of respect that comes with them, society will have to be prepared for outbreaks of anger or even violence. (cited in Mangan, 2012, p. 121)

If we look only at the United States, new college graduates have been especially victimized by what has come to be known as the Great Recession. The Center for Labor Studies at Northeastern University found that as of 2012, 54 percent of young adult college graduates (with a bachelor's degree and under twenty-five years old) were either jobless or underemployed (Weissman, 2012). Tellingly, the center was closed just two years later, due to lack of federal grant money and the failure of private funders to invest sufficiently to form an endowment. However, The Federal Reserve Bank of New York's most recent figures for underemployment among college graduates are still troubling. As of August 2017, 43.4 percent of recent college graduates remained underemployed (2018). Two economists, David Bell and David Blanchflower from the University of Stirling and Dartmouth College, respectively (2018), have concluded that in both the United States and Europe the issue of underemployment has now replaced unemployment as a major factor on dampening wages following the Great Recession. They somberly conclude that "even though the unemployment rate has returned to its pre-recession levels in many advanced countries, underemployment in most has not" (2018, p. 1). What makes this trend especially troubling is that the student loan default rate in the United States has increased dramatically between the early 2000s and 2014; and nearly one-half of the student borrowers will struggle to pay back such loans by 2023.

Understandably, these trends have the potential to become more social and political than economic. In fact, report titled *The Global State of Democracy: Exploring Democracy's Resilience* (2017) concluded that inequality tends to exacerbate political polarization as well as undermine trust in democratic processes.

In the United States, the figures are better. Despite unemployment continuing to improve, and prior to the advent of Covid-19 pandemic, there were nine U.S. states with over 21 percent in underemployment four years after the onset of the economic crisis: Illinois, Hawaii, North Carolina, Oregon, Florida, California, Michigan, Nevada, and Mississippi (Shah, 2012, p. A4). As of 2017, these figures had declined considerably, with only five states topping 10 percent underemployment (Alaska, Connecticut, Nevada, New Mexico, and West Virginia). Nationally, underemployment overall has seen a steady decline, from its peak at 17.1 percent in December 2009 to its current low of 8.1 percent (Bureau of Labor Statistics, 2018). It is worth noting that in 2018, hourly jobs accounted for about 60 percent of the U.S work force, and more than 90 percent of new net jobs remain hourly.

Although the overall trend was improving, until Covid-19 hit the United States in February 2020, the major problem that the underemployment issue poses for young adults entering the labor force remains salient: the dismal reality that young workers graduating during economic downturns "are unable to fully shift into better jobs, at least for the first 15 years of their careers" (cited in Biggs, 2012, p. A13). Lisa Kahn of Yale University expanded even further stating, "Recovery is excruciatingly slow [for these young college graduates]. . . . [E]ven 15 years following graduation, their pay [remains] 2.5% below normal" (cited in Biggs, 2012, p. 13). As a recent Brookings Institution study reported, the millennial generation had reduced median and mean wealth in 2016, compared to any similar aged cohort between 1989 and 2017, since the Great Recession of 2007–09 (Gale, Gelford, Fichtner, & Harris, 2020). When taking into account the COVID-19 pandemic, the average millennials will bear enduring economic hardships in the form of lower income and lower wealth, such as in delay in buying homes. "Proportionally, the even younger generation, known as Zoomers, suffered worse than all [other previous generations]. A third of their jobs were vaporized in two months in 2020" (Van Dan, 2020, p. 5). The problem for millennials is especially acute for the African American and Hispanic populations, given that these groups have historically suffered the impact of systemic discrimination. While, overall, millennials are the most educated in history in the United States, their careers have suffered another economic shock due to COVID-19 that will have important impacts on their wealth accumulation (Gale, Gelford, Fichtner, & Harris, 2020).

The Economic Policy Institute echoed earlier this same trajectory when it concluded that about 70 percent of the nation's college graduates have experienced wage declines since 2000 which, after inflation, have become even more pronounced since 2007 (Greenhouse, 2013). One scholar who has studied this problem in great depth put it in these candid terms: "[T]oday's new college graduate on average will lose $40,000 in inflation-adjusted income over the next 15 years" (Biggs, 2012, p. A13). And while it is true that increasing educational attainment overall has raised wages for those workers, we must not lose sight of the fact that most Americans still lack a college degree to begin with (Shambaugh & Nunn, 2017). Presently, 52 percent of millennials are classified as underemployed, and 29 percent of Generation X fall into this category. And in the United States, for those who did go to college, student debt has climbed to a staggering record high of $1.5 trillion.

This trend is even more troubling when the data on underemployment are disaggregated. Closer examination shows that the economic costs of underemployment have fallen disproportionately on workers with lower incomes, thereby contributing directly to an even greater concern than underemployment: the growing problems of income and wealth inequality in the United States (Stiglitz, 2015; Sum & Khatiwada, 2010). Most large wage increases, particularly since the 1970s, have gone to those already at the top of the national income distribution, while wages at the bottom half of the distribution have declined or remained stagnant. To reverse this trend will require a reexamination of increasing the minimum wage, improving the educational system, promoting worker bargaining power, and encouraging pro-mobility and entrepreneurship policies (Shamburg & Nunn, 2017).

Although the income gap between the rich and the poor is increasing in most industrialized countries around the world, some of the largest increases are in the United States (Stiglitz, 2015, 2017; Sum & Khatiwada, 2010). It is this latter point that merits examination, because its relevance grows when we explore what this gap exemplifies:[3]

- In the 20 years leading up to World War II, the top 10 percent accounted for 45 percent of pre-tax income. This declined to 33 percent during the 1940s and remained fairly constant until the 1970s. Since the 1970s the income share of the top decile has increased rapidly surpassing its previous levels at 49.7 percent in 2007. This declined slightly following the recession, standing at 47.9 percent in 2010. As of 2014, this figure has dropped only slightly, to 47 percent (Piketty, Saez, & Zucman, 2016).

- In the period from 1980 to 2014, there were dramatic shifts in real income corresponding with economic expansion, two recessions, and the current (slow) recovery. Strikingly, the top 1 percent has seen its pre-tax income grow by 205 percent, while the population as a whole has seen only 61 percent growth . . . and the bottom 50 percent has seen a mere 1percent growth (Piketty, Saez, & Zucman, 2016).

- From 2007–2010, while the percentage drop in real income is highest among the top 1 percent due to losses in capital gains, the bottom 90 percent were adversely impacted more than the top 10 percent, which was the reverse of the 2001 recession. Gains in real income were also unevenly distributed whereby the top 1 percent incomes gain 11.6 percent, while bottom 99 percent incomes gained only 0.2 percent. This pattern will most likely continue without dramatic changes (Stiglitz, 2012a, 2015).

- And finally, for "those at the bottom of the income distribution, there have been no gains at all. Real incomes for the lower half of the distribution have stagnated. The same picture emerges if we look at wages. Median real earnings for full-time year-round male workers have not grown since 1974 (Quiggin, 2012, p.155; Stiglitz, 2017). In 2012, "the income of the typical U.S. family fell or was flat in almost every [U.S.] state . . . with the drop in places where the economy had been hit hard by the housing bust." In short, the income level of a typical family has fallen to levels last seen in 1995, "a long and pernicious slide means it will be a generation before Americans regain the peak income levels reached at the close of the 90's" (Dougherty & Mathews, 2012, p. A1; Stiglitz, 2017). Overall, the share of wealth in the U.S. economy is rising to those in the the high end of the income distribution. That is, "the top 20 percent held 77 percent of total household wealth in 2016 . . . [and] the top one percent alone hold more wealth than the middle class" (Sawhill & Pilliam, 2019, p. 1).

Although hardly thorough, these studies indicate a sobering economic pattern: that income and wealth inequality in the United States has, sadly, reached a historic high and represents a troubling trend both economically and politically (Tooze, 2018; Friedman, 2012; Noah, 2012; Stiglitz, 2012a). Larry Bartels summarizes this worrisome situation in the following stark terms (2016, pp. 14–15):

> Whether we focus on the share of income going to the top 5% of taxpayers or the share going to the even richer top 1%, [these trends] suggests that current levels of inequality rival those of the Roaring Twenties before the Great Depression wiped out much of the financial wealth of the nation's reigning upper class. By this metric, America's New Gilded Age is a retrogression of historical scope.

But as disconcerting as this problem seems to be, equally vexing is the issue of the American aspiration of upward social mobility, which is such an integral component of the American folklore and may no longer hold as much validity as it once did. As Jacob Hacker and Paul Pierson (2011) contend, there are studies showing that American mobility has declined over the last generation as inequality has risen. They extrapolate from the data that

> [c]ompared with other rich nations . . . U.S. intergenerational mobility is surprisingly low, in part because the gap between income groups is so much bigger. The American Dream portrays the United States as a classless society where anyone can rise to the top, regardless of family background. Yet there is more intergenerational mobility in Australia, Sweden, Norway, Finland, Germany, Spain, France, and Canada. In fact, of affluent countries studied, only Britain and Italy have lower intergenerational mobility than the United States does (and they are basically even with the U.S.). (2011, p. 29; Chetty, Hendren, Kline, Saez, & Turner, 2014)

Miles Corak (2010) has shown that as income inequality increases, social mobility tends to fall, a phenomenon that is now referred to as the "Great Gatsby Curve" (Freeland, 2012). The disconcerting aspect of this situation, when viewed historically, is that income and wealth inequality could be more or less tolerated as long as it is accompanied by a *belief* in social mobility. However, such aphorisms as "land of opportunity" and "children will be better off than their parents" are increasingly viewed with skepticism. In May 2012, a *Wall Street Journal*/NBC News poll reported that 63 percent of Americans were expressing doubt that their children would truly be better off than their generation. As of 2017, a Pew Research Center report found that this figure had dropped by only 5 percent, to 58 percent of the population, despite five years of falling unemployment rates and economic growth (Stokes, 2017). This rather distressing view was given empirical validity by a Brookings Institution study (Haskins & Sawhill, 2009) that focused on men whose fathers resided in the bottom fifth of the income distribution. This study concluded that "42 percent of American men with fathers in the bottom fifth of the income distribution remain there as compared to: Denmark, 25 percent; Sweden, 26 percent; Finland, 28 percent; Norway, 28 percent; and United Kingdom, 30 percent.

[Hence] . . . starting out poor doubles the risk of ending up poor" (cited in Quiggin, 2012, p. 163). In another analysis of children born in the 1980s and 1990s, the data projected that "68 percent of whites—but only 34 percent of blacks—will make it to the middle class (defined . . . as an annual income of $68,000 for a married couple with two children) by age of forty" (Wessel, 2012, p. A6).

It is not my intention here to ascertain the reasons for this decline in social mobility, but to clarify that the economic tendency of a growing income and wealth inequality represents a major barrier (although there are others) to social mobility. That is, "the slow growth and decreased social mobility of the last decade," Luigi Zingales (2012, p. A19) of the University of Chicago surmised, "have damaged the free market's reputation as a creator of prosperity." In a surprising tone, he speculated that the implications of this process might lead to something even more dangerous: increased economic and political resentment—a prediction that has been darkly realized in the tide of populism, and a distortive view of publicness that swept the United States during the 2016 presidential election (Judis, 2016). While the long-term implications of the Great Recession are still being debated, I think Zingales's assertion posits an important factor—although he never explicitly states it—that has enormous implications for public affairs: the role of positional goods in the market system.

Fred Hirsch (1976) first coined the term *positional goods* and predicated his theory on the notion that there are social limits to growth—social limits that present a major challenge to our present market economy and society. To understand some of Hirsch's valuable insights, I need to first comprehend the difference between the material economy and the positional economy. The material economy, Hirsch insisted, is the production of goods and services that can be increased indefinitely without loses in quality and with continued productivity in the economy. More specifically, "[I]t is defined as output amenable to a continued increase in productivity per unit of labor input" (Hirsch, 1976, p. 29), and represents goods whose enjoyment does not depend on the number of others who are also consuming such goods. Positional goods, on the other hand, are services, goods, work positions, and other social relationships that are valued because "the satisfaction they yield [is] possible only for a minority" (1976, p. 23). The enjoyment of positional goods is predicated on a social scarcity or the nonpossession of such goods by others. Some positional goods are fixed (e.g., leisure and suburban living) and competition for these positional goods does not, as such, necessarily lead to non-optimality (Matthews, 1977, p. 576), whereas other aspects of positional goods are based on income and social status. As such, the positional economy is the production of those limited social goods, and the intense meta-monetary contests undertaken to control them.

The critical point here is that positional goods cannot be democratized because such goods are intrinsically scarce and, therefore, competition for them represent(s) a zero-sum game that can be wasteful.[4] Hirsch is clear that positional goods are typically consumed by higher income groups in society and if they were obtained by a larger segment of the population, they would lose their status and value. Hirsch somewhat delicately emphasizes throughout his analysis the gulf between those who can obtain positional goods and those who cannot, despite rising real income. In fact, as Hirsch surmises, the interactions between material sectors and positional sectors become ultimately inimical. "Instead of alleviating the unmet demands on the economic system, material growth . . . exacerbates them. The locus of instability is the divergence between what is possible for the individual and what is possible for all individuals. Increased material resources enlarge the demand for positional goods, a demand that can be satisfied for some only by frustrating demand by others" (1976, p. 67).

The theoretical backdrop to Hirsch's arguments is his trenchant contention that the market only functions well if tempered by moral probity. Rather than being a value-neutral system, the market, he claims, promotes largely individualistic, economically driven actions, which, in turn, erode the societal norms that have historically allowed the market to operate successfully. The decisions and transactions made by individuals within the market system have a procilivity to be isolated, decentralized, and made without knowledge or consideration of their cumulative effects. He goes on to state that individuals often make small decisions that are seemingly beneficial for themselves but can have potentially damaging impacts on the broader society (the tyranny of small decisions).

It is within this context that Hirsch presents a dilemma for us in our modern market society: as more people compete for positional goods, or hope to achieve these goods in the future, there might develop a frustration or confrontation over the distribution of such goods "unless advanced countries are able to agree on methods of collective allocation for the intrinsically scarce goods sought by people in an affluent society" (Bakunin, 1977, p. 814). A sobering consequence of this situation is that the access to such goods becomes a breeding ground for potential social conflict, "for it persuades people that they are entitled to those positional goods which are, in a competitive market, the prerogative of a small minority only" (ibid., p.

813). And because advances in a market economy do not resolve distributive issues, they might emerge as sharpened conflict over the distribution of positional goods (Mason, 2000; Poltke, 1986; Carvalho & Rodriques, 2006; Schneider, 2007). Not surprisingly, economic and political elites are in an advantaged position compared to others to obtain such position goods, thus exacerbating an inherent tension between aspirations widely shared and the actual opportunities aspired to that remain restricted and unequally distributed (Hirsch, 1976, p. 110).

Raising a related point in terms of positional goods as status, Herbert Grubel (1978, p. 152) highlights the example of education:

> The problem [of status] arises from the fact that positions at the top of the social and economic hierarchy are limited, while economic growth has permitted increasing numbers of people to obtain the education and income which in preceding periods were sufficient to reach these positions of leadership. As a result many university graduates and economically successful persons are frustrated because of their failure to obtain the relative status which they had expected to achieve. As in the use of other types of positional goods, economic growth cannot solve but in fact intensifies the problem . . . [since] there are social limits to growth.

Likewise, Hirsch recognized that positional goods encourage social waste by reducing the level of welfare available to all, which results "from an imposed hierarchy that confines socially scarce goods to those at the highest rungs of the distributional ladder, disappointing the expectations of those whose position is raised through a lift in the ladder as a whole" (1976, p. 6). If Hirsch's analysis is even partially accurate, it fundamentally challenges the central premise that economic growth provides a way in which to achieve egalitarian outcomes—and to accomplish this with little, if any, social discord or resentment. Moreover, Hirsch's overall arguments directly confront the assumptions about the viability of the social underpinning of the market economy, especially in an era that tends, to a large degree, to strengthen self-regarding individual objectives. Notwithstanding the controversial implications of this argument, it does pose a nagging (and legitimate) point: that perhaps limited social mobility, underemployment, and income and wealth inequality intensify the role of positional goods and their deleterious impact on society. But, even more pointedly, we need to acknowledge both in public management/administration and public policy that the social nature of positional goods is—in a very real sense—creating new tensions within the market economy in particular, and society in general.[5] Further, these tensions could become even more acute in light of the economic and political residue left by the economic crisis of 2008. One need only look to President Trump's appeals to "Forgotten Americans"—generally white, rural voters disadvantaged by the postindustrial development of our economy and experiencing a never-before-achieved degree of disenfranchisement—during the 2016 election. In the eyes of many critics, these appeals flew on the wings of cultural, rather than economic, substance. Yet, it is arguable that these appeals played no small part in Trump's victory, hammering home political frustrations, economic fears, and resentment of political elites who have the ear of powerful policymakers.

As such, positional goods denote more than an economic and political dilemma, they represent the growing power of those who can monopolize positional goods and exert the political muscle to ensure the continued extraction of necessary favors from the policy process (Dymski, 2006). Such a perspective (and power) does come at cost: the greater the ability to monopolize and restrict positional goods, the more unequal policies will tend to become, contributing to a diminution of legitimacy and respect for the institutions of government (Dymski, 2006). While this point may be overstated, Jacob Hacker and Nathaniel Loewentheil (2012, p. A3) have claimed that "as income inequality has translated into rising political inequality, it has been harder and harder to act on sensible prescriptions that would increase middle-class living standards, security and opportunity as well as overall economic growth." Yet their real point is not so much economic but political when they wryly conclude: "[E]nsuring that today's economic winners do not dominate our political process may be the most important way to improve the quality of economic life in America" (2012, p. A3). Stiglitz (2012b, p. 8) put it in even more explicit terms: "Political inequality leads to economic inequality, which leads in turn to more political inequality, in a vicious spiral undermining our economy and our democracy." In the popularity of the campaign messages of both Donald Trump and Bernie Sanders, the urgency of this point to the voting public became clear. And, in the aftermath of 2016, the consequences of a presidency committed not to easing income inequality but to perhaps exacerbating it could not be more evident, or more disturbing.

In the economic crisis of 2008, which demonstrated so starkly the deleterious fault lines in our modern economy (particularly regarding its individualistic ethos so engendered by the market) it is worth pondering the warning of de Tocqueville who feared that such individualistic tendencies, if left unchecked by the lively influence of civic associations, could result in a form of aristocracy. That said, we in public affairs—whether we admit to or not—must address an uncomfortable and controversial proposition that can no longer be ignored: that perhaps "the crisis of government is a general crisis of the liberal capitalist form of society" (Sullivan, 1986, p. 25). In short, that the rise of powerful economic actors in the policy process as described by Wolin (2010) and others, and the dominance of the neo-managerial norms that undergird it, are the symptoms of a distortive notion of publicness that has emerged so vividly in public affairs.

This crisis of government, Sullivan (1986) reiterates, is largely due to the underlying and pervasive Hobbesian assumptions that promote an instrumental view of social relationships in the modern polity. As uneasy as this contention makes us feel, we know that public institutions will continue to operate in the milieu of a turbulent market economy trying to provide social stability to those who fall victim to the market's shortcomings, even in the midst of the cornucopia of plenty that the market supplies. Unfortunately, this all takes place in an era of increasing public cynicism against government and its public institutions. Although public cynicism hardly began with this economic crisis, it has certainly contributed to a growing public disillusionment with both government and corporations alike. This public disillusionment, as de Tocqueville indicated, can beget certain public sentiments that have the possibility of becoming the very preconditions of despotism. More than ever, de Tocqueville's observation is worth taking seriously. What is so sorely needed today is further debate and research examining the efficacy of what would constitute a more democratic economy, as well as the feasibility of cooperative projects that promote a "civic discovery" and "civic dignity" and mitigate the rougher edges of an instrumental, utilitarian politics of public life (Cruikshank, 1999; Barber, 1984; Ramos, 1981).

This may sound too utopian, if not downright unrealistic, for both fields that are primarily concerned with the implementation (and administration) of policies borne out of the real world of politics. But if we have learned anything from this economic crisis, especially given some of the more disturbing implications that continue to reverberate through society, it is that the stability of public trust is subject to historical vicissitudes (Jacobs & King, 2009). As the state's administrative capacity is being contested, a larger debate should be looming—a debate first proposed by Lynton Caldwell

(1996)—concerning the revival of statecraft as a way to reexamine the role of the state in a democratic polity in addressing the important issues of the day. This focus on statecraft, Caldwell emphasizes, should stress advancing the "social learning processes" (his phrase) between the citizenry and public institutions, as well as creating new policy venues to rethink many of our domain assumptions concerning the efficacy of our public policy approaches. Caldwell is vague about what this would look like in practice, but he asserts that an intellectual exercise in statecraft is long overdue in public management/administration and public policy. He also notes that such an exercise is uniquely propitious in times of crises. As a result of the economic malaise of underemployment, income and wealth inequality, limited social mobility, and the winner-take-all politics so prevalent in our times, we may have no other choice but to finally take Caldwell's challenge seriously and make it an integral part of what we do and who we are.

Delimitation of the Market and a Discussion of Public Accountability

> The immediate problem, then, is how to manage politically a civilization . . . heavily dedicated to the accumulation of wealth when the limits and indeed internal contradictions of that goal are becoming more apparent.
>
> —William Sullivan

"The market," Andrew Bard Schmookler (1984, p. 314) reminds us, "is a selective listener." He goes on to explain, however, that the market "can attend to some kind of human needs far better than to others. The market specializes in what can be exchanged in discrete transactions. This embraces a considerable variety of goods and services. But it also excludes a great deal, including much of the flesh and blood of human social life." Schmookler's compelling point is important for all its apparent simplicity. Regardless of the mounting criticism that has been heaped on the fallacy of unregulated free markets (especially dealing with the financial sector), there has been a paucity of discussion about the actual limits of what the market can do (and do well), and about how to restrict the utilitarian market mentality from dominating the modern polity itself (Block & Somers, 2016; Ramos, 1981; Candler, 2010; Sullivan, 1986; Giddens, 1994; Habermas, 1973; Ventriss, 2010; Adams & Balfour, 2010; Kuttner, 1997).

This latter issue is especially crucial to both public management/administration and public policy due to the market's intrinsic ability to transform social choices into a commercial ethos or what Jules Henry (1963) referred to as the inevitable "monetization of values." This transformation was eloquently explored by Karl Polanyi (1944) who argued that the modern market is not embedded in social relations, but instead that it is "social relations [that] are embedded in the economic systems" (p. 57). This transvaluation requires us, as Michael Walzer (1983) suggested, to consider a "boundary revision."

Walzer claims that the market (and the value-system of which it is a part) needs to be confined to a particular sphere of life in order to facilitate the viability of a "plurality of spheres." Walzer, it should be noted, is not arguing to "undo" the market and its legitimate role. Rather, his point is that the market should not become the cardinal category for ordering individual and social life. Unfortunately, Walzer never analyzes how this could be realistically achieved, particularly in light of the erosion of normative constraints that might have helped mitigate such a ubiquitous market influence on modern society (Cerny, 2008; Frank, 2001; Giddens, 1971, 1981; Jessop, 1993; Polanyi, 1944; Ritzer, 2004; Ventriss, 1998; Nisbet, 1988, 2013; Sandel, 2012). Herein lies an emerging issue: what we are seeing is a precipitous and steady decline in the erosion of precapitalistic norms that, ironically, "underlie a benign and efficient operation of the self-interest principle operating through market operations" (Hirsch, 1976, p. 11). Guerreiro Ramos recognized the implications of this "moral depletion" (Hirsch's term) and why it was necessary to develop a countervailing approach to nurture publicness. He posited that a "para-economic paradigm," if implemented, might provide a way out of this difficulty:

> [T]he para-economic paradigm can only come into being as a result of confrontive endeavors on the part of actors whose personal project is to resist the intrinsic trends of the market-centered society. Yet the objective of the para-economic paradigm is not to obliterate the market mechanism, but to save only the unprecedented capabilities it has created, albeit for wrong reasons. Properly delimited, the market does serve the goals of a multidimensional model of human existence in a multicentric society. (1981, p. 135)

What Ramos recognized some time ago—and very few in public affairs have acknowledged since—is that we need to come to terms, both theoretically and pragmatically, with what a countervailing power would actually look like in face of "the constitutive role of the market and the commodification that has penetrated every component of our everyday existence" (Ventriss, 1998). Rethinking the influence of the market on economic and civic affairs will surely be a challenging task in that it will imply directly confronting the legitimization of America's core cultural values of economic opportunity and self-reliance (Bartels, 2016; Sullivan, 1986).

Admittedly, whether this is realistic in the present political environment of "predation" defined as the "systemic abuse of public institutions for private profit, or, equivalently, the systemic undermining of public protection for the benefit of private clients" (Galbraith, 2008, p. 30) is certainly subject to further debate. Assuming some validity behind Galbraith's analysis, the challenge we face is that when the modern market is left to its own tendencies (as displayed openly in the economic crisis of 2008) it can eviscerate its own normative underpinnings, "which requires norms, habits, or sentiments external to itself to hold [the market] together, to ensure the very political stability itself that capitalism needs in order to strive" (cited in Judt, 2007, p. 24; see also: Durkheim, 1966; Muller, 2002; Schumpeter, 1942; Bell, 1976; Dumont, 1977; Giddens, 1971). Here Durkheim (1966) was right: if the market system loses some of its some elemental moral influence (and purpose) then little can be done to abate economic behavior that could eventually lead to anomic behavior or, worse yet, to undermining the common good. Among the normative constraints that are so crucial to the market system are trust, integrity, honor, loyalty, cooperation, and obligation (Bourdieu, 1977; Durkheim, 1966; Hirsch, 1976; Bell, 1976; Nisbet, 1986).[6] For example, according to Rueschemeyer and Evans (1985), absent these normative constraints, transaction cost could become very high indeed, adversely hindering the efficient allocation of resources.

One of the more vivid and recent examples of this moral depletion occurred in 2008 as the economic situation became more dire. Several major banks found themselves in circumstances whereby "trust between banks eroded and fictitious leveraged liquidity disappeared" (Harvey, 2010, p. 30). As this trust evaporated among the banks, deleveraging started to rapidly unfold, resulting in enormous devaluations and loss of bank capital (Financial Crisis Inquiry Commission, 2011; Phillips, 2009; Harvey, 2010). According to Partnoy and Eisinger, "[A]s trust diminishes the likelihood of another [economic] crisis grows larger. The next big storm might blow the weakened house down" (2013, p. 64). The paradox of this situation is obvious and central to what I am arguing: "[T]he ubiquitous market behavior that constitutes our modern liberal market society has eroded the very moral codes that would prevent it from becoming a corrosive form of utilitarian capitalism" (Ventriss, 2010, p. 411), thereby allowing the market mentality to spread to every aspect of society (Giddens, 1971; Hirsch, 1976; Polanyi, 1944). If the economic crisis of 2008 demonstrated anything, it showed that while the market system depends on normative meanings, albeit often clumsily practiced in economic affairs, these meanings cannot be reproduced by the market itself (Macpherson, 1962; Mandel, 1976; Ventriss, 1998). If this notion is accurate, the issue before us is whether it is possible to preserve institutions outside the market mentality (part of a boundary revision) where other substantive meanings and purposes can still carry weight in public affairs (Giddens, 1994; Ramos, 1981).

But do we in public management/administration and public policy have any substantial role to play here? I suggest two key functions. First, in arresting (if possible) the sabotaging of the market's own moral foundations, and second, in facilitating what Edmund Burke (1971) called the noncommercial basis of society. On this latter point, both Walzer (1983) and Ramos (1981, p. 158) are relevant because they understood that delimiting the scope of market influence would require "[that it] be regulated politically and delimited as an enclave among other enclaves constituting the total social fabric." Notwithstanding the implementation barriers to achieving this policy goal, Ramos and Walzer do infer a critical role here for us in public affairs in any boundary revision debate. That is, any such boundary revision will require the reconceptualization of both fields' inexorable ties to a "cognitive politics" in which the penetration of a market-centered approach to public affairs has taken on a strong hold concerning the direction of both fields[7] (Adams & Balfour, 2010; Kouzmin, 2009, 2010; Ventriss, 1998, 2000, 2010; Farmer, 2010, Ramos, 1981).

To a certain extent, this discussion on the limits of the market has been raised regarding whether in particular public management/administration has at least some responsibility in this economic calamity's impact on so many citizens' lives, here and abroad (Green, 2012b). Although this is, no doubt, an intriguing debate, there is a more poignant issue that should warrant our collective attention: the discussion of the limits of the market must go hand in hand with the broader acknowledgment (and debate) of the inimical erosion of normative constraints on contemporary economic behavior and what that substantively means for public affairs. If there is any one key factor that should be remembered from the economic crisis of 2008, even with the myriad of differing explanations concerning how this crisis occurred, it is that when market relations become nothing more than contractual relations based on self-interest alone, the administrative and policy consequences can be potentially dire. As Durkheim (1966, pp. 203–204) put it: "[Interest] can create only an external link between [individuals]. . . . [W]hen interest is the only ruling force each individual finds himself in a state of war with every other . . . [because] nothing is less constant than interest . . . it can only give rise to transient relations and passing associations." As we wrestle with determining what the limits of the market can, and ought, to be in public affairs and our role in that debate, it will become quite apparent that the market alone cannot adequately provide—nor should it provide—the necessary normative policy lexicon and discussion of publicness that is so eagerly needed in today's modern polity (Anderson, 1990; Sen, 1999; Sandel, 2013).

Following on a related theme, one of the more amazing aspects of the economic crisis of 2008, given the questionable behavior of key actors, is that not one major banking official has been indicted for legal wrongdoing.[8] This is puzzling to many because it is widely known that Wall Street failed to directly address fraud in late securitizations (as they are called) which probably constituted more than 50 percent of the mortgages that were illegally obtained (Bencivenga, 2009). Others have pointed out the perverse incentives in the securitization process itself with the default risk being knowingly passed on to others. One decade out, in a time where rent-seeking behavior is still prevalent and moral hazard among the "too big to fail" investment banks is as potent as ever, many are raising their voices in concern about the moral consequences of such behavior on society. Adams and Balfour (2012, p. 332), for instance, have postulated that after decades of deregulation we have entered what they refer to as "praetorian capitalism . . . a corrupt and venal set of institutional relations." While Adams and Balfour are careful to stress that this praetorian capitalism has both creative and destructive elements (reminiscent of Schumpeter's notion of creative destruction), its more nefarious characteristics are illustrated by allocating risk away from investors and onto others, including the government and the public. They summarize: "The more pervasively corrupt and venal institutions and organizations become, the more people mistrust them. Institutions become the last place that individuals look for the nurturing of affirmative public values; instead they see institutions as a setting in which only the foolish or stubborn act with high ethical standards" (2012, p. 333).

What is paramount to note and what this economic crisis has so dramatically highlighted is the following imperative: the critical need to promote among our institutions and administrators/analysts the ethics of deliberation (providing normative reasons for a given policy decision that are not solely limited to purely technical or analytical considerations) and the ethics of accountability (providing a concrete basis for identifying which official(s) or institution(s) actually are responsible for implementing or formulating a policy) (Thompson, 1980; Ventriss, 2012a). What is suggested here is that these two conditions are crucial, as John Dewey (1927, 1935) correctly understood, because "our faith in [both public and private] institutions must never run so deep that it prevents us from seeing the extent to which they [may] degenerate into something antidemocratic" (cited in Rogers, 2009, p. 224). Presently, what is so disconcerting in many of the discussions I have examined so far is the general lack of attention to ascertain the normative implications of "publicness" regardless of whether it takes place in the public, private, or nonprofit sectors. This idea is echoed in Dewey's notion of the public, which merits mentioning once again, as consisting "of all those who are affected by the indirect consequences of transactions to such an extent that it is deemed necessary to have those consequences systemically cared for" (1927, p. 89).

For all the tactical insights contained in Dewey's famous statement, he poses an intriguing but controversial point that has genuine theoretical and practical import for us: Is there any fiduciary responsibility to hold (public or private) institutions accountable for providing an ethical rationale for their decisions, making explicit the lines of accountability and defending their policy decisions with complete transparency before the public? The significance of this question has particular merit because in an economic crisis that shattered so many lives it raises the highly charged issue of what actually constitutes, or should constitute, "democratic accountability" at a time when the policy process itself renders more or less invisible the power of dark money in contemporary public affairs (Mayer, 2016; Bowles and Gintis, 1986).

The Challenge of Managing Political/Economic Involution

> The contemporary impasse on who gets what and the associated impediments in the operation of the market economy can be seen as the surfacing of an embedded historical process. A long latent conflict is coming to a head.
>
> —Fred Hirsch

While, as mentioned previously, Fred Hirsch's (1976) book *Social Limits to Growth* has shed light on some fundamental questions about the very nature of the market system, his argument below illustrates the continued relevance of his ideas in the aftermath of the economic crisis of 2008:

> Market capitalism has never been the exclusive basis of the political economy in any country at any time. That has been its strength. It was the marriage of market capitalism with state regulation that produced a hybrid politico-economic system with the necessary resilience and plasticity to survive. But the new skin grafted on to western capitalism to provide it with stability and support appears to have papered over a continuing and perhaps growing stress in the foundations of the system. (1976, p. 118)

Similarly, Guerreiro Ramos indicated in even more polemic terms that our challenge today is part of much broader conceptual blind spot that rarely gets the attention it deserves:

> Governmental policy makers do not seem to realize sufficiently that American society is generating imaginative schemes of resource allocation which, were they bolstered by adequate systematic policies, would represent antidotes for the flaws of the economy in its present dystrophic state. Like the physician who treats a patient with a medicine which aggravates his disease, these policy makers try to correct, with traditional market correctives, the distortions of social life used by the market system. (1981, p. 160)

Both of these thinkers, in their respective ways, elucidate a critical issue that is politely dismissed in the empirical and theoretical discussions of many of today's major policy problems: that "the central ambiguity of liberal philosophy arises from the contradiction between its moral content of protecting the dignity of the individual and the categories of thought it has employed to elaborate and establish that idea" (Sullivan 1986, p. 18). Or could it be that it is inherently difficult for us, whether it be for ideological, political, or historical reasons, to partake in seriously questioning the underlying leitmotifs that exalt the overarching validity of market values so prevalent in public affairs, thus reverting to policies that emphasize an incessant focus on procedural managerial incentives that will supposedly sustain and smooth over the rougher edges of the liberal market economy (Adams & Balfour, 2012; Hacker & Pierson, 2011; Ventriss, 2010)? Richard

Goodwin, the former advisor to President Johnson, reflecting on his own experience in government, indicated that often this procedural managerial approach to policy disguises a certain abdication that we too often take for granted: "that changes in policy—which now dominate what passes for public dialogue—will not arrest a process of decay that results from deepening flaws in the structure that sustains our society. It is like debating what color to paint the house, and how to remodel the porch, when the foundation is crumbling" (1992, p. 8). In short, the upsurge of privatization and deregulation, the primacy of neo-managerial norms that it has at once ushered in and been built upon, cannot be halted by the same methods that have enabled its rise.

I will argue here that the economic crisis is going to exacerbate the arduous challenge of managing political/economic involution that can be briefly described as a kind of managerial fatigue, so to speak, whereby even the most technical/rational approaches run "the risk of becoming internally complicated [in that] inventive originality . . . becomes eventually both politically and analytically exhausted in its efficacy in promoting social equity and [at the same time] the stabilization of growth" (Ventriss, 2010, p. 407). Political/economic involution, in other words, highlights a propensity by which the administrative mechanisms of the modern state find it difficult to effectively (or successfully) mediate the various economic and political stresses of the market in all its variegated manifestations (Tooze, 2018; Bowles & Gintis, 1985; Cerny, 2008; Candler, 2010). Specifically, I refer to political/economic involution as a process of advancing administrative and policy condensation, whereby failing to address the inherent anomalies of the market neoliberal framework, of which it is a part, policies increasingly become more internally complicated (and often contradictory), hence making decision making unduly laborious and circuitous in nature (Boonstra & Van Den Brink, 2007; Ventriss, 2010). One scholar, with a critical eye on legitimacy, stated it in this manner:

> In spite of all its methods of legitimization and various provision for social welfare [and economic remedies], the modern industrial state is finding it increasingly difficult to disguise the widening discrepancy between promise and performance, between its supposedly egalitarian ethos and the glowing inequalities in income, status, and power. It is this very discrepancy and its administrative and ideological ramifications which lie at the root, the everyday crisis of legitimacy. (Camilleri, 1977, p. 201)

On a related aspect of this point, Erica Schoenberger (1997), an economic geographer at Johns Hopkins University, may have put her finger on a central problem and its haunting policy implications for the future: we have to face the somber reality in this new interconnected global economy that the structural tensions in the market system may no longer be resolved within its own framework. If accurate, the result of this state of affairs is that we endure conditions of political and economic instability with "a heterogeneous patchwork of economic and political [approaches] reflecting opposing interests and contradictory value-systems . . . [as well as] institutional responses . . . to the underlying economic disaster which [policymakers] are powerless [to transform]" (Camilleri, 1977, p. 198). Robert Durant (2011, p. 9) added his own voice to this perspective in contending that there has emerged a disturbing trend in the United States "by which prior reforms and policies create legislative and administrative structures that produce biases within the system privileging some policies and interest groups and diminishing or marginalizing others." Durant does not hesitate to draw this rather provocative and intriguing conclusion, saying further that

> [t]his tendency toward "lock-in" not only creates repeated "self-reinforcement" and a "reproduction of institutions," but also, and paradoxically, it amplifies the allure of market solutions. Citizens see a less direct connection between government and the meeting of their needs, and they thus become less mobilizable to support funding for government programs. At the same time, as the complex and opaque implementation structures produced increase the transaction costs of citizen engagement with government, they see it as more remote from them than ever and less worthy of political support. This continues until a new crisis breaks out because of the inevitable excesses of, in effect, loosely regulated or even unfettered markets (e.g., the 2007–2008 global financial crisis). At that point, calls for government initiatives ensue. And the next round of reforms ensures, starting the cycle again. (2011, p. 10)

What Durant circuitously hints at here, but does not explicitly state, is that our traditional managerial, neoliberal perspective could be becoming increasingly exhausted, especially since 2007–08, because of its intellectual and pragmatic fixation with the prevailing managerial thinking of a market rationality, a point intimated by many others (Adams & Balfour, 2009; Ritzer,

2004; Vanderburg, 2005; Ventriss, 2010). This "locked-in" mentality exhibits a tendency for political/economic involution in that there is a tendency to view all political problems as primarily managerial issues/questions rather than as issues deeply embedded in the broader political, economic, and societal arrangement of power (Eichengreen, 2016; Morgenson, 2011; Ventriss, 2000; Erie, 1977; Ramos, 1981; Lustig, 1982). One way of viewing this process, then, is that when the central problem becomes the fundamental conflict between substantive issues of participation, social equity, and democratic citizenship and an economy that has become an arena of structural inequality, public discord, and demands upon governmental resources, mere policy tinkering within a market/managerial mindset may not be enough in meeting the grievances of diverse constituencies (Duncan, 1989).

This policy involution, given the validity of its assumptions, presents a vexing task for us in public affairs because the state, as Offe (1976, pp. 34–35) has succinctly pointed out, "attempts to politically regulate the economic system, but without [publically] politicizing it." Given this reality, the economic crisis of 2008 has, for all intents and purposes, intensified the role of public management (and nonpartisan policy analysis) within the mediated context of promoting—as it must—the flawed idea that societal issues can be resolved alone with the application of the proper technical expertise and organizational (and managerial) efficiencies. This inclination, however, has merely legitimized the continued amplification of market solutions into the public sector (Box, 2010), while neglecting "the underlying structural and ideological leitmotifs that [may] have caused this crisis in the first place" (Ventriss, 2010, p. 417; Harvey, 2009; Durant, 2011; Kouzmin,2009; O'Conner, 1987).

In fact, Lawrence Jacobs and Desmond King (2009) have suggested that the growing incoherence of governmental policy since 2007–2008 has put front and center the troubling issue of policy legitimacy itself:

> The legitimacy problem is that the state's imperative to sustain core industries like finance and automotive collides with its requirements to maintain its standing as a government for and by the people. This collision of opposing necessities may eventually show up in surveys of public trust in the political system; it also manifests itself in the incoherence of government policy and the confusion of government . . . officials who find themselves both advocating for policies to sustain business while also approving policies to respond to the natural consequences. (2009, p. 282)

The way forward from this present maelstrom in understanding this process is not by confining our analysis to the supposed relevance of path dependence nor by any models of punctuated equilibrium (as valuable as these theoretical approaches can be at times). Rather, it is by trying to ascertain the actual dynamic administrative processes of attempting to manage economic change without precipitating any further policy incoherence, while simultaneously striving to maintain a resemblance of policy continuity that does not undermine the global circuit of capital.

The management of this dual role, especially since 2008, is noteworthy as a result of a new balance between public and private authority (and responsibility) and how that balance is being presently recalibrated. As Randall Germain correctly acknowledges, "[t]he recalibrations of the public-private authority nexus may be expanding the scope of public regulation and shrinking the sphere of private calculation, but it is doing so with the best interests of private capital in mind" (2009, p. 667). And here is the crucial point: regardless of whether the issue has involved the U. S. Treasury's policy of buying toxic assets or the European Union's instituting approaches to bring more nonbanking institutions under its regulatory framework (Tooze, 2018; Harvey, 2010, Germain, 2009), the focus has been—and will probably remain—on regulatory reform (or reduction of such financial regulations) instead of any fundamental reform of private institutions (and the power they wield in the political process) and the need for more effective venues of public accountability (Pauly, 2009).

Political/economic involution will probably continue as long as economic policies remain to be categorized as merely issues of administration (Hummel, 2007; Merrifield, 2002). Some scholars have claimed that such a view represents nothing more than the depoliticization (or economization) of policy issues (O'Connor, 1987; Harvey, 2010; Galbraith, 2008; Ventriss, 1998). And yet, it could also be argued that we are experiencing is in fact a "repoliticization" of issues in which both fields will become more visibly entangled in managing short-term policies commensurate to the continuation of technical and formal administrative procedures (Offe, 1976). In many respects, again in both fields we are already adapting to fulfill this need. As mentioned previously, with the emphasis on the professionalization of public affairs programs coupled with the norms of neo-managerialism, researchers and practitioners alike tend to pursue chiefly technocratic policies, which are policies understandably well intended, but which probably give only a modicum of thought to any renewed focus on publicness.

One of the ramifications of "this situation . . . could put public administration [and public policy] in the awkward position of being no longer viewed as a neutral tool of the state but as an integral part of the re-politicization of a managed economy whose distributive effects [may] not be borne equally" (Ventriss, 2010, p. 418; Jacobs & King, 2009; Macartney, 2009). Specifically, under these circumstances, public management/administration will have to serve as a "normative stabilizer" (to use Durkheim's famous words), attempting to hold together the rules of the game as well as the structural tensions of a changing market economy. The crisis of 2008 represents a critical turning point in the evolution of both fields (in the United States, anyway). That is to say, because of public management/admnistration's and public policy's intellectual aversion toward social and value conflict in society as exemplified in diverse schools of thought such as scientific management, new public management, public choice theory, and human relations, we will find ourselves continuously struggling to manage the inherently conflicted implications of political/economic involution in these uncertain times. How we can effectively deal with this state of affairs is anyone's guess, particularly with the rising tide of populism that would undermine any normative notion of publicness. Assuming the present trajectory of the policies developed so far in this crisis, one thing is certain: the challenge of managing political/economic involution will probably not get much easier with time.

Economic Crisis and the Value of Historical Inquiry

> [Historical understanding] is the opportunity of seeing a passage of the past in terms of hitherto neglected relationships and of being able to imagine it freshly and more perspicuously.
>
> —Michael Oakeshott

The late Paul Samuelson, best known for his classic economic textbook and as the first American Nobel Laureate in Economic Science, was influential in demonstrating the importance of mathematical modeling in understanding and analyzing economic phenomena.[9] One year before he died he gave an interview reflecting on his long and distinguished career. In that interview, Samuelson mentioned that his advice to any new graduate student in economics would be quite different than what he would have given in his younger years. He would now emphasize a healthier respect for the study of history, "because that is the material of which any conjectures or testing will come" (Clarke, 2009, p. 18). Concomitantly, Nouriel Roubini and Stephen Mihn, echoing Samuelson's insight on this exact point, made the following observation:

> Samuelson is right—economic history is important, for more than theories of efficient markets and rational investors would lead one to believe . . . history is useful precisely because its raw material can inform and inflect economic theories. It injects gritty, real-life detail into elegant mathematical models like those devised by Samuelson and his peers. That's a good thing: an almost religious faith in models helped create the conditions for the crisis in the first place, blending traders and market players to be very real risks that had been accumulating for years. History promotes humility, a quality that comes in handy when assessing crises, which so often come on the heels of arrogant proclamations that ordinary economic rules no longer apply. (2011, p. 59)

From a slightly different methodological angle, Paul Krugman offered this rather somber explanation as to why there was such a serious lapse in prevailing economic thinking in anticipating this economic crisis, even with all the analytical acumen being displayed in this "queen" all of social sciences:[10]

> As I see it, the economics profession went astray because economists, as a group, mistook beauty, clad in impressive-looking mathematics, for truth. Until the Great Depression, most economists clung to a vision of capitalism as a perfect or nearly perfect system. That vision wasn't sustainable in the face of mass unemployment, but as memories of the Depression faded, economists fell back in love with the old, idealized vision of an economy in which rational individuals interact in perfect markets, this time gussied up with fancy equations. The renewed romance with the idealized market was, to be sure, partly a response to shifting political winds, partly a response to financial incentives. But while sabbaticals at the Hoover Institute and job opportunities on Wall Street are nothing to sneeze at, the central cause of the profession's failure was the desire for an all-encompassing,

> intellectually elegant approach that also gave economists a chance to show off their mathematical prowess. (2009, p. 37)

Although these insights are compelling, one may question what they have to do with public management/administration and public policy. After all, the key decision makers who most likely played central roles in the conditions leading to the economic crisis of 2008 probably had professional and academic backgrounds in business administration, economics, and law. The aforementioned notwithstanding, the economic crisis of 2008 reflected more than a series of bad and reckless policy decisions by certain key actors and institutions. It also exposed a worrisome trend festering in public affairs: a growing fixation on the inherent superiority of technical and analytical approaches to public problem solving that has, over time, essentially driven out the theoretical value of historical inquiry and social theory. This intellectual tendency has led us to ignore what Dana Villa (2001, p. 2) argued is so pivotal to any substantive human inquiry. Villa referred to this approach as "elenchus"; that is, a critical inquiry of those unexamined political, economic, and administrative assumptions that can lead to moral and value distortion. Put simply, if there is any salient lesson to be directly learned from this economic crisis, it is the importance of avoiding the conceptual perils of methodological hubris when confronting "wicked" societal problems facing the modern polity (Adams, 2011; Adams & Balfour, 2012).

Following a similar line of thinking, Raadschelders (2000) and his colleagues have insisted, convincingly, that public administration scholars, in particular, have largely deemphasized historical research as part of their methodological repertoire. This view is supported, in part, by an analysis of articles published in the *Public Administration Review* from 2000–09 that showed a marked increase of quantitative statistical analysis and, at the same time, a troubling tendency for the continued marginalization of "the historical context and epistemological foundations of the [disciple]" (Raadschelders & Lee, 2011, p. 19). Yet this result should come as no surprise. This historical lacuna, especially public in administration/management, has increasingly become even more acute and accordingly has been noted at different times by such scholars as Caldwell (1955), Waldo (1948), Adams (1992), Adams & Balfour (2009), Karl (1976), Luton (1999), Neustadt & May (1986), Raadschelders (1998, 2000, 2005), Ventriss (2000), Schachter (1998), Stivers (1999), and Roberts (2012). Put bluntly, the analysis of policy issues is increasingly becoming divorced from its substantive foundations, as I argued in chapter 1. In the aftermath of the economic crisis, and its enduring implications on society, a historical perspective will become essential in understanding the grave consequences it can have on publicness and its changing meaning in public affairs.

It is interesting to note that it was Joseph Schumpeter, the influential economic theorist best known for his concept of creative destruction, who forcefully contended that to properly understand any economic subject it was essential to analyze the historical and sociological context of those factors that affect economic growth, especially because such contexts relate directly to the phenomenon of economic activity itself (McCraw, 2007; Viner, 1954). Schumpeter's words below go well beyond his own discipline of economics:

> I wish to state right now that if, starting my work in economics afresh, I were told that I could study only one of three [theory, statistics, and history] but could have my choice, it would be economic history that I would choose . . . it is, I believe, *the fact that most of the fundamental errors currently committed in economic analysis are due to the lack of historical experience more often than to any other shortcoming of the economic equipment.* (1954, pp. 12–13; my emphasis)

Schumpeter's sensitivity to the historical context and its significance to social and economic inquiry has been exemplified in Alasdair Roberts's (2012) provocative work *America's First Great Depression*. In this book, Roberts draws obvious attention to our present fiscal situation and how the economic crisis of 1837 was also similarly launched by real estate speculation, lax regulations, and a banking crisis. Policy change arose from the sober vicissitudes of this crisis, including the adoption of new constitutional debt requirements by six states, while another eight states instituted borrowing limits. But, according to Roberts, the arguably more precarious outcome of the economic upheaval was a crisis of "civic order" resulting in civil unrest in the Northeast and the deleterious erosion of trust in public institutions as well as increasing mistrust between companies and workers. Roberts gives an illuminating historical examination of how numerous states borrowed monies abroad, especially from Britain, to finance an array of infrastructural activities that would promote and open new markets. When the economy collapsed in 1837, foreign creditors wanted payment for their loans, forcing some states (very reluctantly) to raise property taxes. Ultimately, foreign relations between the United States and Britain became strained "and America had learned a hard lesson about the limits of popular sovereignty with a globalized economy" (Roberts, 2011, p. G4).

For our purposes, what is noteworthy about Roberts's meticulous historical analysis is not so much the validity of his conclusions, but instead his attention to the interplay of the global economy and the changing economic dynamics occurring domestically, and the political detritus of such developments within the body politic. This is a prescient reminder of why the inclusion of a historical dimension is critical to any legitimate inquiry (coupled with appropriate empirical data) about the important nexus between the changing notion of publicness and economic issues (Roberts, 2010).

Moreover, in another fascinating historical analysis, Elizabeth Tandy Shermer, in her careful (and extensive) examination of the history of financing in America, postulated that the historical evidence is relatively clear on one particular point: "[I]t was regulation that created and policed the banking system and was [largely] responsible for America's remarkable mid-twentieth-century economic growth" (2012, p. 83). Regrettably, she concluded, in general, Americans have not learned the important economic lessons from our past.

My point in raising these examples is that by downplaying the significance of historical inquiry, we essentially restrict both field's theoretical (and pragmatic) questions/issues to what Nicos Mouzelis (1973) depicted as the organizational and shop levels of analyses.[11] What tends to be neglected, following on Mouzelis's perspicacious point, is the consideration of a macrosocietal level of analysis that focuses on such factors as the role of government in a global economy, the changing and historical nature of political economy dominated by certain institutional actors and its impact on the policy process, and the institutional history and political culture of regulatory reform, just to mention a few examples. Ironically, this economic crisis might just remind us that what makes our fields of social inquiry somewhat unique among the social sciences is the following: "that given the importance of both normative and empirical questions to the field, public administration [and public policy] as an intellectual enterprise must operate on all three levels of abstraction (sub-organizational, organizational, and macro-societal) in order to construct a viable, albeit conditional, theoretical base" (Ventriss, 2000, p. 310). Our intellectual relevance in the future, as we confront some of the broader social, economic, and administrative aspects of the Great Recession, may depend on how effectively we can appropriately integrate all three levels of analysis without disintegrating into a form of intellectual myopia that comfortably (and politely) overlooks the larger and more fundamental questions/issues that will ultimately emerge from the sheer scale and scope of this economic crisis.[12]

A Final Thought

> Democracy . . . spreads through the body a restless activity, superabundant force, and energy never found elsewhere, which, however little favored by circumstances, can do wonders. Those are its true advantages.
>
> —de Tocqueville

It has become almost commonplace in American and European public management/administration to recite the shibboleths of the intrinsic strengths of a managerial liberalism and the utilitarian perspective that underlie most of the intellectual and pragmatic importance of what we do and who we are. To a large degree, public management/administration and public policy (at least in the advanced industrialized countries) must often deal with the unintended effects of a market society, and, equally important, provide the requisite institutional and analytical infrastructure, so to speak, in implementing policies passed by legitimate authoritative decision makers. Fittingly, many would contend that this is exactly the way it should be (Lynn, 2012).[13] But one can still ask the question whether this understandable defense merely cloaks the tendrils of a "stalled ideology" that makes us even more of an enigma to the public we serve (Wolin, 1994, 2008).

The economic crisis has pushed to the surface the intellectual subterranean tendencies that have been around for some time (e.g., neo-managerialism, instrumental rationality, the growing academic insularity, the depoliticization of issues of public concern and corresponding rise of a corporate approach to governance, the emphasis on procedural reforms, the stress on group adjustment in managing conflicts, and the mortgaging of administrative and policy thought to economics). And, dare we say, the increasing narrowness of comparatively inconsequential research and a general distaste for asking the big, and often controversial, questions of the modern polity?

To the general public, these tendencies (and debates) are likely to be regarded as highly idiosyncratic and as having little, if any, direct bearing on the public services that citizens depend upon in their daily lives. No doubt, there is some truth to this view. But, on the other hand, there is nothing idiosyncratic about maintaining a strong theoretical prism in addressing social issues that provides a more comprehensive view of policies and their impact on the public; or assessing the cost of any obfuscation of the underlying assumptions of various policy approaches and their implications on how power is being displayed in society; or acknowledging the paucity of research on the delimitation of the market and general absence of any viable alternative nonmarket frameworks; or pointing out the economic detritus left behind in this crisis representing a tocsin of just how disruptive things can get in the body politic; or finally, sparking the needed moral debate on the ripple effects of this crisis, a debate that goes well beyond a discussion of mere illegalities, conflicts of interest, and deception.

It is beyond the scope of this chapter to offer any specific suggestions to the challenges presented here. Ostensibly, it is more crucial at this juncture to have us rethink certain trends and theoretical inclinations and, hopefully, to critically deliberate on what has happened to public management/administration and public policy. Regardless of where this debate takes us, and the issues we ultimately find to be the most salient to explore, I think we will never be quite the same again.

Yet, it is worth mentioning that in virtually every article, book, and research report and article that one reads, the word *crisis* inevitably appears in denoting just how serious the consequences were—and continue to be—following what happened in 2008. One of the key lessons that emerged from this historical event was the attention national governments needed to give to effectively balance the fragile relationship between coordination and oversight and in providing enough autonomy to promote innovation within the modern economy (Cassidy, 2009). For us in public management/administration and public policy, the impact of this situation can be hardly described as an intellectual minor event. But, as briefly noted earlier, the Great Recession has displayed our intellectual sensibilities as primarily quotidian in nature; that is, we defined this deeply troubling event as more or less a technical problem, albeit a major one in this instance, in that as agents of the state there was little that public management/administration (or public policy) could have done beyond the analytical and managerial expertise we are called upon to competently demonstrate. This notion is an understandable and legitimate response, but it is hardly satisfying to those who contend that there is a distinct reason why we call ourselves "public" administration rather than "administration of the public" or "public" policy instead of "policies for the public." Again, to reemphasize, this is not merely a matter of semantics, but rather it implies a vital societal purpose and substantive approach to our role and meaning in public affairs—our very relationship to publicness and to critical democratic thought (Ventriss, 2012b; Fischer, 2003; Bevir, 2010; Ramos, 1981). What is noted here is that public affairs, both intellectually and pragmatically, in dealing with the issues mentioned here should, at a minimum, attempt to rediscover the importance of publicness and how it can be impacted. While any such rediscovery will not itself serve as a panacea to many of the societal issues created by what happened in 2008, it could nudge us in the right direction to further clarify our role in seeing publicness in more than just administrative and market terms. Hopefully, it could help in facilitating a public language and a public social science that can foster a more dynamic civic relationship to the public we serve.

In other words, what I tried to clarify here is that while there are a myraid of worthy approaches to our most pressing issues of the day,[14] John Dewey correctly pointed out that is paramount to examine value distortions and their public consequences. All things considered, Dewey knew that "what is given is an inquiry which taxes reflection at the uttermost" (1903, p. 61). Few have stated it better.

Although it is true that memories of any major economic or political event tend to fade with time, and that old habits die hard, it is nevertheless hoped that a mosaic of innovative ideas will emerge that can encourage both fields to move in new directions, not in order to dismiss what has gone before, but rather to instill in us a renewed confidence in where we need to go and why. T. S. Eliot (1971, p. 145), perhaps, stated it best as we contemplate what lies before us:

> And the end of all our exploring
> Will be to arrive where we started
> And know the place for the first time.

Conclusion

This chapter marks the first of three investigations that, I believe, are significant issues/problems facing both fields. In this chapter, I used the enduring effects of the 2008 economic crisis as a site to examine changing economic forces and their consequential impact on public and community life. And I discussed the impact of this crisis on publicness, paired with critical democratic thought, and the challenges this crisis poses to both the intellectual mission and pragmatic implications for those committed to public service.

The first section of this chapter examined the most evident consequences of the crisis: rising income and wealth inequality; underemployment; and declining social mobility in the United States. I also suggested that Hirsch's concept of "positional goods" can help us understand how these outcomes challenge economic policy. I argued that in a market economy in which positional goods play an important role, it raises an array of distributive concerns in the present political and economic environment of unequal democracy, at least in the United States.

In the second section of this chapter, I investigated the pathways needed to restore democratic values to the U.S. economy through public affairs—and the challenges to doing so. I drew on Schmookler and Ramos to sketch perspectives on how to counterbalance the transactional ethos of current market centric policies. The vision of these thinkers is compelling, but also challenging to conceive of in sufficient detail to implement. I argued that to do so, we in public affairs must focus our research on how to arrest the moral deterioration of modern markets and help facilitate a noncommercial understanding of social values.

To accomplish this, I turned to Adams and Balfour, and others, to understand the depths of what I refer to as policy involution. These thinkers suggest that a singular emphasis on market values, and the subsequent policy approaches developed as part of this process, has in effect undermined the government's ability to justify policy actions on norms that are not overall instrumental in nature. Accordingly, I called for the centrality of an invigorated publicness in exploring other policy alternatives that might or could emerge.

Undoubtedly, fostering a deliberative and normative foundation dealing with economic policies of a late market society such as the contemporary United States is an ambitious endeavor. Guerreiro Ramos and Schoenberger in their respective arguments both caution that policy involution (although they do not call it by that name) often results in merely a collection of policy patchwork that does not address the underlying source that created the problem in the first place. One possible approach, I argued, is to ground such calls for deliberative policy justifications in a historical perspective. If the 2008 crisis is any indicator, the quantitative approaches to economic policy have demonstrated their methodological shortcomings in explaining economic trends and designing policies to be pursued. Historical analysis, coupled with other methodological approaches, may be a better way of understanding how publicness is impacted in this changing and volatile global economy.

7

Public Affairs in the Epoch of Space

Challenges to the Public Sphere

> The present epoch will perhaps be above all the epoch of space. We are in the epoch of simultaneity: we are in the epoch of juxtaposition, the epoch of the near and far, of the side-by-side, of the dispersed.
>
> —Michel Foucault

> A model of political culture appropriate for our situation will necessarily have to raise spatial issues as its fundamental organizing concern.
>
> —Frederic Jameson

For at least the last several decades, there has been an active and lively debate among urban sociologists, environmentalists, policy analysts, human geographers, and urban planners about the importance of space[1] as related to such crucial issues as urban change, citizenship in an era of globalization, economic development, and economic and political restructuring. While this debate has consumed much ink in the literature of these disciplines, little attention on this subject can be found in the major journals of public management/administration and public policy. This modicum of interest in spatiality among public management and policy scholars is somewhat surprising given that the debate on this subject has important implications for both disciplines in two basic ways: (1) it introduces (and draws attention) to the theoretical importance of space and how this concept raises critical policy and administrative issues concerning the public sphere in a global economic environment, and (2) it forces public management/administration and public policy to consider the concept of space as an important factor in formulating any viable social and political theory, particularly in regard to the changing nature of the state and how citizenship and publicness is taking on a more spatial (and global) dimension.

These two points constitute important issues that will inevitably involve both fields in addressing some rather controversial ways that have not occupied much attention up to this point. One such issue, for example, will involve the role of public organizations managing, or attempting to manage, the spatial implications of a global economy that is restructuring the political and economic landscape of our democratic polity as well as of other advanced industrial countries (Mazzucato, 2015; Harvey, 2006, 2010; Albrechts, 1991). Such an effort will require nothing less than confronting the politically contentious issue of how the mobility of capital is impacting our public spaces (i.e., communities) and the role of citizens in trying to exert democratic control over these public spaces in a volatile, unpredictable global economic environment (Lefebvre, 1991). However, increasingly we are seeing placeless services such as Amazon eliminating local place-based services that are spatially limited to a particular market area. To be sure, this attempted control could take the form of nationalistic populism that might be exploited for cynical political purposes—a trend that has recently emerged in many countries (Moffitt, 2016). As noted by Clarke and Newman (2017, p. 108), this growing nationalistic populism emerging in many countries, particularly in the United States and the United Kingdom, is based on a paradox in which the "forgotten individuals" channel their political resentments, ironically through a group of political or economic insiders, of "outsiders" who are elites who know how to manipulate these populist sensibilities for political and economic gain.

This spatiality, moreover, is also manifested in how social media can channel communications across time and space instantaneously, such as by Facebook and other, similar media outlets, among different publics, thus creating a public space via media platforms that expose users to a variety of messages for immediate consumption. This communicative spatiality can facilitate social and political networks in mobilizing public action and debate, but concomitantly it can serve as a manipulative tool in colonizing the user's lifeworld in converting a public space into a social media environment comprised of contrived and distorted information. Hence, these digital social media, while connecting various publics instantaneously, must be understood within the broader contradictions of social media power (Dijck & Poell, 2015).

For example, Twitter, Facebook, and other social media platforms are being increasingly confronted with the challenge of how to mediate the flow of information between the governed and those who govern them, particularly when dealing with authoritarian governments. Moreover, because these social media platforms are by definition public spaces, what happens when inappropriate or offensive language is used? To cite only one example from the United States, in 2019 seventy civil rights groups petitioned Facebook to halt what they regarded as its racially biased content moderation system. These issues are becoming more pronounced because from 2010 to 2015 social media platforms have become integrally entangled with professional activities such as health care and education as well as citizen involvement and protest organizations (Dijck, Poell, & de Waal, 2018). Publicness is crucial here due to the growing reality that cultural, social, and political activities are now part and parcel of the techno-commercial infrastructure of social media platforms (Gillespie, 2018). In effect, what we have is a media ecosystem of public spaces that can not only shape public values, but manage to sidestep basic questions of their public role and responsibility (Schneier, 2015). The troubling aspect, therefore, of this trend is that this technology with such enormous power to affect public spaces, and our very sense of publicness, is now being controlled by a few major corporations.

Given these trends, this chapter will examine some of the issues (and debates) of the theoretical and practical implications of spatiality in public affairs. There will be no attempt to argue that by exploring the importance of sociospatial factors it will in any way resolve the problems dealing with the theoretical viability of public management/administration or public policy. Rather, the purpose here is to pry open—or at least try to—new theoretical doors to broaden our understanding of the human environment in which we operate. Such is the nature of the challenge and opportunity before us—a challenge that will endure for some time.

Space and Globalization

> People live in places, power rules through flows.
>
> —Manuel Castells

> The recovery of space for . . . community life should be a priority of citizens and governments . . . [for] space affects [and], even shapes, people's lives.
>
> —Alberto Guerreiro Ramos

At first glance, the attempt to discuss such an ambiguous term as "space" in respect to the disciplines of public management/administration and public policy may seem rather odd. Yet, one manner in which to comprehend its importance is to reflect on the statement of Thomas Johnson, who at that time, as president of Chemical Bank, voiced these words before the stock market crash of 1987. If there is a financial crisis, he commented, "there is a possibility of a nightmarish domino effect as every creditor ransacks the globe attempting to locate his collateral" (cited in Smith, 1990, p. 161)—words that still hold true in the wake of the economic crisis of 2008. As melodramatic as this may sound, Richard O'Brien (1992, p. 96), echoing sentiments similar to Johnson's, asserts that we need to understand that we are experiencing nothing less than the parallel integration of finance and economics "and [that] the connecting rod is the massive and freer flow of capital." While these statements are a quarter-century old, their arguments continue to have relevance (Klein, 2009; Harvey, 2014, 2012, 2006; Lefebvre, 1991; Fox, 2009; Brenner, 2003; Dicken, 2007; Panitch & Konings, 2008; Wolf, 2009).

But, how does the continued relevance relate to the notion of space and the complex issues we face in public affairs? The answer is actually quite simple: what we are experiencing (in historical terms) is not just the massive flow of capital moving quickly across the globe, but also, and more fundamentally, a restructuring of the production of space, which is reshaping our political and economic lives.[2] In other words, while capital or economic space has become more mobile, our social spaces (cities and communities, for example) are fixed in particular places and hence have become, more than ever, vulnerable to changing global market forces of technology and communications that can reshape the spatial order of localities. Many years ago, one scholar succinctly put it this way: "Capital is mobile. Detroit is not" (Child-Hill, 1984, p. iii).

This phenomenon has hardly escaped the attention of scholars examining these new economic developments and their spatial implications. For example, it is widely acknowledged that cities (and other subnational levels of government) are linked, for better or worse, to the global economy. This is especially evident in what are now aptly called "world-cities" such as New York, Tokyo, Los Angeles, Chicago, Houston, Paris, London, Detroit, and São Paulo (to name just a few) that serve as headquarters for transnational corporations, financial centers, major transportation nodes, manufacturing centers, international institutions, and research and educational centers (Harvey, 2012; Friedmann, 1986; Hall, 1984; Perry, 1987; Sassen-Koob, 1985, 1986, 1987; Smith & Feagin, 1987; Soja, Morales, & Wolff, 1983; Thrift, 1987). While the ascendant dominance of world cities in the global economy is hardly a new development, there is another but related trend that has emerged that should not go unnoticed. Due to structural changes in the global and national economy that have facilitated the internationalization of capital and production and freed corporate capital investment from previous dependencies on local agglomeration economics (McNally, 2011; Reich, 2015; Storper & Scott, 2016; Smith, 1989; Peet, 1987), this spatial dispersion of capital has, ironically, led to "locality becoming the key place for the regulation for the production/reproduction nexus" (Swyngedouw, 1989, p. 40).[3] Erik Swyngedouw, a professor of geography at the University of Manchester, has summarized this point nicely by explaining that because we have entered an era of *hyperspace* (his term) "in which capital can flow at the twinkle of an eye from one place to another, . . . [this trend] makes locality again . . . the place of regulating daily social and economic life in the face of [globalization]" (1989, p. 40). Swyngedouw (1992) has referred to this process as "glocalization" of the local/global interplay.

Assuming the validity of these assertions, these new spatial developments pose important implications for public management/administration and public policy: we are witnessing not only an economic restructuring[4] that is manifested in the geographical dispersion of new production systems and capital at the global and regional level (which has contributed to uneven development), but to a political restructuring in a response to this spatial trend (McNally, 2011; Phillips, 2009; Cooke, 1986a, 1986b, 1988, 1989a, 1989b; Cox, 1989; Gottdiener & Komninos, 1989; Harvey, 2012; Logan & Motolch, 1987; Mayer, 1992; Komninos, 1987; Stiglitz, 2002, 2010, 2013, 2015; Smith, 1988). This trend has been extensively documented not only in the United States but in European countries such as Belgium, Greece, Italy, Portugal, and Spain (Stiglitz, 2013, 2015; Harvey, 2010; Courlet, 1989; Krätke, 1992; Moulaert & Willekens, 1987). This political restructuring has been defined as a shift away from the traditional policy goals of localities that aim to provide the general conditions of production and encourage the redistribution of value by increasing social wages for the working public, to the promotion of a good business climate and the subsidization of growth in the service of capital (Reich, 2016; Galbraith, 2008; Gottdiener & Komninos, 1989; Harvey, 2014; Milanovic, 2005). The crucial issue here is that the emergence of entrepreneurial subnational governments (since the 1980s) must be viewed within the broader context of how public spaces are being politically mediated, whether by intention or not, that has essentially weakened the capacity of citizens to question the normative implications of economic restructuring that might be contributing to social and spatial inequalities. Consequently, with the rise of entrepreneurial subnational economic strategies, new alliances have been forged between entrepreneurial state policymakers (and their policies) and glocal business elites. The consequential implication of this trend is that the publicness of decision making itself is depoliticized to the extent that entrepreneurial strategies do not appear as politics at all; "rather it is viewed as merely the inevitable managerial adaptation of a responsible state government to new economic (and international) realities" (Ventriss 2000, p. 93; Harvey, 2014). The challenge to us in public affairs is that as the production of space has changed so has the notion of publicness. In short, we are seeing a reconstructed idea of publicness defined increasingly in terms of consumption rather than in trying to expand political and economic rights of citizenship in this era of political and economic uncertainty. In other words, the process of what is called the politics of policy containment is occurring with more frequency, in that discussion of key policy issues are largely confined to certain managerial and ideological dicta consonant with the market-centered motifs of key public and private decision makers (Ventriss, 2002; Muller & Ventriss, 1985).

This spatial dispersion of capital to different local areas around the globe has been attributed, among other things, to the ineffectiveness of national regulation of capital, the transnational strategy of multinational firms dealing with sharpened international competition, and the changing international division of labor (Foster & Magdoff, 2009; Milanovic, 2005; Storper & Walker, 1989; Lipietz, 1986; Cochrane, 1991; Stohr, 1990). That is to say, as subnational levels of government have become more critical actors in this process, they have found themselves, to a large degree, disempowered and subordinated to global forces. Manuel Castells (1985, p. 31), for example, has summarized this development in the following polemic terms that continue to resonate even today:

> [P]erhaps, the most striking effect of the new international economy on cities and regions is the loss of their autonomy vis-à-vis the worldwide economic actors that control their activities in terms of a global logic largely ignored and uncontrollable by local and regional societies. A rapidly changing economic space determined by economic units whose size and transnationalitv places them above social pressures and political controls is a tendency that, favored by the internationalization process . . . attempts to impose the abstraction of a space of strategic decisions over the experience of place-based activities, cultures, and politics.

Castells highlights a point here that cannot be so easily brushed aside: the restructuring of space has become, and will continue to be, a critical policy issue for localities as they strive to maintain some control over their territorial places. In fact, what has emerged is a new kind of *spatial politics*—a politics that must ultimately confront the dilemma posed by the difference between "placeless power" and "powerless places" (Harvey, 2012; Low & Smith, 2006; Henderson & Castells, 1987; Bookchin, 1992; Cox, 1997; Abers, 2000; Albrechts, 1991; Brenner & Theodore, 2003). The crucial issue here is that with the emergence of the "entrepreneurial" local and regional governments trying to incessantly attract new businesses via copious financial incentives offered to such enterprises, this has essentially reduced the role of ordinary citizens to mere passive actors in questioning the efficacy of such efforts that might be contributing to new forms of political and spatial inequality (Combes & Thisse, 2008; Wei, 2015; Ventriss, 2002).

Is this restructuring of space really anything new, though? Many prominent scholars have argued that we have indeed entered a new era. Allen Scott and Michael Storper (1986, p. 6), for example, suggest that it is "through the interaction of industrial production and money capital, [that] internationalization has now emerged as a relatively external pressure on the organization of production, work, and territory in all countries." Most of the arguments echo Scott and Storper's (1986, p. 6) analysis, contending that "the historical realities of capitalism began with a crisis of profitability [concerning] production in the developed nations." These views are predicated by and large on the assumption that, beginning in 1973 with termination of the Bretton Woods agreement and the ascendancy of capital mobility, transnational firms began to reorganize production, management, and distribution activities into multiple operation units spread geographically throughout the world (Combes & Thisse, 2008; Stiglitz, 2010; McNally, 2011; Fox, 2009; Lipietz, 1986; Harvey, 1988). This new strategy, it is argued, has ushered in a new era of spatial economic restructuring that has changed the urban landscape of advanced industrial countries.

Briefly stated, the argument goes something like this: following the breakdown of the Bretton Woods agreement in the 1970s, the mobility of capital became even more acute due to the lack of any national regulation on its movement, thus leading to an intense competition for capital and global currency speculation.[5] At the same time, U.S. competitiveness in manufacturing was starting to decline and multinational production systems had to alter their flow of shipments and payments in response to fluctuating exchange rates. Because of the depreciated dollar, American assets became a bargain for European and Japanese firms, therefore, positioning other nations' multinational companies in the lucrative U.S. domestic market. Furthermore, it was during the period of the early 1970s that demand for mass-produced goods started to stagnate because consumers sought more diversified and higher quality products in a new competitive international marketplace. And finally, in the 1970s locational constraints became lessened due to technological and communication innovations as well as the desire by major U.S. transnational corporations to reduce factor costs in order to bolster declining profits (Dicken, 2007; Scott & Storper, 1986; Harvey, 1989; Foster & Madgoff, 2009; Panitch & Konings, 2008). According to this line of logic, it is no wonder that "interspatial competition intensified and the particular position of a locality within the international division of labor, which set certain constraints, [became] viewed as an asset to be exploited in ways that were decided locally" (Dunford & Kafkalas, 1992, p. 7; Sassen, 2014; Harvey, 2006). These new economic trends have resulted, as the advocates of this argument proclaim, in a historical disjuncture that is reflected in the shifting geographies of investment, production, and urban space.

Although this analysis might seem convincing to some, other scholars—while openly sympathetic to many of the views presented—have expressed reservations about the historical validity or the reasoning behind the some of the explanations previously mentioned. Susan and Norm Fainstein (1989, p. 22), to cite only one example, have maintained that it is often forgotten that "decentralizing tendencies have existed throughout the history of capitalism, even at the apogee of the nineteenth-century European manufacturing city." Next, they argue that the internationalization of capital actually emerged with the rise of the great trading companies of the seventeenth century. And, more importantly, the deindustrialization process that many attribute to the mobility of capital might, in fact, have more to do with the emergence of the economic influence of the Far East countries. Fainstein and Fainstein (1989, p. 24) conclude that "throughout the history of capitalism and its periodic restructurings, we can identify a number of creative destructions that manifest themselves *spatially* as well as within social relations that, in turn, affect social and productive relations." Other theorists, with a somewhat different twist to their arguments, have also presented alternative explanations to this new economic trend and its spatial dynamics on our cities and regions (Wolfe, 2009; Harvey, 2010, 2018; Jessop, 1990; Gertler, 1988).

Whatever may be said about the merits of these different arguments and theoretical positions, it can be safely stated that our knowledge of the dynamics of internationalization of capital and its sociospatial implications on subnational levels of government is still incomplete. But one thing is certain: *the restructuring of space is being forged by the global forces of both capital and transnational corporations, and state responses to these developments have produced a new global/local interplay* (Smith, 1989, p. 190; Piketty, 2014; Smith & Feagin, 1987; Ventriss, 2002).

This global/local interplay can be clearly seen in the United States in the ways state and local governments have actively participated in international economic affairs, in what has been referred to as "global microdiplomacy" (Duchacek, 1984; Ventriss, 1994).In 1988, for example, more than 750 American cities had developed various trade development agreements with about 1,200 cities in eighty-six countries (Luke & Ventriss et al., 1988). In 2015, U.S. state governments maintained forty overseas offices or representatives in seventeen different countries (Pennsylvania, for example, has seventeen overseas offices, followed closely by Florida, Colorado, Georgia, Illinois, Louisiana, Maryland, and Missouri). Moreover, exports play a critical role in the economic health of states. For example, "[The value of total goods and services exported in 2014 reached a record $2.3 trillion and supported 11.7 million jobs nationally." Jobs supported by exports grew more than 107 percent in New Mexico from 2009 to 2014, followed by Arkansas and Hawaii (66 percent) and South Carolina and Washington (38 percent) (Council of State Governments, 2015). More recently, this trend has continued, albeit in a different way, after the U.S. withdrawal from the Paris Climate Accords, with California, New York, and Washington having formed a domestic effort to combat climate change, the U.S. Climate Alliance. This alliance aims to keep state governments relevant even in the face of the U.S. federal government no longer abiding by the Paris Accords. This approach is similar to the regional Greenhouse Gas Initiative, an East Coast interstate compact between states and Quebec (Congressional Research Service, 2019).

Although the trend dealing with export promotion and international offices abroad has subsided somewhat due to state government cutbacks, when we analyze these trends along with other aggressive state and local economic development strategies from the 1980s to 2016, it is no wonder that a shift has occurred toward what has been previously noted as the rise of the "entrepreneurial state/city." This "new entrepreneurial approach" on the subnational level is not only mushrooming in the United States (Mazzucato, 2015; Fosler, 1988), but is widespread in Europe and Asia (Porter & Faust, 2009; Morgan, 1992; Mayer, 1992; Swyngedouw, 1989). In short, national spatial policies are being balanced by discretionary strategic policies at the subnational level. While these strategic policies are proliferating at the local and state level, the more general question of who commands control over our economic and social spaces by those promoting such strategic policies has gone largely unanswered (Harvey, 2012; Swyngedouw,1989). For public affairs, this raises some serious research and policy questions that will demand, one hopes, some critical examinations. These issues include the following:

- Given the spatial nature of economic restructuring that is taking place, what policies need to be formulated that can realistically address the globalization of capital and production systems that is reshaping our cities, regions, and public spaces? Put candidly, do we need new political and economic regulations that can better manage the internationalization of capital that has often led to uneven development? And if such regulations are needed, how can we address the relationship of social equity to economic development in this age of the local/global interplay?
- How can public organizations and citizens mediate the local or regional conflicts that will inevitably occur as a result of spatial politics?
- And finally, how can we in public affairs redesign public spaces that appropriately delimit the more corrosive implications of an increasingly market-centered mentality on our local communities and social media platforms?

The issue for us in public affairs is that by raising "spatial issues as an organizing concern," it draws our attention to the politics of sociospatial processes and the implied effect of these changes on the everyday lives of the public and the meaning of publicness. Guerreiro Ramos (1981) was right: the recovery of space should be a central concern for citizens and governments alike. However, if we are able to grasp the significance of this concept, it must be somehow linked to social theory. Let us now turn our attention to how such linkage might be possible, and its importance to the theory and practice of public affairs.

Toward a Spatial Social Theory

Prophesy now involves a geographical rather than historical projection; it is space not time that hides consequences from us.

—John Berger

Theorists, especially in geography, urban and regional planning, and sociology—and those who contend that space is best understood in terms of it being a social construct—have been wrestling for some time with how it may be possible to conceptually link space to social theory and practice (Brenner, Jessop, Jones, & Macleod,2008; Merriman et al., 2012; Soja, 1989, 2011; Harvey, 1989; Urry, 2004; Giddens, 1984; Sayer, 1989; Massey, 1996). In the search for this linkage, such theorists have thought it necessary to reexamine the classic works of thinkers such as Weber, Marx, and Durkheim. The contemporary theorists, for the most part, have discovered that such classic thinkers devoted little, if any, theoretical attention to the notion of space. At best, the concept of space had to be inferred from their works, in relationship to the broader social issues they were attempting to analyze.

Scholars in both public management/administration and public policy, on the other hand, have exhibited little interest in what some might claim is just too abstract a concept, and, more significantly, too unrelated to the theoretical and applied mission of both disciplines. Guerreiro Ramos and Charles Goodsell, of course, are exceptions to this rule. Unfortunately, both Goodsell's (1988) and Guerreiro Ramos's (1981) ideas about the importance of spatiality have been largely ignored. If space is mentioned at all in either discipline, it has come from the earlier works of Fred Steele (1973), Edward Hall (1966), Robert Sommer (1969), Arendt (1958), Habermas (1962), Domahidy and Gilsinan (1992). Other than Arendt, Habermas, and a few others, the proclivity in public policy and public administration has been mainly focused on the spatial dimensions dealing within organizations or on the usage of space in specific social settings. Moreover, these works in the public policy and public management/administration literature have not tried to link space to social or political theory in any definitive manner.

Saying this, the question that immediately comes into mind is: Why try in the first place to relate spatiality at all to social theory, and what relevance could it possibly have to such pragmatic fields devoted to the study and practice of public affairs? The answer to this legitimate question can be stated as follows: the saliency of linking space to social theory is that public policies implemented by public agencies (and their impact on various publics) play a central role in how spaces are managed in the policy process. In other words, public agencies must inevitably deal with the political, economic, and normative implications of this new epoch of flexible space as they directly impact the "publicness" of community life. This implication of this process is being played out in the tension between the political rights of citizenship and the economic rights of those who control the power of capital and what places it should flow to. However, this tension, as noted earlier, can manifest sometimes in regressing to a crude form of populism that, ironically, displaces such tension into a political style that is antiintellectual, antiimmigration, and nationalistic, and a political rhetoric emphasizing identity politics (Moffitt, 2016).

In this respect, the challenge of developing a social theory of space is directly related to both the issue of citizenship and the meaning of publicness, the shifting dynamics of spatial arrangements, and the role of the state in adapting to the diminution of spatial barriers in a global economy. Before elaborating on these themes, we need to first discuss the relevance of two prominent social theorists (a sociologist and geographer, respectively) who have tried to integrate sociospatial processes to social theory: Anthony Giddens and Edward Soja. Of course, there are other thinkers that could have been chosen, but these are two of the most highly cited thinkers dealing with this integration. Let us, briefly, discuss their approaches in turn.

Generally speaking, most geographers and planners were pleasantly surprised to find such an eminent social theorist as Anthony Giddens trying to make some theoretical sense of the concept of space. As early as 1979, Giddens was criticizing most social theorists for regarding space as merely a "vacuous backdrop" in which social action unfolds. Giddens wrote (1979, p. 202):

> I want to lodge a further claim, which is that most forms of social theory have failed to take seriously enough not only the temporality of social conduct but also its spatial attributes. At first sight, nothing seems more banal and uninstructive than to assert that social activity occurs in time and in space. But neither time nor space have been incorporated into the center of social theory; rather, they are originally treated more as environments in which social conduct is enacted.

It is worth noting that Giddens's (1985) original attraction to the notion of space stemmed from his belief that spatiality must be seen as part and parcel of the "problem of order," which is at the heart of any viable social theory (Saunders, 1989). "As [Giddens] sees it," Peters Saunders asserted (1989, p. 218), "the problem of order can be conceptualized as the problem of how social systems are bound and integrated over time and space." To make this claim stick, Giddens makes a distinction between what he calls social integration and system integration. The former depends, Giddens explained, on the continuity of everyday life and routinized interactions in the company of others. Thus, social integration requires what he awkwardly referred to as "co-presence," meaning face-to-face interaction. Conversely, system integration refers to actors who are not co-present; interactions that are spread over temporal and spatial distance (what Giddens calls time/space distanciation). Since the eighteenth century, Giddens argued, system integration has become more predominant primarily as a result of communication and transportation innovations, as well as the growing economic interconnectedness between countries and people who may never come in contact with one another. Giddens states that space must be regarded as a part of both social and system integration.

The key issue for Giddens (1984, pp. 35, 185), congruent with his theory of structuration, is how "the limitations of individual presence are [being] transcended by the stretching of social relations across time and space." While this is only a brief sketch of the outline of his theoretical perspective, his general conclusion can be summarized in this manner: that time-space transformations have eroded the very fabric of social activity, and, more critically, have stripped time-space routines (social integration) of their "moral and rational content," thus reducing the substantive meaning of space to a "commodified form" of a "created environment" (Giddens, 1981 pp. 153–154). This transformation of space has radically changed the very meaning of public places for people. As Giddens goes on to emphasize, this transformation of space (and time) has also resulted in what he refers to as a structural contradiction (or friction) between public and private influence over the meaning and purpose of how space is used and how localities control (or, fail to control) their political, social, and economic future (Dikec, 2012; Merriman, 2012; Massey, 2005).

Given this situation, according to Giddens, what makes the concept of space so critical to our understanding of the economic and social environment is that its changing meaning is related to "the advent of industrial capitalism that [has] . . . radically altered the connections between social life and the material world" (Giddens, 1985, p. 146). The ubiquitous influence of the market economy, Giddens maintained, has led to the commodification of everyday life and the deterioration of our social spaces. Simmel likewise argued that the influence of a market economy has placed "us at a distance from the substance of things; they speak to us as from afar; reality is touched not with direct confidence but with fingertips that are immediately withdrawn" (cited in Gregory, 1989, p. 212). Giddens's[6] warning to us about the changing meaning of space is worth noting: "What tends to disappear is the meaning of places for people . . . space is dissolved into flows . . . life is transformed into abstractions, cities into shadows" (cited in Gregory, 1989, p. 203).

With a different theoretical emphasis, the late Edward Soja (1989) argues for a reassertion of a critical spatial view into social theory addressing, among other things, the imbalance of time over space. Unlike Giddens, Soja positions his analysis within the context of a critical postmodernism—a postmodernism that has put spatialization in a new trajectory along three paths: post-Fordism (an economic environment in which capital is not only more mobile, but where industrial systems have become more flexible in order to deal with the disorganized nature of a market economy), posthistoricism (the importance of space in comprehending political and economic changes), and postmodernism (the advent of cultural and ideological changes that have reconfigured our postmodern culture of space and time). The key concern for Soja is that space must always be understood within the broader context of economic and political restructuring. Soja further indicates that it is possible and desirable to develop a "spatialized ontology" (his phrase) that can appropriately balance time, space, and social being. He equates this ontology to "the making of history with the social production of space" (Soja, 1989, p. 11). He is particularly influenced here by the works of the late French philosopher Henri Lefebvre (1976, 1991) who saw the modern city as a "space of differences." Lefebvre makes an interesting distinction between two forms of space worth emphasizing: social space, which involves the everyday spatial activities of citizens, and abstract space (or production of space), which is molded by the relations forged by the institutions of capital. What both Lefebvre and Soja are trying to argue is that "the production of space increasingly constructs social differences" (Smith, 1989, p. 12). Soja goes even on to argue that spatiality situates social life. In somewhat awkward terminology, Soja (1985, p. 6) writes:

> [Spatiality] is an active arena where purposeful human agency jostles problematically with tendential social determinations to shape everyday activity, particularize social change, and etch in place the course of time and the making of history. . . . To be

> alive is to participate in the social production of space, to shape and be shaped by a constantly evolving spatiality which constitutes and concretizes social action and relationship.

However, it is for Soja the appropriation of space and the economic and political struggles over its use that now has a direct impact on the differential distribution of space as a social product (Casey, 1998; Zieleniec, 2007; Jones, 2009; Lefebvre, 1991; Harvey, 1996). It is in this line of reasoning that Soja tries to suggest to his audience that what we call postmodernism may in fact represent nothing more than a restructuring of modernity. For example, Soja (2014) argues that the city of Los Angeles exemplifies the postmodern city as characterized by spatial segregation, fragmentation, and dissociation. It is an urban space that has become socially reproduced to reflect a melange of complex and contradictory social relations. To Soja, Los Angeles not only represents the archetypal postmodern city in which sociospatial life is becoming more fragmented and incoherent, but also serves as an example of how our social spaces have lost their substantive meaning and purpose. While Soja is careful to point out that economic restructuring will vary from region to region (and from country to country), space will nevertheless continue to maintain its political significance as more and more cities and regions are affected by the changing flows of capital, labor, production systems, and information. The restructuring of space, as Soja reiterates, will force us to examine such issues as the spatial division of labor, uneven development, social justice, and the rise of the postmodern city. Soja (2010) contends that without such an examination, our social theories will always be incomplete in comprehending the spatial changes that are altering our political lives.

As instructive and insightful as these two approaches are in pinpointing the critical importance of space to social theory, there are serious omissions in their analysis. For example, the major lacuna in Giddens's analysis is his neglect of the social production of space and how the mobility of capital may be contributing to uneven development (Gregory, 1989; Harvey, 1996; Smith, 1990). Moreover, Giddens does not link his rich analysis with the changing meaning of citizenship or the nation-state in a global economic environment. Given his insightful examination of spatiality, it is an interesting theoretical omission. On the other hand, the criticism of Soja's analysis, in part, has questioned his theoretical adherence to Marxism. This devotion, as Michael Dear (1990) argued, has caused Soja to give undue emphasis to the economic sphere over the equally important political and sociocultural spheres. In sum, Dear is claiming that Soja has reduced the concept of space to a singular meaning: the relations of production of capital. To be fair, while Soja seems to fall into this theoretical trap, he is merely claiming that the economic sphere (or the market economy) tends to be very effective in diverting our attention from developing a critical perspective that would confront those who are expropriating control over economic and social spaces. Yet, Soja's theoretical outlook does tend to ignore the role of the public in addressing the issues he has labored so hard to uncover. The issue of citizenship and the changing meaning of publicness, for instance, are strangely missing from his arguments. Although one can criticize Soja for relying too heavily on Marxist concepts, he does—as even his critics admit—a masterful job in demystifying the economic forces that are clearly eroding the substantive grounds on which our political structures and processes rest. Like Soja's, Massey's (2009) analysis is correct in emphasizing that space and power are interconnected in the sense that they are both products of complex relations, networks, links, and exchanges that extend from the level of our daily lives to the global impact of financial institutions.

As ambitious as these two conceptual views are in trying to link space to social theory, there is still an incompleteness about their analysis. This is not to imply that we should dismiss Giddens's and Soja's analyses; rather, we need to build upon their insights. It may strike some as an anomaly that it is public affairs which brings a particular insight in enriching their analysis.

The Relevance of Public Affairs to Spatiality: Coming Full Circle

> We determine what the world has been by the anxious search for the means of making it better.
>
> —George Herbert Mead

The debate concerning the importance of space can be properly credited with providing both disciplines with a better appreciation of the problems of dealing with economic restructuring and its spatial implications and the ways space could be linked to social theory. Both public management/administration and public policy have a particular relevance in broadening the discussion of spatiality that has only been briefly hinted to before: the changing nature of citizenship and the nation-state. For instance, again, David

Held (1989, pp. 8, 230) has spelled out the dimensions of these far-reaching changes in citizenship and the nation-state in this trenchant manner:

> While there is still insufficient evidence to conclude that the very idea of a national economy is superseded, the internationalization of production, finance and other economic resources is unquestionably eroding the capacity of the state to control its own economic future. At the very least, there appears to be a diminution of state autonomy, and a disjuncture between the premises of the theory of the sovereign state and the conditions of modern economies. . . . [More importantly,] the idea of citizenship and the theory of democracy has to be rethought in relation to substantial changes in political, social and economic life which derive from, among other things, the dynamics of the world economy, [and] the rapid growth of transnational links . . . a project scarcely begun today. (my emphasis)

This analysis implies a mandate to reconceptualize both citizenship (and, by implication, publicness) and the nation-state within a new spatial meaning—a meaning that is intertwined with the process of globalization and a spatial redefinition that transcends the view of citizenship as exclusively confined to the nation-state. We see this spatial redefinition of citizenship in the migration of displaced publics fleeing economic and political discord. This is not to imply that citizenship can be somehow stripped of national sovereignty, but rather that citizenship and public spaces are now subject to new forces that can serve as venues for potential social conflict and international economic processes (Harvey, 2006, 2010; Sullivan, 1986; Vincent, 1986; Held, 1989). Citizenship, in other words, is becoming increasingly intermeshed with decision making involving multinational governance frameworks and nation-states, a development being played out in a dramatic manner in the ongoing Syrian civil war.

There is a flip side to this changing spatial meaning of citizenship and the state. For instance, an international body such as the International Monetary Fund (IMF) can impose severe economic austerity programs on less-developed countries (and developed countries such as Greece) with payment deficits, resulting—as a condition of any continuation of loans to that country—in mandating an array of policies ranging from drastic cuts in public subsidies and expenditures to a devaluation of the nation's currency. The obvious dilemma here is that the state and its citizens (and the political community in which citizenship is embedded) can lose any modicum of control in directing their own future policies. Under these circumstances, the citizens' social and economic spaces can be dramatically altered by another international organization's own notion of what should constitute economic reforms—reforms that can have serious negative spatial and temporal consequences for the citizenry. The point here is that the nation-state and citizenship now exist in a mosaic of networks and web of spatial interactions where foreign and domestic affairs are difficult to separate (Mellor, 1989; Manning, 1977; Reich, 1991).

Although no doubt it is true that not all nation-states and their citizens are being impacted in the same manner by these global forces, nevertheless David Held's observation should not go unheeded. Citizenship and the state are taking on a new meaning, albeit slowly, in our increasingly global environment where spatial barriers are being redefined and renegotiated. Yet, this new spatial environment in which citizenship, and the nation-state, finds itself is not without its contradictions:

> The more global interrelations become, the more internationalized . . . our money flows, and the more spatial barriers disintegrate, so more rather than less of the world's population clings to place and neighborhood or to nation, region, ethnic groupings, or religious belief as specific marks of identify. . . . [Thus,] the geopolitics of place tend to become more rather than less emphatic. Globalization thus generates its exact, opposite motion into geopolitical oppositions and warring camps in a hostile world. (Harvey, 1990, p. 428)

What is hinted at here can now be more directly stated: that those who directly work in public affairs, as an academic and professional field, will be, willingly or not, in the forefront of how to democratically deal with the changing social significance of space and its consequences for the citizenry that the public administrator and policy analyst serve. Furthermore, this changing meaning of space (and time) in an emerging global (and domestic) economy will pose new pragmatic challenges for public management/administration and public policy. Such challenges might include the issue of how the public can maintain some degree of democratic control over its economic and social spaces without lapsing into a dangerous form of unbridled nationalistic populism or civic boosterism and, from a theoretical perspective, how we can conceptually integrate the concept of space (and time) into our analyses of public affairs itself. To some extent, it can be argued that the integration of space into our analyses is already being done (at least implicitly) by studies focusing on the issues of redlining and the allocation of scarce capital in support of inner-city neighborhoods and the role of capital in rebuilding, or attempting to rebuild, social spaces that have been devastated by urban decay. While this may be true to a certain degree, the majority of such studies—at least in the mainstream public management/administration and public policy literature—have mostly neglected to critically question those who control the capital in the first place and how the power relations manifested in this control impact the everyday spatial lives of the public (Massey, 2009; Ventriss, 2000; Smith, 1990).

Interestingly, both fields occupy a unique intellectual niche in which to deal with these issues. For many, the spatial issues raised in this chapter directly involve the future role of the citizenry (and its sense of publicness) in the recovery of its economic and social spaces, and, just as importantly, the relationship of the public and the state in dealing with the interplay of local and global forces on political life. The centrality of these concerns (along with others), as Guerreiro Ramos (1981) emphasized, should prompt the field not only to consider time and space as critical factors, but also the notions of technology, size, and cognition. As mentioned previously, Guerreiro Ramos believed that the consideration of these factors provided a way in which to design different social systems congruent with the multidimensional needs of the public. Even though Ramos can be correctly criticized for presenting a somewhat romanticized approach, he did recognize that one of the central tasks for those of us in public affairs is the need to include spatial factors within our understanding of publicness, for no other reason than that they involve issues of fostering a more democratic society. Guerreiro Ramos's message is more important today than ever before. Yet, a more basic concern needs to be posed: Can we in public affairs overcome our parochial thinking in exploring the political and economic forces that are, in a very fundamental way, reshaping our space and time? Any viable response to this critical point will inevitably imply coming to terms with the meaning (and role) of democratic politics in a changing political and economic milieu—a milieu that is becoming both more fragmented and, ironically, more interrelated at the same time (Storper & Scott, 2016; Harvey, 1990, 2006).

Certainly, even in a highly interconnected world the linkage between citizenship and the nation-state in global affairs will continue to remain a powerful force. But, at the same time, the pervasive influence of a market economy has radically restructured the temporal and spatial dimensions of our social and political existence. And here is the pivotal point to keep in mind: What is at stake for us in public affairs may be nothing less than the way we can incorporate "publicness" into our definition of time and space so that it is not merely reflective of economic forces adherent to a particular political-economic trajectory of development.[7] For, as social anthropologists remind us, different cultures and societies exhibit different conceptualizations of space and time (Hall, 1966; Moore, 1986). However, such conceptualizations of time and space can be appropriated and dominated by powerful forces that can reshape the meaning and purpose of these social constructs[8] (Dikec, 2012; Massey, 2009; Elden, 2007; Smith, 2008; Harvey, 1990, 2010; Lefebvre, 2000;). It is within this context that Foucault's message that "the present epoch will be above all the epoch of space" can now be better understood. What Foucault did not mention is that this new "epoch of space" has ushered in a new role for public management/administration and public policy in regulating the growing diminution of spatial barriers and its consequences for the citizenry and the nation-state. To update Soja's trenchant point, perhaps we need to become more cognizant of how struggles and conflicts over the changing nature of space will require a new kind of participation in public affairs—as daunting as that task may seem. Such a participation in this new endeavor will require, as Held has inferred in his analysis, a theoretical rethinking of a "public" citizenship along new spatial and temporal terms—a rethinking long overdue in public management/administration and public policy.

A Final Reflection

> Everything flows. Give me a place to stand.
>
> —Heraclitus

Heraclitus, the Greek philosopher who is best known for his dialectic view of reality, wrote these words, which succinctly capture much of the central themes raised in this chapter: the growing tension between the mobility of economic space, coupled with the important advent of social media, and the normative impact of this mobility on social spaces. While some may argue that the emphasis on space (as a social construct) might be overdone, there is still a haunting issue that cannot be so easily ignored or obscured. That blunt issue is the restructuring of space and its impact on communities, which raises, by definition, the politically charged issue of whether communities (or any other subnational level of government) can be empowered to organize control over their "place," particularly given the fierce competition for capital and the dominant role of the market over our lives.

If we can agree that this point strikes a nerve, the debate concerning the changing meaning of citizenship and the modern state has to be expanded to include spatial issues that explicitly raise whether those who own (dare we say) the "capital" have any sense of citizenship and obligation to the polity other than the desire to accumulate more capital. Or, to put it even more pointedly, should citizenship itself be rethought to include economic and political rights that can provide the meaning of publicness with some democratic control over economic and social spaces even in the face of constraints that can be imposed by the private appropriation of capital? As controversial as this may seem, it goes the very raison d'être of citizenship, the public sphere, and the role of the state in this new epoch of space.

Given the policy and management ramifications of these volatile issues, public management/administration and public policy cannot afford to dismiss the concept of space. But, in many respects, this is really beside the point. For the economic and political restructuring of space and its implications will inevitably come to rest on our doorstep anyway, as most public issues eventually do. This time, however, we cannot afford the risk of being ill-prepared for this eventuality both from a theoretical and pragmatic perspective—for to do so, one can argue, might just negate the "publicness" of what we purport to be as respective fields of public affairs.

This is not a call to some kind of conceptual playfulness, or a utopic scenario falling on deaf ears, but rather a call to examine how we can better integrate new considerations into our economic and political decision making in a world being defined more and more in spatial and temporal terms.

Conclusion

In this chapter, I introduced the issue of space as an overlooked but important lens through which to understand the challenges facing public affairs in an age of economic globalization and political discord. I asked readers—particularly practitioners—to consider how the spatial dimensions of our markets and governments impact the practice of public affairs. I called on readers,particularly researchers, to reflect on how space might factor into any viable, normative theory of the public. I also explored how social media (and related technologies) are expanding the notion of publicness in a communicative space that has both positive and negative ramifications in its societal implications.

In the first section, I introduced space as a public affairs concern through an economic lens. Noting the ever-faster movement of capital around the globe that has come to characterize late modernity, I juxtaposed the regulatory and entrepreneurial challenges facing flexible private entities with those facing publics and their institutions. I quoted Hill in reminding us that "Capital is mobile. Detroit is not." This one-liner captures the fundamental challenge facing the public (and policymakers) in a time when economic forces are shaping our public spaces.

Following this introduction, I examined how both the mobility of capital and the changing nature of space as an interplay between global, mobile economic actors and spatially static public entities has ushered in a new, lopsided power dynamic of "government entrepreneurship" in which the latter seek to court—rather than regulate—the former.

I then turned my attention to two preeminent thinkers whose work has important implications for the study of space in public affairs. Sociologist Anthony Giddens gives us the insight that limits to spatial interactions, which historically occurred in real time, are being stretched over vast geographies and time frames by new technologies. And geographer Edward Soja called us to rethink space in the context of each historical moment, to accommodate the constant restructuring of politics and economies and their consequences for how space functions in public life.

I concluded the chapter with an optimistic challenge. If we can restructure how we relate to space through public affairs, we may also be able to restructure the fragmentary underlying social dynamics evident in today's spatiality. I note that oversights in both Giddens and Soja's analyses beg to be addressed in this new task; Giddens neglects the social production of space, and Soja over emphasizes the economic sphere relative to sociocultural and political spheres. But, if we in public affairs can remind ourselves that citizenship and public spaces are now implicated in global social conflicts and economic processes, we may begin to appreciate how important it is to understand the implications of spatiality on public affairs.

8

A Critical Analysis of the Role of Citizen Involvement in Public Affairs

A Reexamination

It is interesting to note that much of the administrative and policy literature on public participation—regardless of the different venues it plays out in—assumes that, by definition, citizen involvement contributes to reflexive deliberation, discursive democracy, effective representation, and consensus building in the public sphere (Nabatchi & Leighninger, 2015; Deleon & Ventriss, 2010; Ventriss, 1985; Thomas, 1995; Barber, 1984; Bohman, 1998; Fung, 2006; Guttman & Thompson, 2004; Nabatchi, 2010). This should come as no surprise given that communication and reflexivity are two concepts now at the heart of contemporary theories of late modernity (Ventriss, 2016; Carpini, Cook, & Jacobs, 2004; Sørensen, 2012; Fung & Wright, 2003; Barber, 1984; Habermas, 1996; Beck, Giddens, & Lash, 1994). These two concepts, moreover, are often discussed in the literature as an integral part, or within the context, of communicative rationality: a theoretical condition under which individuals can debate and substantively discuss issues free of ideological distortions, where the normative benefits of deliberations are high, and where the fruits of this unencumbered communication are inherently rational (Habermas, 1984). Concomitantly, the most widely used application consistent with the concept of reflexive modernization is the concept of the citizen as a stakeholder in the policy process. Citizens—stakeholders, in other words—are primarily defined by their differences. Citizens identify their "stake" by reflecting on opposing claims, or by their ability to take the perspective of the other (Mead, 2010). Assuming the validity of this assumption, effective management leading to rational outcomes requires decision makers to bring all stakeholders together to deliberate on positional differences in a nonthreatening communicative environment. As a result, a growing body of the literature on both public participation and collaborative management suggest approaches to ensure effective public involvement in the policy and administrative process (Bryson, Quick, Slotterback, & Crosby, 2013; Fung, 2006; Forester, 1989, 1999; Saward, 2000; Wondolleck & Yaffee, 2000; Beierle & Cayford, 2002; Sorenson, 2012; Dryzek, 2007; Hirst, 2000; Bohman, 2007).

But what if this is only half the story? To put it in somewhat different terms, what if the citizen stakeholder approach to public policy and public management obscures as much as it reveals? The public participatory approach and its assumptions about fair and open communication have such a powerfully intuitive appeal to the theories and institutions of democracy that critical scrutiny of these concepts appears needlessly academic. It is no wonder that much of the literature concerning the public participation process, therefore, seeks techniques for more effective involvement, and searches for ways to overcome the constraints to effective participation in the public sphere. But truth be told, the communicative and participative process in public affairs is inherently limited by a complex array of social selective pressures in public deliberation. Moreover, while citizen involvement is certainly an improvement over the "high priest" models of technical expertise in the organizational culture of public agencies, assumptions about fairness and equity among different stakeholder groups are ideals rarely achieved. Consequently, a consensus in the public sphere is like a transitory mirage, contingent on the constellation of actors who happen to rise to the surface of ongoing public conflict and debate. In other words, what is often missing in the discussion concerning the efficacy of citizen participation is the view of publicness "that constantly explores the underlying assumptions and implications of a political hegemony that can mold our thinking to be uncritically quiescent and conformist . . . that prevents the citizenry from achieving any alternative (and viable) vision of public freedom and action in the modern polity" (Ventriss, 2002, p. 292).

If this contention is valid, what is being left out? What current administrative theory does not tell us may be most instructive. For example, Habermas's concept of the ideal speech act treats communication as the most elemental component of human interaction. His theoretical starting point is that humans are social beings because they communicate. Yet, Habermas's theory pays inadequate attention to variation in communicative effectiveness. Like Marx, whose critique of capitalism offered a nebulous vision of what socialism might look like after the demise of the market, Habermas offers no clear image of communicative rationality in the context of an ideal speech act, when people's communicative effectiveness varies so widely. His theory fails to tell us why people choose not to talk in public settings, even when the occasion is clearly relevant to their interests, and even when public agencies have been diligent at creating nonthreatening environments for debate. This oversight reveals an essential gap in the literature of public participation: that formal organizations (who often use such approaches to legitimize their policies) are by and large instrumental vehicles of control who too often disguise their power in normative clothing (Pateman, 2012; Cooke, 2006; Deleon & Ventriss, 2010; Cleaver, 2004; Ventriss, 1985; Cooke & Kothari, 2001; Morgan, 1986; Hummel, 2007; Ramos, 1981; Burrell, 1980).

The controlling nature of institutions that superficially tout the virtues of participatory process is evidenced in the existence of structural forces that limit the reflexivity of contemporary society. For example, managers of public organizations lament the fact that the people can only become participants if they come forward to make a claim. Consequently, the managers are often legally or legislatively mandated to exhaustively search for potential stakeholders to participate in the deliberations over resource allocation. Yet, the allocation of resource goods necessarily frames the context whereby citizens can be identified. Public representatives must therefore qualify as stakeholders before they can enter the deliberative process. Conversely, there are systematic ways that people become excluded, marginalized, or disqualified from this participative status, despite the best-intentioned efforts of some agency managers to be inclusive. It will be argued that the citizen involvement framework as employed by formal organizations frequently limits the scope and contentiousness of conflict, and narrows the boundaries of possible change, all under the guise of democracy and "fair and open" deliberation. Or, as Guerreiro Ramos (1981) would argue, can the issue of public participation sometimes merely become an organizational strategy that diverts our attention from critically examining the underlying cultural, political, and economic forces that created the social or environmental problems in the first place?

For the purposes of this analysis, the focus will be on how formal organizations have implemented citizen involvement as a way to enhance their environment managerial agenda embedded in a utilitarian, market ethos. Given this situation, perhaps what warrants exploring is not so much any new approach to a citizen participative process in environmental decision making (as important as this issue may seem), but rather the articulation of a critical approach for a broader political and theoretical understanding that recognizes the realities of gender, class, and ethnicity as well as the relationship of an environmentalism that links "natural" and "human" environments (Gibson-Wood & Wakefield, 2012; Hornik, Cutts, & Greenlee, 2016; Gottlieb, 2005; Deleon & Ventriss, 2010).

To tease out some of these crucial issues, the emphasis will be on two social thinkers: Jürgen Habermas and David Harvey. While I recognize this is only a small sampling of social thinkers that could have been chosen for analysis, Habermas (more as a pragmatist than a critical theorist anymore) and Harvey (as one of the leading scholars in human geography) have fostered, albeit from somewhat different theoretical venues, much debate about the roles of Habermas's ideal of communicative rationality and Harvey's spaces of hope (as he called them). Specifically, Habermas was selected for this analysis because of his focus on the public sphere and his enduring influence concerning communicative action in facilitating public discourse. From another perspective, Harvey (as the most cited human geographer in the world) raises an array of critical issues concerning the reconceptualization of social change to environmental (and social) issues in an era besieged by a pervasive market ethos. It will be argued that the forces of change and conflict in contemporary society cannot be so easily contained under a public participation approach in addressing environmental concerns, or for that matter any policy concern. In short, there may be a fundamental disconnect between an increasingly reflexive society (Giddens, 1999) and its ability to talk about—and change—its differences.

Habermas and the Managerial Citizen Involvement Approach: An Environmental Perspective

> Democracy is a useful tool for peaceful reconciling conflicting interest conflicts among . . . functional groups, for taking reading of the level of contentment of the people so that technocratic administrations can monitor their own performance, and for legitimating the . . . administrative state behind a facade of mass participation. The rub is that . . . the national bourgeoise's concern is purely instrumental and implies no normative commitment to the concept of popular power.
>
> —David Becker

The Utilitarian Past

The natural resource management profession in the United States is, to a large extent, facing a crisis of legitimacy. Managers were once granted free rein to apply their biological expertise to environmental restoration, habitat protection, land-use regulation, and resource production. Today, however, traditional constituencies and newly emerging opposition groups constantly challenge management policy and decisions—and in many cases with good reason. As communications technology has made access to natural resource science easier, and as trends toward interdisciplinarity in the environmental fields have encouraged new voices to weigh in on matters of management, public comment is in many ways more informed and more evidently valid than ever before. However, increasing contentiousness surrounding natural resource management is not always a function of enlightenment. Increasing political and cultural polarization, coupled with trends toward anti-intellectualism in many facets of American culture, have fueled aggressive pushes for deregulation (Farrell, 2016).

To the resource management professional at the end of his or her career, this new contentiousness is particularly ironic. The legacy of resource management in the United States is filled with successes: landscape restoration, species recovery programs, public ownership of environmentally important lands (parks, forests, wilderness areas, and wildlife refuges), provision of culturally important hunting, fishing, and gathering traditions, and a supply of resource commodities provided through the tools of scientific management. Yet the utilitarian principles that nurtured the resource management profession through much of the twentieth century increasingly are being challenged by a postutilitarian mood that questions the foundation of contemporary environmental management.

These utilitarian principles of resource management in the United States had their beginning in the Progressive conservation movement of the early twentieth century. Gifford Pinchot's experience in the 1890s working on German plantation forests provided the seeds for his vision of scientific forestry. Thirty years later, Aldo Leopold was articulating a similar vision of "scientific" game management. Their goal was to use the methods of science to efficiently produce natural resources in a way that met both current and future needs. This progressive vision was based in the Enlightenment belief that the more humans can know and understand their world, the better able they are to shape outcomes to their desired purposes and uses. With this belief, science and technology became the tools whereby people could make the natural world more stable and ordered, and generate a predictable flow of resource commodities.

Yet, in spite of a century of success stories, management of the natural world has not become more stable and ordered. Managers are more frequently engaged with the public over contentious and controversial proposals and decisions. And managers have found that to be at all effective in this changing social context, they must be attentive to staying ahead of, or keeping up with contemporary public demands for natural resource provision. Biological or technical expertise no longer suffices as the primary prerequisite for the profession. Managers must also be adaptable, creative, flexible, responsive, collaborative, intuitive, and entrepreneurial. These adjectives, however, hardly suggest stability and order.

The Utilitarian Response

The tools used by the resource management profession to confront contemporary demands and controversies are largely acquiescent to the assumptions and frameworks of the profession's utilitarian past and the formal organizations of which they are a part. In dealing with public conflict, managers primarily use a "systems" metaphor (Morgan, 1986). They assume that just as the natural world conforms to biological systems dictated by laws of nature and cause and effect relationships, the social world likewise conforms to laws and predictable cause and effect relationships, which can be empirically observed.

Two elements of this social systems approach are key concepts in dealing with public controversy. First, the concept of social value is used to help understand competing public claims in environmental conflicts. These social values were the centerpiece of Parsons's (1971) systems-based theory of structural functionalism. Moreover, they were the normative glue that held together the personality system, the social system, and the cultural system of any society, and provided the normative direction for coordinated action among diverse interests. Second, the concept of citizen participation is a way of categorizing the variety of interests that exist in a pluralistic society, and a way of explaining the behavior of individuals as they act in concert with identifiable value positions or ideologies. Values, then, are the psychological elements of the social system, and citizens are the elements of the social system that turn values into action. In this context, values and citizens fit easily within resource management's utilitarian framework. Participative analysis is a pragmatic heuristic that facilitates the identification of specific tasks or actions with concrete and measurable outcomes. The strategy for environmental managers inevitably becomes focused on values clarification, stakeholder identification, and public involvement with the goal of compromise and consensus (Nabatchi & Leighninger, 2015).

This approach appears consistent with the ideals of participatory democracy, where conflict is resolved by principles of fairness and inclusiveness in the policy process, particularly under assumptions of communicative rationality. Consequently, it is not hard to understand why public participation is receiving considerable attention in public agencies. For many public agencies, public participation is legislatively mandated in the policymaking process. As a result, public participation has become an active area of scholarship in recent years, and managers have become keenly interested in how to do it better. The traditional public hearing is giving way to a variety of new techniques such as focus groups, scenario development, and collage processes (Kasemir et al., 2003; Beierle & Cayford, 2002; Fung & Fagotto, 2009) to name a few, each of which relies on a participative analysis to organize the public. The goal of these techniques is to help diffuse actual or potential conflict and to lend a sense of public ownership in the policymaking process. In short, the goal of public participation is to transform the human dimension of natural resource management into a more orderly administrative and policy-driven process.

Communicative Rationality and Social Transformation

Many public participation scholars in the natural resource field draw their analytical and prescriptive frameworks from Habermas's influential theory of communicative rationality. However, this theoretical heritage is only partially realized in practice. Habermas's vision of a communicative society in late modernity offers a smooth and intuitive transition from the utilitarian rationality of the modern age. His theory fits easily with ideologies inherent in democratic pluralism: interest groups/stakeholders, fairness and equity, and equal access to the policymaking process. But this goes beyond interest group politics carried out within the bureaucratic structures of party politics and a culture of expertise. It envisions a more diverse and inclusive form of discursive democracy that draws on more sophisticated reasoning and debate among a broader array of stakeholders in a contemporary reflexive society. Yet, the application of Habermas's theory in the natural resource field has also been selective, emphasizing the parts that are consistent with the field's utilitarian past, and deemphasizing the critical theory parts of communicative rationality that are suggestive of a postutilitarian transformation. This selectivity is expressed most clearly in citizen involvement strategies.

In practice, Habermas's theory of communicative action has not realized its potential as critical theory. There are at least two reasons for this. First is the way that Habermas positioned his thought within the broader domain of critical theory. His early training in the Frankfurt School of Social Research and his concern with alienation in modern society clearly qualify him as a critical theorist, even though his later works have taken on more pragmatic overtones. And while his idea of "decolonizing the lifeworld" offered a transformative vision for contemporary society, the mechanism of change,communicative rationality, departed dramatically from the mechanisms of transformative change inherent in most critical theory.

Habermas's conceptualization parts ways with his Frankfurt School mentors, who argued that the promise of the Enlightenment—human progress through rationality—has failed or at least fallen short. The contradictions of science, industry, and technology in the modern age, they argued, have brought about widespread alienation, and have positioned society on the brink of economic disaster and impending chaos. For better or worse, revolutionary change was inevitable, albeit different from Marx's conceptualization. The ensuing literature on postmodernism offered a variety of diagnoses of the contemporary situation from postindustrialism, poststructuralism, social constructionism, and nihilism, each arguing, in turn, that a dramatic social transformation was under way that was every bit as momentous as the transition from feudalism to modernism.

Habermas, however, had a different interpretation of contemporary social change. He rejected the notion that modernism was in decline, and argued instead that the promise of Enlightenment progress was still a viable orienting principle for "late modern" society. Habermas, in part, built this argument on Weber's (1978) discussion of rationality. Weber argued that human rationality had evolved historically through four stages: (1) traditional rationality, where action is determined by ritual, obligation, or habit, (2) affective rationality, where action is driven by emotion or feeling states, (3) values based rationality, where action is determined by duty, morality, or religious sentiment, and (4) instrumental rationality, where action is determined by calculated outcomes. Habermas argued that the instrumental rationality, which characterized industrial society, was giving way to a fifth type of rationality: communicative rationality, where action is determined by an increased capacity for individual reflexivity and a society that can, hopefully, engage more frequently in public discourse. However, this communicative rationality may in fact do little to abate the structural distrust that many of the different publics have in their governmental institutions, even though political trust tends to be relatively stable in those countries where the institutions are perceived as efficient, inclusive, and for the most part free of corruption (Van der Meer, 2017; Van der Meer & Hakhverdian, 2016).

At first glance, thinking and talking more about issues of public concern do not provide a very compelling foundation for a theory of contemporary life. It was Habermas's notion of the lifeworld that energized his theory. Habermas again built on Weber and his iron cage metaphor, an analysis of instrumental rationality during European industrialization that was rather pessimistic. This analysis of modern bureaucracies predicted a "polar night of icy darkness" where corporations and state bureaucracies would confine public decision making and policy formation to more progressively rigid forms of instrumental rationality. The mechanization of production and the codification of management in bureaucratic procedure would reduce most forms of human interaction to means-ends relationships, and subject individuals to strict forms of functional determinism in their everyday lives. Habermas characterizes these outcomes of instrumental rationality as the "colonization of the life-world." But Habermas did not see these outcomes as inevitable, and suggested an alternative based on the distinction between the rationality of administrative and market systems and the rationality of the "life-world" or public sphere. According to Habermas, the progressive differentiation of productive and administrative technologies through the imperatives of instrumental rationality creates a specialized culture of expertise, whose internal logic and history separate it from other cultural spheres of knowledge and action. In modernity, the distance between expert cultures and the public sphere has inexorably widened. But it need not continue to, as some have claimed.

Under communicative rationality, the public attempts to reassert itself against the trends toward colonization of the life-world. And, through dialogue in a fair and nondistorted setting where people can speak without fear of intimidation, retribution, and embarrassment, the potential for an effective resistance exists. In this setting, the public becomes free to imagine and invent public policy and action through collaborative and inventive ways that are not constrained by rigid bureaucratic procedure or institutional obligation. In short, this process describes Enlightenment notions of rationality made better through communication rather than a search for efficient instrumental outcomes.

Citizen Participation and the Utilitarian Acquiescence

The problem, of course, is that Habermas does not offer a very clear vision for how communicative rationality will bring about a social transformation in late modern times. Exactly how does society go about reconfiguring the relationship between bureaucracies and the public sphere under communicative rationality? This shortcoming is the second reason why his theory, in practice, has not realized its potential as critical theory and why some have claimed his recent approaches have eroded his previous critical proclivities. A number of emerging literatures argue explicitly that significant transformations of existing institutional and economic structures are not necessary. For example, ecological modernization, from sociology and ecological economics, makes similar assumptions: that contemporary environmental problems can be solved within established market, political, and organizational structures. Both subdisciplines, for example, rely on principles of communicative rationality and citizen participative analysis in executing a problem-solving approach to environmental problems. Yet, public participation per se cannot produce social transformation when one is looking for solutions that work within existing institutions and prevailing market ideologies.

In practice, public participation has become an ideology in and of itself, with many—but not all—of the elements of a fully developed social theory. Most resource management agencies engage in some form of public participation when making policy or implementing actions. Motivated by the belief that more communication produces better decisions, the idea of a stakeholder in any debate or management decision has become a reified concept. Identify the question, identify the stakeholders, and put them in the same room to talk. Under these circumstances, citizen involvement runs the risk of becoming a process dictated by those who control what is feasible to pursue.

By removing the transformative potential of Habermas's theory of communicative action—its call for and empowerment of reflexivity—citizens' participation has become simply one more tool of instrumental mechanism used to understand competing claims for the provision of public goods. This approach, in all its varying manifestations, operates from a modernist framework, where participants in a dispute are assumed to make rational judgments about allocation options that will maximize their personal or collective benefit, and then act in a way that will maximize their political influence in the final allocation outcome. From a manager's perspective, this analysis operates within a system of utility. When questions or conflicts arise, managers must specify action alternatives with measurable outcomes. Public participation, then, provides a task framework that proceeds within the parameters of a systematic actionable problem and decision context. Not surprisingly, managers also use the tools of science to demystify policy and administrative disputes. They assign distinct value orientations to competing members of a controversy in an effort to find some grounds for consensus building. In sum, managers muster the tools of modernity to systematize choice and justify the "zero-sum" game inherent in management decisions, perpetuating the colonization of the life-world rather than emancipating it.

Stripping away the transformative potential of communicative rationality forces public participation into a consensus project, which enables incremental change at the cost of true transformation, effectively perpetuating the status quo. Resource management practitioners seek to achieve a degree of social acceptability for projects and decisions through discussion, concession, and compromise. The doctrine they follow suggests that by airing differences, exploring alternatives, and providing clarifying information, citizens are able to work toward an acceptable solution that maximizes the benefits of the decision and spreads the costs of the decision more equitably to all. Information and education are prominent tools of this framework, where conflict is diffused by persuasive appeals that draw on science, expertise, and experience. Conflict, in effect, is a controlled process of consensus making where stakeholders have already agreed on the parameters of the issue and are working in good faith toward a solution. Yet, for all of its noble aspirations, this perspective delimits the scope of conflict to narrow and manageable contours of stakeholder conformity, influence, and persuasion. Change comes in tiny increments that may not match the speed of contemporary social transformations.

Equally problematic, ignoring the transformative potential of communicative rationality in favor of a consensus approach to public policy and public management are the processes inherent in instrumental rationality pervasive in formal organizations (Hummel & Stivers, 1998; Ramos, 1981). State theory (Poulantzas, 1978) argues that there are structural reasons that often lie outside the awareness of managers of state agencies that lead them to favor the interests of the wealthy and disfavor the interests of the working class. More recent iterations of state theory (Block, 1987; Jessop, 1990, 2007; Smith, 2000) have dropped much of the class analysis in their observations that agencies of the state are themselves an interest among many in an ideological struggle over the allocation of resources, naturally predisposed to form alliances that advance their own (often unacknowledged) value claims.

In other words, state agencies are never disinterested parties in public debate. So, when conflict over resource allocation arises and managers specify the problem and devise an action strategy, they do so selectively in a way that is dependent on their ideological (and instrumental) commitments. Thus, public participation is inherently influenced by the framing of managerial ideology used by resource managers. Based on that ideology, as many citizens are systematically excluded from public debate as are included in the public participation process. But the ideology of citizen involvement as often practiced by formal organizations, with its roots in instrumental rationality, obscures the link between action and ideology (Ramos, 1981). In this respect, participatory approaches are limited in face of powerful institutional actors and often can do little in revealing "the wider power relations in society" (Deleon & Ventriss, 2010; Kothari, 2004).

To reinvigorate the transformative potential of Habermas's communicative rationality, resource management agencies must find a way to embrace the "conflict" that is raging around it—and to recognize their own role as value-driven participants in it. To regain their institutional legitimacy, management agencies must develop a culture of risk that embraces innovation. Agencies who tenaciously defend the logic of its core services, and who seek to "educate the public" behind a veil of utilitarian ideology, will find themselves spending more and more time dealing only with "people problems." To achieve Habermas's ideal of decolonizing the life-world, perhaps, we must engage the public in new ways, reflective of "an environmentalism that is democratic and inclusive, an environmentalism of equality and social justice, an environmentalism of linked natural and human environments, an environmentalism of transformation" (Gottlieb, 2005, 1993, p. 320). Let us now turn to David Harvey, albeit from a more controversial perspective, to examine some of these key issues.

Toward Critical Spaces of Hope

David Harvey offers interesting and provocative insights concerning the interdependency of social and environmental change. Harvey posits that what remains as one of the lacunae concerning the prevailing analysis of both environmental and social issues is our reluctance, or conceptual inability, to shift "from an argument about protection or management of the natural environment to a discussion of social movements in response to the urban and industrial forces of the past hundred years" (cited in Harvey, 1996,

p. 186). Robert Gottlieb (1993, p. 306) has succinctly argued this point, which is worth quoting at length:

> The common claims of movements based on experiences affected by the realities of gender, ethnicity, and class offer the potential of a political base strong enough to confront the sources of economic, industrial, and political power and their role in environmental destruction. Gender, ethnicity, and class are not distinct from one another in people's lives: women work in hazardous jobs and care for men and children who may return home from contaminated workplaces and schools; people of color, both men and women, discover that they are living in poisoned neighborhoods where their babies eat lead chips, and they can find jobs only in fields or factories where the hazards of uncertain employment intersect with the hazards of the work itself. Industrial practices contaminate workers, and industrial wastes contaminate neighborhoods, water, and air. Differences in power based on distinctions of gender, ethnicity, and class mean that some people disproportionately suffer the effects of economic and environmental decisions, and other people disproportionately reap the benefits of those decisions. As those who are most at risk join the environmental movement and expand its definition, their participation also broadens the possibilities for social and environmental change.

Here, Harvey and Gottlieb are drawing attention to the reality that such a shift in thinking goes well beyond any call for administrative tinkering. While there is no attempt here to analyze all the key contributions of Harvey's complex thinking on environmental and other, related issues, there are, however, some important insights he offers that have a direct bearing on the discussion of a participative approach that "has taken center stage in the play of influences that determine how society will manage and protect the environment" (Beierle & Cayford, 2002, p. 1). In no uncertain terms, David Harvey tells us that regardless of what the administrative and policy literature tells us concerning the participative processes of stakeholder advisory committees, citizen juries, public hearings, face-to-face deliberations, facilitated mediations, or any other hybrid approach, if we leave untouched the political, cultural, and economic infrastructure of power we inevitably obscure the societal forces that are presently shaping our lives.

In this regard, Harvey would applaud Iris Marion Young's (1990, p. 127) normative observation that the "purpose of critical normative theory is to offer an alternative vision of social relations which . . . conceptualizes the stuff of which the experienced world consists . . . with a view of its possibilities, in the light of their actual limitation, suppression, and denial. Such a positive normative theory can inspire hope and imagination that motivate action for social change."

Human Practices and the Market Ethos

One of the pivotal concerns for Harvey is that environmental groups—often under the rubric of promoting more citizen involvement as an end itself—over time become increasingly institutionalized and bureaucratized as they view social power as merely an extension of an "enlightened business as usual" outlook. These environmental groups forget, according to Harvey, that any critical approach, in order to have an impact on daily political practices, must find a manner—a point raised in chapter 7—"to embed it in the materialities of place, space, and environment" (Harvey, 1996, p. 45). He further articulates the trenchant view that "we need critical ways to think about how differences in ecological, cultural, economic, political, and social conditions get produced . . . and we need to reevaluate the justice/injustice of the differences so produced" (Harvey, 1996, p. 5). His analysis provokes an intriguing insight: that the nature of space and its relationship to issues of social justice is never politically neutral; rather, human practices ultimately shape and create different conceptualizations of space. Hence, the dynamic institutional forces that mold our political existence are an integral part of broader social processes and spatial forms that convert our practices congruent to the market imperative and commodification of public life (Ventriss, 1985; Ramos, 1981). If one follows this logic, as indicated in chapter 7, Harvey's argument denotes that space and temporal dimensions are merely social constructs that vary from place to place and from one historical era to another.

To understand these different social constructs goes well beyond the "conventional" participative techniques employed by public agencies; rather, one must incorporate, he asserts, a "historical geographical materialist" approach, which "entails searching for the material causes of space-time perceptions and understanding the mechanism behind the material causes" (Merrifield, 2002, p. 7). Borrowing heavily from classical Marxism, Harvey argues that modern capitalism by definition is always creating new technologies and systems of production in the pursuit of even more capital accumulation. It is in opposition to this capital accumulation and the subsequent normative implications it poses for modern society that Harvey enumerates his position. That is, any critical inquiry by the citizenry should not be based exclusively on issues of class or even on a substantive belief, but instead should emerge from a coalition of different groups operating outside of the formal organization with a common purpose of opposing any form of social injustice. In other words, citizen involvement programs often employed by agencies or environmental groups rarely incorporate a program to achieve social justice from a political economy perspective that would take note of how power is constituted through the ideological and material processes of society. Here Harvey echoes Guerreiro Ramos's (1981) contention that formal organizations are sometimes contrived social systems that promote (and protect) their instrumental goals.

The Need for Citizen Spaces of Hope

David Harvey has argued that in our increasingly global economy we find more and more contradictions whereby "people are increasingly connected to the rest of the world through increased ease of migration and economic trade, [and consequently] people are now increasingly concerned with their own local identity" (1996, p. 7). Put bluntly, while the forces of globalization manifest themselves in a variety of ways, it is ultimately specific places and spaces that feel their effects (Harvey 2010, 2007; Dicken, 2007; Lipschutz, 2004). According to one astute scholar, such thinking implies the following ramifications for the role citizens play in our modern polity:

> [T]he claims that environmental politics are local . . . can be understood . . . as a disconnect between the individualist orientation of capitalism as a social order and the structural features of capitalist political economy. We make our choices in the market, and in our everyday lives, on an individual basis, often with little thought to how they may affect or be linked to other individuals nearby and far. Such choices . . . are not simply the product of our individual desires or needs. They are connected to structures, and those structures affect the environment and have global reach. The structures are not particularly amenable to change through action by individual agents; acting alone, each of us can hardly have an impact. Collective political action is

> required to modify or transform such structures, and it may best be initiated where agents are offered the greatest opportunity to act, in localized settings where praxis is possible and practical, rather than in national or international ones where no one is interested in structural change. (Lipschutz, 2004, pp. 143–144)

Harvey picks up on this notion by arguing that public participation programs—even with the best intentions as practiced by agencies—usually are unable to find an "optimism of the intellect" (as he calls it) to confront the perspective that there is simply no viable alternative to the prevailing status quo other than succumbing to the utilitarian rationality of the market itself (Harvey, 2000). We seem to become, Harvey maintains, captives of the "institutional and market mentality" of the world we inhabit, leaving no "spaces for hope." He asks a fundamental question: Is the issue of fostering a democratic ethos in the environmental policy process (or the policy process in general) really linked inexorably to citizen involvement alone or could the real issue we face merely be that we no longer have any viable (and visionary) perspective for social change? Here, Harvey is deeply indebted to Roberto Unger's (1987, pp. 359–360) viewpoint:

> The visionary is the person who claims not to be bound by the limits of the tradition he or his interlocuters are in . . . notice that visionary thought is not inherently millenarian, perfectionist, or utopian. It need not and does not ordinarily prevent the picture of a perfected society. But it does require that we be conscious of redrawing the map of possible and desirable forms of human associations, of inventing new models of human association and designing new practical arrangement to embody them.

The message to those trying to promote citizen involvement is clear: in a world of political and economic uncertainty any participatory process that does not permit citizens to become active agents in critically acting upon social reality will, in the end, be only partaking in a form of political tinkering or acquiescence—a utilitarian ideology that leaves untouched the dominant (and prevailing) power relations in society. While it is true that Harvey is often not associated with proposing any critical administrative or policy theory per se, he does represent a perspective closely aligned to critical modernism that questions orthodox managerial thinking as manifested in its empiricism, instrumental rationality, and its lack of attention to how citizens develop their thinking and action predicated upon their network of social/power relationships (Fung & Fagotto, 2009; Roberts, 2008; Görgens & Van Donk, 2011; Clegg, 1979, 2013; Marsden, 1993; Hickey & Mohan, 2004; Rahman, 1995). In fact, Harvey reminds us that citizen participation itself, as employed by the utilitarian needs of public organizations, is merely part of what is called the "organizational imperative"; that is, an emphasis on hierarchical obedience, technical rationality, stewardship congruent to hierarchical elites, and a pragmatism devoted to expediency (Scott and Hart, 1989). Under these circumstances, Harvey avers, citizens have already lost their capacity to find a language or a voice having any substantive impact on society. Harvey's inferred point merits our attention: only a revised notion of publicness that takes a critical and confrontive approach to social reality can ever begin to create social spaces whereby citizens initiate what Arendt (1977) called "islands of freedom" and Fraser's (1992) notion of "subaltern counterpublics" whose role is to promote the ideal of participatory parity.

Jürgen Habermas and David Harvey, in their own specific and penetrating analyses of the societal forces impacting our lives, have raised a crucial point often overlooked by those advocating for more citizen involvement in the policy process.They contend that the political and institutional milieu of power tends to divert, or at times displace, the critical examination of environmental and social change to issues of what can be called a managerial stakeholder analysis. What I mean here—particularly in response to Habermas's and Harvey's erudite examination—is that participatory approaches often tend to merely "manage" conflict within the legitimate parameters of the prevailing status quo. In this regard, a politics of policy confinement takes place; that is, the containment of policy alternatives commensurate with the conventional managerial and instrumental ethos of formal organizations (Muller & Ventriss, 1985; Ventriss, 2002; Ramos, 1981; Hummel, 2007).

What both Habermas and Harvey have articulated, although from different theoretical angles, is reminiscent of what Hannah Arendt voiced about the dynamics of power, action, and politics: "Power is actualized only where word and deed are not parted company, where words are not empty and deeds not brutal, where words are not used to veil intentions but to disclose realities, and deeds are not used to violate and destroy but to establish relations and create new realities" (1958, p. 200). It should be noted that Habermas and Harvey would never dismiss out of hand the relevance of participation/stakeholder approaches, but rather would see these approaches as "limited" tools of public engagement that would do precious little to confront the constitutive basis of a managerial, neoliberal governmentality. In other words, a reconceptualization of publicness is called for that is embedded in critical democratic thought. A new kind of critical politics is called for, and new spaces of hope are needed, to provide "the organization of people as it arises out of acting and speaking together" (Arendt, 1958). More importantly, for both Habermas and Harvey the issue of citizen participation—putting aside its idyllic meaning for those who wish to legitimately foster a more democratic leitmotif in modern society—can too often become nothing more than an "ideological mystification" that diverts our attention from the efficacy of promoting broader social change. In this sense, they would agree that there is a critical point where social, environmental, and political theory must eventually merge. In the end, they have given us much to think about as we ponder the political, environmental, and administrative challenges would foster a more democratic ethos in the public arena.

So where do we go from here? I questioned earlier in the chapter whether we have focused enough of our attention on what created the problem in the first place, even when we believe it is crucial to initiate, with the best of intentions, the plethora of participatory techniques, procedures, and frameworks in order to include the public. Most of these participatory approaches presuppose by and large that conflict is always to be avoided, to be redirected into a public consensus that can be integrated appropriately into administrative processes. What this perspective avoids is an acknowledgment that conflict—and I mean here constructive conflict that is always nonviolent and representative of the common good—can be instructive in itself by raising issues that are not merely administrative. For example, this conflict may point to issues and approaches that ought to, and should, be on the policy agenda, which previously have been disregarded. Moreover, such conflict may invoke legitimate concerns that point to the underlying problems, which are perhaps part and parcel of the prevailing structures of power. Whatever the case may be, I think John Dewey's observation is correct that conflict can often play a productive purpose in democratic policymaking. Frank Bryan (2004, p. 253), in his extensive study over a thirty-year period of citizen participation in New England, put it best: "My findings suggest . . . that as politics is a part of human nature, conflict is as necessary to democracy as winter is to spring." Perhaps what is warranted in our participatory strategies is a framework to channel this conflict in a way that better questions the domain assumptions of policies that the public can openly debate.

Conclusion

In this book, my analysis began with a look at the core assumptions behind the notion that citizen involvement must translate to better policy. I suggested that the core beliefs of this stance, the idea that deliberative and communicative approaches to decision making are rationally and normatively sound, has been subverted by a pervasive utilitarian ethos endemic to globalized Western democracies. Under these conditions, I argued that a range of pressures operates to limit who among a public can engage in citizen involvement with decision making, and how they understand engagement to affect policy. Resultingly, citizen involvement can become little more than a tool, which public institutions use often to gain credibility and legitimacy for their agendas.

To understand this subtle disenfranchisement, I brought Habermas's notion of communicative rationality into dialogue with the realities of environmental management in the twenty-first century. I argued that Habermas's vision for an ideal state of discourse unfettered by unjust hierarchies, which elevates powerful expressions of experience to the forefront of public debate, has yet to be realized. Instead, many environmental institutions have adopted the trappings of this ideal—an active citizen base, and public discussion processes—and assimilated them into their utilitarian and technocratic traditions of resource management. The result is a distorted communicative rationality that fails to empower the public to envision and articulate normatively rigorous alternatives to the status quo.

Continuing in this vein, I introduced insights from Harvey's scholarship to contend that the technocratic and utilitarian approaches to environmental policy, developed to allocate and maintain abundant resources, have failed to acknowledge the broader economic and political forces that impact the public. Again, I called for a bolder vision of citizen engagement in policymaking as an antidote to this trend. I cautioned that under current conditioning factors in environmental management as well as in other areas of policy, the capacity for institutions to accept more than incremental changes to their operating policies is probably minimal.

In closing, I considered the possibility that an approach to citizen engagement and communicative rationality must think about the ways to integrate—as difficult as that may sound—constructive conflict of citizens embedded in the common good as a promising path forward. I suggested that such an orientation might help nurture the optimism needed for citizens to imagine policy transformation and the perspective to ground that visioning in normative considerations. As such, I argued that our challenge in both fields today is not merely to promote citizen involvement, but rather in promoting citizens involvement in conceiving of and helping to formulate alternatives that are not diverted into token modes of public engagement.

9

Conclusion

Reflections of a Sympathetic Critic

> There are these two young fish swimming along and they happen to meet an older fish swimming the other way, who nods to them and says, "Morning, boys, How's the water?" And those two fish swim for a bit, and then eventually one of them looks at the other and goes "What the hell is water?"
>
> —David Foster Wallace

I

I have always enjoyed this quote because it reminds me, and should remind us all, of how often we take for granted what is historically given, what appears to us as obvious, and what we accept too often without question. This book has tried to take David Foster Wallace's prescient insight to heart—to nudge us to ponder some fundamental questions in this era of political and economic uncertainty. The questions I have posed are hardly the last say on these matters. They are questions, properly understood, in response to the broader milieu of societal interdependency, rapid economic changes (both domestically and globally), a ubiquitous social media, and the rise of public distrust and cynicism regarding democratic institutions in the United States and elsewhere. These are questions, hopefully, that constructively challenge preconceived ideas, and the political and economic assumptions that legitimizes such ideas, not just for purposes of initiating productive change, but to deepen our awareness of how easily we can sometimes become acquiescent, willingly or unwillingly, to a uniformity of academic and professional opinion. Often this uniformity of thought takes the form of habitually shifting our attention away from examining societal problems as an integral part of larger political and economic inequalities embedded in society.

Many in public affairs would describe this convergence of factors, and its implications for the field, as a crisis of the highest order. But, when discussing these trends, I have tried in this book—as best as possible—to avoid the word *crisis* entirely, which has become an overused term to the point of becoming a cliché. Too often those who have used the word forget that, in Chinese, a crisis refers to both "danger" and "opportunity." Saying this, I have attempted to analyze certain dangers and opportunities that we face in public affairs. I maintain that we have placed too much emphasis on a procedural rationality that has narrowed, rather than broadened the moral syntax of public affairs, a managerial politics usually ensconced within the interstices of governmental institutions. By doing so, we have inevitably underestimated the powerful economic and symbolic forces (and actors) in modern society that can undermine any substantive role of publicness. Consequently, what we observe is a citizenry increasingly devoid of the independent thought needed to question the prevailing status quo, driven more by partisan loyalties and social identities, and guided more by preconceived ideas and partisanship, than by the validity of any evidence informing them on policy issues (Achen & Bartels, 2016).

Given this reality, I have argued that a revitalized notion of rationality and a renewed notion of "publicness" are sorely needed, a publicness that implies a Socratic citizenship that is not part and parcel of any "behaving system" that uncritically encourages obedience as part of a consumer herd in exchange for political acquiescence. It is a public rationality, in other words, which confronts those political, economic, and social forces that make plurality a mere fiction mediated in a cultural environment that encourages passive citizenship. This public rationality has the following characteristics:

- A public rationality is a critical and confrontive approach to social reality. The emphasis of a public rationality is on the ability to question the domain assumptions of those political and economic hegemonic forces shaping public life.
- A public rationality acknowledges that truth claims can be—and often are—historically and contextually contingent.
- A public rationality cannot be equated with history, society, the modern state, or an organization. Rather, it is a rationality

that attempts to contain the socializing forces of instrumentality on the individual in order to explore the social and political leitmotifs impacting the modern polity.

- A public rationality is fundamentally a "maieutic process" whereby citizens partake in a critical learning process that examines the underlying normative assumptions of policy choices.
- A public rationality also attempts to create and open new theoretical doors in exploring the efficacy of "social spaces of hope" or an "oasis in a desert" as a way to spread new enclaves for public action and public reflection.
- And finally, a public rationality recognizes that public action is rooted in the intersubjectivity and social practices of public life. (Ventriss 2002, p. 293)

In this sense, public rationality encourages us to continuously question the various political, social, and economic value systems that might be contributing to societal injustices. Dana Villa (2001, p. 38) stated it succinctly, stressing this very point: "[V]irtually every moral [or political] belief becomes false and an incitement to injustice the moment it becomes unquestioned or unquestionable"

Understandably, there have been copious debates in both public management/administration and public policy on such issues as citizen engagement, collaborative networks, public values, and the new public service. But these debates, as important as they are, have usually ignored the issue of modern power and the questioning of those deeply embedded political, cultural, and historical forces that are presently shaping civic life. Truth be told, these debates are mainly insular academic and professional discussions that were never meant to include the general public in the first place. Certainly, some would argue that there is good reason for this situation, given that these deliberations are inherently too technical and too complex for the general public to fully understand.

I think this rationale is not an effective response anymore, as reasonable as it may seem. We cannot, of course, do without experts. Obviously, we know experts can—and do—make mistakes. But, as Gary Wills (1979, p. 121) correctly asserted forty years ago, in words that have lost none of their timeliness today: "Everyone in our society seems to resent elites—but only certain elites. We are all elites; [curiously] we are all anti-elites." Wills correctly recognizes a stark and ironic reality that has significance for those of us directly involved in public affairs: assuming that we are operating within a democratic context, we are, like or not, an integral part of what some have called democratic elites. This democratic elitism comes at a price, however. That is, we must shoulder the ominous responsibility of balancing policy and managerial expertise with continuous democratic accountability, and a critical analysis of what role we might or ought to play in society. A Sisyphean task, but a necessary one. This book has tried to categorize some of the key problems before us, leaving us now to turn our attention to a basic, but essential question nestled among the obstacles I have painstakingly laid out: Where is the "opportunity" to do something quite different that gives us more of a substantive direction and sense of responsibility toward where we need to go? To respond to this salient question, I will now depend on my experiences and reflections over several decades as an educator concerned with public affairs during these troubling times.

II

I have been teaching public policy (and other, related courses) for almost forty years at such institutions as Johns Hopkins University, University of Southern California, University of Oxford, and the University of Vermont. The overwhelming majority of my students, while empirically rigorous and inquisitive toward the subject matter at hand, have been largely recalcitrant about critically questioning the underlying historical and epistemological premises of the ideas and concepts they are learning. Granted, this observation is based on my own professional experience and not on any empirical analysis that I am aware of. I could be wrong here. Yet, I do not think I am. I have heard from too many colleagues over several decades similar sentiments, although expressed in a somewhat defensive manner, about the consequential pedagogical and theoretical costs of this trend.

Arthur Felts put his finger on this important and related point when he argued that both public management/administration and public policy are inexorably linked to technical expertise and purposive-rational organizations oriented toward efficiency. Under these conditions, should we really be surprised that students seldom engage in serious critical reflection? Felts (1994, pp. 19–20) put it this way:

> The implications of this [tendency] are clear enough for [any] critical theory of public administration. Minimally, it suggests

> that public administration [and policy] theorists should be very careful when they begin to formulate a model of administrative imperatives or norms vis-à-vis the political system. Administrators cannot per se fill a political breach left open by a legislature and executive branch that increasingly finds itself unable to rule even on the grounds of a technical mastery of the "system" without further contributing to the suppression of a symbolic interest in communicative interaction. Administrators can only perform a substitute political function in a system that has already begun the process of eliminating of practical considerations by redefining them as technical ones.

To get around this situation, no doubt, will be a difficult task. Furthermore, we have to heed a salient warning that Dwight Waldo issued nearly forty years ago that continues to be particularly relevant today: "For if public administration [and public policy] is not knowledgeable and honest about its limits, it will inevitably suffer not just for its sins of waste and ineffectiveness, but from the bitterness of faith misplaced and hope unfulfilled" (1980, p. 46). One of the key issues we need to confront, both pedagogically and conceptually, is the zealous penchant for only procedural managerial and policy reforms (as important as they are in public affairs) over the pursuits of inquiries that may reside in the history and cultural fabric of society itself (Sandel, 1996; Wolin, 1960; Arendt, 1958). In my experience, most of my students tend to cloak their questions when touching upon any of the fundamental assumptions of what they are learning, with questions of managerial efficacy coupled with the appropriate normative overtones justifying their purpose. One can hardly blame them for taking this approach. To do otherwise is to take a chance on advancing one's career or dismissed as being unrealistic.

In other words, what I think is missing from most of our discussions in our classrooms and conferences is the acknowledgment of a political epistemology that filters conflicting values and interests commensurate to the dominant thinking of the day. We must, or should, begin to search for the limitations of our presuppositions of social reality, our theoretical biases, and our own deficiencies of our respective societies. In this regard, Karl Mannheim has something significant to contribute to this perspective: what he referred to as "non-immanent ideas." Non-immanent ideas are political or social ideas "that people accept, but which are not intrinsically more rational than many other alternative ideas which they might have accepted." (Cited in Landan, 1978, p. 202).

What Mannheim was maintaining is that a focus on non-immanent ideas encourages the scholar to emphasize the historical and cultural reasons why certain ideas have prevailed at a certain time compared to other equally effective ideas available during the same historical period. Mannheim, I believe, should be central to any serous inquiry: it is an inquiry that shifts our research attention to explore not only our own domain assumptions, but to assess the ethical implications of those non-immanent ideas that could be serving as an ideological prop in legitimizing a certain episodical administrative system (Ventriss, 2000, p. 513; Ramos, 1981). If nothing more, this suggestion by Mannheim may motivate us in a direction that opens new theoretical doors that we have been reluctant to open.

The different issues argued here are part of an enduring debate that has a long and distinguished history, as exemplified in the some of the writings of Hume, Kant, Dilthey, Nietzsche, Weber, Polanyi, and, more recently, Jürgen Habermas, Ian Shapiro, Sheldon Wolin, Michael Walzer, Dwight Waldo, and Hannah Arendt. These disputes will most likely outlive us all—as they should. But ultimately, we may find that we can only do so much when confronted with those broader societal influences and cultural norms, and, more importantly, in what we can really expect from ourselves and our students in enriching civic life. Waldo's warning about the potential for hubris is worth noting where our efforts are concerned, even with our best intentions of improving the conditions of society. The struggle before us is daunting because there is a built-in tension between maintaining a viable intellectual autonomy to explore potentially controversial public issues, while adhering to the prevailing dictates of the modern state. I have found that this is one topic that has received only a modicum of attention, if any, in our journals, at our conferences, and most likely in our classrooms as well. From my experience, both seasoned and young scholars, regardless of their respective intellectual perspectives, will have to wrestle with both the theoretical and professional implications of this perennial tension. It is an inquiry long overdue. Dealing with this tension, I contend, will mean upholding in no uncertain terms an intellectual integrity that is unafraid in asking needed controversial questions concerning some of the most urgent policy issues of our time.

Perhaps, when all is said and done, and after all that has been written here, what is achievable at this particular time is a more modest approach that is not so grandiose in its intended macro-societal effects. This is not to negate other issues I think we need to consider in the future. Rather, it is a call for recognizing the necessity and validity of different approaches to meaningful change in public affairs. I am referring here to Arendt's (1977) notion of what she called "islands in a sea or an oasis in a desert." These are places where one can nurture—in our universities, in our local communities, and in our neighborhood organizations—those public spaces whereby concerned citizens might have the opportunity to experience publicness as part of an "elenchus process" of Socratic inquiry that delimits the influence of instrumental and market values on public discourse. Some will, undoubtedly, claim that this is nothing more than a pipe dream unlikely to occur in an era when the notion of publicness has been largely appropriated by market values. Given that we live in a world of growing political illiteracy, one can argue that the prospects for widespread "public debate informed by democratic values and critical reason are dim" (Isaac, 1998, p. 56). In short, How can we possibly achieve even this modest endeavor when surrounded by a sea of political instrumentality?

In response, I would argue that these modest oases in the desert can exist, and do, and not just in the United States. For example, the Springtide Collective is a Canadian nonpartisan organization connecting Nova Scotians to alternative ways of doing democratic politics; Civinomics is an initiative in Santa Cruz, California, giving citizens crucial information to assist them in formulating and suggesting their own policies commensurate to their unique needs; Smart Citizen tries to collect data about various citizen activities to foster more engaged communities throughout the Netherlands; Sensing City is an organization in New Zealand that collects data in facilitating citizen engagement and in promoting the livability of its major cities. As important as these vibrant civic initiatives seem to be, inasmuch as they are surrounded by a sea of instrumentality they are still at best sporadically and randomly scattered throughout the political landscape, although understandably existing more often in established democracies.

I wish I had a more concise, pragmatic answer to the question of how to further nurture these "islands in the sea." In this regard, I offer no new typology or specific policy model to consider. However, I do ask us to ponder Arendt's (1968, pp. ix–x) suggestion, written in a poetic tone that is neither patronizing nor romanticizing in its desire to have us seriously consider the value of having "oases in the desert":

> Even in the darkest of times we have the right to expect some illumination . . . from the uncertain, flickering, and often weak

> light that some men and women, in their lives and in their words, will kindle under almost all circumstances and shed over the time span that was given them on earth.

This illumination is, however, presently being tested during the COVID-19 pandemic. As I mentioned in the Foreword, the COVID-19 pandemic underscores how widespread political and economic uncertainty can often foster sustained confusion and obfuscation in formulating policies for "wicked" societal issues. More tellingly, this unprecedented global pandemic has exposed the fragile fault lines of our market society (i.e., United States), particularly given the inherent tension between implementing needed public health priorities while trying to mitigate as much as possible the consequential economic repercussions of such health policy initiatives. This complex and thorny problem stands in the haunting shadow of the following disquieting political reality: "Our own liberal institutions have proven not to be as robust as many imagined, with ascendant far-right movements, intensifying inequality, endless war, and feckless cultural and political elites undermining confidence in the durability of democracy itself. The invisible hand of history, the market, or Reason have failed to guide us to universal peace and prosperity" (Reitter & Wellmon, February 14, 2020, p. B 19).

Many, I suspect, will find this provocative assertion as overdrawn. That aside, the COVID-19 pandemic represents not only how a health crisis of this magnitude can change political preferences in the decision-making process (Tooze, 2020), but the enduring effect this catastrophic pandemic has had on the workforce in the United States (and elsewhere) who lost their jobs in hotels, restaurants, bars, and retail stores (and other related industries) impacting millions of workers. In the United States, these workers were disproportionately female, minorities, young, and those lacking an education beyond high school. Most economists have somberly predicted that the unemployment rate in the United States could reach a peak of more than 20 per cent. Not surprisingly, these same economists anticipate a long and slow return to pre-pandemic employment levels and economic growth.

As Elizabeth Kolbert (2020) laments, a health pandemic tends to be divisive in its social impact. Following on that theme, given the reality of racial segregation, redlining, poor housing, and less access to healthcare (and other related issues), is it any wonder that in Chicago, where one-third of the population is African American, two-thirds of the eighty-six who died by COVID-19 (in March 2020) were African American. Similarly, the Centers for Disease Control and Prevention (CDC) has reported that in fourteen

States African Americans accounted for 33 percent of the hospitalization rate, although only making up 18 percent of the population surveyed. Put simply, "In a country [United States] that was highly unequal in many ways before it had a confirmed case of Covid-19, other disparities will be sadly predictable, falling along racial and class lines, as well as other fateful divides" (Pinsker, 2020, 1). From a global perspective, Oxfam International has estimated that, at a minimum, an additional five hundred million people will fall into poverty due to the rapid spread of COVID-19. And Kristalina Georgieva, the International Monetary Fund's managing director, reported that the world economy could be facing the worst economic crisis since the Depression of the 1930s (British Broadcast News, April 9, 2020).

But this global pandemic, interestingly, may offer a propitious historical moment to encourage new thinking along the lines of a revitalized public philosophy. While a more thorough discussion of this revitalized public philosophy lies beyond the scope of this book, broadly speaking, it would, first, facilitate the view that our collective existence is an integral part of a dense and complex network of social interconnectedness. This social interconnectedness, if properly nurtured, would encourage citizens to express their publicness by designing and engaging in a variety of public enclaves that highlights both their individuality and substantive contributions to community life; second, it would provide incentives for the implementation of policy approaches that acknowledges the differentiated public and social needs of the citizenry, and, in so doing, value the importance of acquiring crucial historical and cultural knowledge of differing publics and their respective substantive social practices; and finally, it would, hopefully, foster an overdue debate on delimiting the market from becoming an all-exclusive category that encompasses all aspects of individual, social, and civic affairs (Ramos,1981).

This public philosophy—assuming the merit of its basic premises for many of the challenges we need to confront—warrants some rethinking on our part, which, among other things, will require a reconceptualization of the meaning of professionalism, an emphasis on social experimentation based on disaggregate policymaking, and a revision of education for public service. These incremental steps alone, I admit, will hardly be enough to accomplish some of needed changes that I have called for in this book. Yet, I maintain these suggestions are nevertheless a step in the right direction as we debate the implications of new pathways and new roles we should, and ought, to consider in this uncertain future we all face.

Hopefully, many will regard this book as an open invitation to explore and deepen our understanding of "those societal play of forces" in this time of political and economic uncertainty; an invitation which I see as a seed that can be planted to encourage others in nurturing those "oases in the desert." Many might find this quest to be an intellectual dead end to those more acceptable and pragmatic perspectives better suited to administrative and policy realities. As we struggle with this challenge and the various theoretical venues it may take us to, we should take to heart this insightful advice from Rabbi Tarfon: "It was not granted you to complete the task and yet you may not give it up" (cited in Gitlin, 1989, p. 438). We have reached that critical moment in public affairs when it is finally time to ask more and more questions in the spirit of "What the hell is water?" This quest is long overdue.

To be sure, I have asked more questions in this book than I have answered. Some of my colleagues will find that what is argued here is as a mere polemic—just another argument against the mainstream thinking in public management/administration and public policy. While there is some validity to this claim, most of these ideas and themes in this book are reflective of my thoughts—and reactions—inspired by what I first encountered as college student in the late 1960s. Those turbulent years, marked by social unrest, cultural change, new social movements, the assassinations of Robert Kennedy and Martin Luther King Jr., and the beginnings of a conservative backlash demonstrated by the rise of Alabama's governor George Wallace to national prominence, foreshadowed and mirrored the conditions that new scholars must grapple with today. All of these events made an enduring impact on my thinking. If we can put aside for the moment some of the negative trends that came out of that era, I believe the historical period gave birth to a whole range of new questions and contradictions that have not been expunged since that time, but rather have gone socially, culturally, and philosophically underground, even as their relevance has continued to grow. That is to say, they are buried underneath presuppositions that regard these contradictions and unsettling questions as best addressed within the confines of managerial expertise, analytical acumen, and the rule of law. On the face of it, this is a compelling argument that is difficult to dispute. In fact, many believe these "presuppositions" are at the very heart of what are perceived as the major social responsibilities of both fields to the citizenry. But is this enough?

My answer to this question is both "yes" and "no." Undeniably, it is a fact that for those who practice in public management/administration and public policy are often limited by legislative statutes or legal rulings about their respective administrative duties and limitations in implementing rules and regulations. I assume that many of my colleagues would assert that to go beyond those mandates runs the risk of undermining the political legitimacy of both fields. On the other hand, both fields are more than mere state functions, more than an administrative arm of the state, and more than an implementing "neutral" tool within public organizations for enforcing legislative mandates and regulations. As I have tried to elucidate in this book, both fields, as practiced and theorized, can be viewed as part of a process of nurturing seeds for democratic inquiry and deliberations in a variety of domains, a valuable and reliable source for the citizenry to consider information about the tradeoffs and the underlying assumptions to policy choices, and, finally, the acknowledgment of the limitations (and potential for hubris) concerning the role of both fields in helping to shape societal affairs.

This does not mean that I am calling for both disciplines to act like social workers or social justice advocates. In other words, our role is not as Platonic guardians of what we might think is best for the public or in deciding what policies should be pursued. Clearly, there is much merit to this viewpoint that echoes the politics/administrative dichotomy. Yet, we cannot ignore the publicness of our role, which transcends governmental institutions. We are also part of civil society—or more specifically, we are part of a larger political and cultural ecosystem, which requires a more expansive role on our part in working with the public on some of the most crucial policy issues facing society. At a minimum, I think this expansive purpose involves three important initiatives we can pursue. These initiatives, previously mentioned, should be regarded, however, only as suggestions in encouraging debate about feasible ways we can broaden both fields' intellectual horizons in this time of uncertainty by: (1) redefining professionalism; (2) promoting civic experiments based on disaggregate policymaking; and (3) rethinking education for public service. My discussion of these initiatives is mainly a theoretical exploration of their importance to both fields. I will briefly discuss them in turn.

When the American Society for Public Administration was formed in 1939, its primary purpose was to reduce the gap between academia and government so professional knowledge could have a salient impact on governmental policy (Stever, 1988). Other professional associations, such as the Municipal Finance Officers (MFOA) and the International City Managers Association (ICMA), likewise stressed that public administration should try to pursue a professional status (Pugh, 1989). Yet, interestingly, in the 1930s with the emergence of professionalism in such fields as public health, social work, and city planning there was hardly any attention given to the inherent conflict between public interest values and the professional values of expertise and efficiency (Erie, 1979). Dwight Waldo (1980) thought the best way to proceed with the issue of professionalism was for public administration to act like a profession even though it could not in reality ever become one in the same sense as medicine or law. This general sentiment for professionalism and its importance to those devoted to public service has been highlighted by such influential scholars as Derek Bok (1975), James Perry (2007), and Frederick Mosher (1968).

On the other hand, Charles Fox (1993, p. 56) voiced concerns that this trend toward professionalism essentially "robs public administration [and policy] theorists of the independence required to imagine more emancipatory conditions of work and governance and the alertness to seize upon emerging trends to coax from them more authentic human interrelationships." Taking on a more controversial tone, Magali Sarfatti Larson (1984, p. 46) has argued that professionalism is in reality about "imparting both general ideology—that is to say widely shared, although possibly shallow beliefs, knowledge, and assumptions—and, at the same time, specific ideologies embedded in limited discourses restricted to the circles of the initiated." From a historical perspective, some have argued that what we are seeing in professionalism is a shift from the rhetoric of a "trustee professionalism" to a rhetoric of an "expertise professionalism," resulting in the marketing and selling of expert solutions, and, in doing so, converting citizens into mere consumers of public programs (Brint, 1994; Evetts, 2011).

While, understandably, there is a plethora of literature on both the merits and weaknesses of professionalism, Alfred North Whitehead observed the following about the myopic intellectual interests associated with professionalism:

> Each professionalism makes progress, but it is progress in its own groove . . . of course, no one is merely a mathematician or a lawyer. People have lives outside of their profession or their business. But the point is the restraint of serious thought within a groove . . . [that is] the imperfect categories of thought derived from one's profession. (1963, p. 78)

Whitehead's prescient point bears examination: Does professionalism in public management/administration and public policy accentuate an intellectual parochialism that fosters scholarly timidity and theoretical retrenchment on key policy issues in order to stay within a perceived professional groove? It is interesting to note that Stephen Bailey (1976) also cautioned that professionalism might encourage, as an unintended consequence, a tunnel vision among administrators and analysts in their duties serving the public interest.

In particular, public management/administration faces a conundrum in pursuing professionalism. Although professionalism is justly proud of freeing itself (at least in the United States) from the shackles of politicization, in public affairs we continue to struggle with the legitimacy of what professionalism intrinsically denotes: the monopolization of knowledge and the application of research-based information to the solution of problems of instrumental choice (Schon, 2001; Ventriss, 1982). If my emphasis on publicness and critical democratic thought has any validity (along with the other issues I have raised), it is time to rethink this quest for professionalism that many believe is so central to both fields. This rethinking will imply what Harry Boyte and Eric Retz (2010, p. 85) so aptly referred to as "civic professionalism" that seeks "our common interests that link professional inquiry and local knowledge production that involve laypeople in the solution of public problems." Albert Dzur (2008) echoed a similar theme that democratic professionals (his term) are those who work with citizens, instead of acting on them. While Boyte and Retz's, and Dzur's, contentions are well motivated, they largely deemphasize the stark political realities of how democratic values are undermined by both business interests and the role of dark money in dictating the tempo of policymaking (Mayer, 2016).

So, what exactly is needed in this rethinking of professionalism? I argue that it is both a new attitude and knowledge that lends itself to a heuristic process—a process that sees professional expertise and knowledge as an integral part of public learning. Donald Schon touched upon this idea in a book that is seldom quoted much any more, *Beyond the Stable State* (1971). In this book, he mentions the importance of being a "learning agent," which he articulates in these perspicacious terms:

> The learning agent in situations of public action must be able to confront multiple, conflicting perspectives on the situation with one another. He [or she] must be able to sustain and work in the interpersonal here-and-now which is characteristic of public action . . . the learning agent must be willing and able to use himself [or herself] as an informational instrumental within the learning situation. His [or her] own abilities to listen rather than assert, to confront and tolerate the anxieties of confrontation,

> to suspend commitment until the last possible moment—all condition his [or her] ability to draw information from the situation while it is in process. (1971, p. 236)

I believe Schon is presenting something we can benefit from in our discussions on professionalism. Here, I am also influenced by his book *The Reflective Practitioner* (1984) and his description of reflection-in-action "that our knowing in is in our action" (p. 49). The question is not whether we are a profession or not, but whether for those of us who study and practice in public affairs we are partaking in a learning process of improving public action through knowledge that critically examines the underlying assumptions and the normative implications of public policies in an intergovernmental and intersectoral environment (Ventriss & Luke, 1988). In short, we need to redefine professionalism in public service as a substantive inquiry that, on one hand, does not negate the importance of promoting managerial efficiency and public accountability, but, on the other hand, incorporates a substantive learning process that can create new possibilities for public action and public dialogue—possibilities that are not exclusively bound to instrumental/utilitarian considerations. It is a redefined professionalism that values our roles as learning agents in sharing the development of a knowledge base applicable to redesigning administrative and policy processes that can unlearn (when appropriate) previous practices and formulate new learning frameworks in order to address ill-defined or "wicked" problems. This focus on rethinking professionalism as learning agents will require cognizance of these challenging factors: (1) devising successful methods of sharing knowledge directly with citizens; making technical information based on a "public language" to cultivate genuine public debate; (2) learning to communicate with nonexperts and becoming more familiar with new modes of communication not solely limited to issues of expediency and efficiency; (3) acknowledging the importance of constructive conflict in which boundaries of power are continuously negotiated with different communities in the pursuit of the public interest; and (4) designing new collaborative spaces that delimit hierarchical goverance in order to allow for joint policymaking for the different publics in a plural-centric policy system (Ventriss, 2016; Sorensen, 2012).

A final note on this part of my discussion: a myriad of interesting and robust research has been conducted on such themes as policy networks, collaborative policy innovations, network governance, co-production, metagovernance, and public values. All of these theoretical approaches share similar and overlapping ideas with my stress on learning agents, but perhaps with the exception of this one cental point: that public organizations, irrespective of their noble intentions and goals, are fundamentally managerial instruments whose central purposes, albeit for understandable reasons, are inexorably centered on institutional growth, survival, and control (Adams & Balfour, 2014; Box, 2014; Ventriss, 2016; Perrow, 1979). In other words, planning with citizens, embracing error, and linking knowledge with action are all undoubtedly significant factors in shared governance and in redefining professionalism. Yet, these approaches may have little impact on those powerful structural political and economic impediments to such perspectives, given that most, if not all, public organizations are still deeply embedded in technical rationality. In this respect, a learning agent, then, is an individual under constant professional tension in resisting becoming a completely socialized actor. In short, a learning agent is one who can delimit instrumental values on the grounds of their ethical sense (Ramos, 1981). In redefining professionalism along these conceptual lines, the issue of monopolization of knowledge and information will ultimately rest on a new dynamic: that professional knowledge is not an esoteric type of knowledge primarily for experts only, but a public knowledge that has genuine substantive meaning when contributing to a learning environment between citizens and social scientists. How to actually create such a learning environment is a challenge worthy of any rethinking of professionalism (Ventriss, 2016; Ventriss & Luke, 1988), which leads to my next point for discussion.

III

Civic experiments, as I use the term here, again refers closely to something that Charles Levine mentioned about how to facilitate policy innovation while building a more concrete relationship between citizens and policymakers. He referred to this process as "building a bridge" that consisted of three strands: innovation, participation, and loyalty. Levine went on to argue that innovation implied experimentation, a process of learning-by-doing in joint problem solving which, in turn, would build in citizens a loyalty to community needs (1984, p. 185).

I think Levine was basically correct on this point. If we take his observation seriously (and I think we should), such experimentation and innovation would be based on the following contextual factors:

- Public action is now increasingly occurring in an expanding and crowded policy environment in which, increasingly, everything depends on everything else, and while power is often not equally dispersed in the policy domain, there is still an acknowledgment of the multiplicity of publics and policy actors involved, or that might be involved, in implementing any policy action (Ventriss, 2016; Ventriss & Luke, 1988; Bryson & Einsweiller, 1987; Fischer, 2009).
- There is significantly reduced capacity for any one governmental jurisdiction or policy actor to effectively act unilaterally to accomplish public goals (Ventriss & Luke, 1988; Ventriss, 2016; Kirlin, 1979; Fung, 2006).
- An enlarging policy domain of often unforeseen, unintended, or indirect consequences increases vulnerability and openness to outside influences, with public officials (and organizations) increasingly dependent on other individuals and networks of organizations outside of their view (Ventriss & Luke, 1988; Ventriss, 2016; Salamon, 1987; Joshi & Moor, 2004).
- The consequences of policy choices and public actions are often far-ranging, delayed, and have indirect or hidden costs beyond the normal externalities; desirable and undesirable consequences are difficult to separate and important and often critical second- and third-order effects of policy choices often go unnoticed (Ventriss & Luke, 1988, p. 346; Ventriss, 2016; Ramos, 1981; Barnett, 2007; Dryzek, 2000, 2006; Kilign & Kooperjan, 2000; Newman & Sullivan, 2004).

Following this related theme, I mentioned earlier what I called disaggregate policymaking. This approach serves as a critical process in achieving both innovation and experimentation in policy. This approach has these important attibutes in designing policy experiments congruent to the public interest:

- Communities have unique experiences and perceptions that can serve as an important information base for the formulation of specific policies for community concerns (as a social knowledge transfer).
- Communities need to communicate their knowledge by effectively organizing people in formulating policy hypotheses that

can be mutually evaluated by policymakers and community leaders.

- Citizens cannot be treated in an aggregate manner. They have distinct needs and interests that need to be addressed and are important components of any substantive feedback between citizens and agencies.
- Individual knowledge must be combined with professionally codified knowledge to facilitate a better fit between public goods and services and the community with its substantive needs (Muller & Ventriss, 1985, pp. 118–119).

These attributes actually fit nicely with Guerreiro Ramos's notion of civic experiments, which characterizes a social system design that attempts "to facilitate the development of initiaitves freely generated by individuals to coalesce them in forms of effective configuration" (1981, p. 127). He reiterates that such experiments are necessary in a multicentric policy system. This experiment he called a "para-economic paradigm that postulates a society diversified enough to allow its members to deal with substantive life issues according to their pertinent intrinsic criteria and in specific settings." (p. 133). That is, different policies, in other words, have to be designed appropriate to the specific needs of particular enclaves, as described in chapter 5. Understandably, there are likely many who are suspicious of the practicality of this endeavor.

Yet, Udo Pesch (2018) and his colleagues have discussed policy experiments strikingly similar to Ramos's ideas. Pesch and his colleagues analyzed local sustainability initiatives involving community gardens, waste reduction systems, and energy cooperatives, all of which experimented with alternative social and economic practices that are more flexible than traditional public organizations. These experiments, they explain, involved the role of technology and the "involvement of citizens in technology development as a way to exert influence over the trajectories and innovation" (p. 18). They summarized their major conclusions this way:

> [Local sustainability initiatives occur when] civic engagement and sustainable innovation meet: [they] can be featured attempts for groups of individuals to gain control over their [specific] environment . . . [thus,] they form a rich pallet of public spaces that explore different practices, identities, and trajectories, doing right to the normative plurality that should be the basis of both democracy and sustainable innovation. (p. 18)

Going back to Levine's original point, an integral part of building a bridge to enhance innovation and experimentation, therefore, should include disaggregating policies that are carefully designed by citizens and policymakers alike in which a plurality of publics communicate their experiences arising from their differences and adjust policies congruent to their specific and unique situations. Of course, more research must be conducted on this matter. For example, can disaggregate policymaking sometimes in fact ultimately lead to policy discontinuity wherein a policy becomes increasingly more disjointed? Is disaggregate policy positively associated with building trust and loyalty between citizens and public agencies? And what would prevent disaggregate policymaking from falling prey to the forces of interest group pluralism (Ventriss, 2016)? Answering these important questions will, hopefully, provide more insights into the value of this approach. All in all, disaggregate policymaking offers an alternative approach in promoting civic experiments, which engages publicness in its inherent plurality. Now let us turn to my last point.

During the Progressive Era in the United States, the disciplines of city planning, social work, and public administration represented what John Dyckman (1978) referred to as an optimistic pragmatism. This optimistic pragmatism, Dyckman claims, is predicated on the notion that the administrator or policy analyst could improve the efficacy of many, if not most, social programs and therefore resolve pressing societal issues with the appropriate application of managerial knowledge and analysis (Adams, 1992; Ventriss, 2000; Stivers, 2010). Whether this belief continues to be valid is, of course, a debatable point. Yet, one might argue that even though there has been copious attention in recent decades focused on such normative topics as the role and meaning of citizenship, as well as other, related substantive issues, these noble endeavors have mostly played an ancillary role in comparison to the amount of attention devoted to technical and managerial matters (Box, 2008; Ventriss, 1991; Hummel, 2007). Certainly, as mentioned previously, educating future professionals for public service requires knowledge of policy analysis, management, budgeting, and other technical matters; there is no argument on this point. But have our traditional approaches to professional knowledge and pedogogy, as noted by Schon (2001), become strongly influenced by technical rationality that, in turn, has narrowed the questions we ask?

In this regard, Frederick Mosher (1986) was right when he argued that universities offer the best hope for making professional education safe for democracy. And I agree that universities should play this essential role. But given the American ambivalence about public management/administration and public policy, Mosher's contention misses a significant issue: Why should universities promote professional education in these fields when there is no explicit philosophy of education that addresses the normative relationship between professionalism and expertise in this "cultural bondage of modernity" (Adams, 1993, p. 130). Sir Walter Moberly (1949, p. 70) outlined the educational consequences of this omission, for both the professional student and the university, which is worth pondering:

> Our predicament, then, is this. Most students go through our universities without ever having been forced to exercise their minds on the issues which are really momentary. Under the guise of academic [and professional] neutrality, they are subtly conditioned to unthinking acquiescence in the social and political status quo and in a secularism on which they have never seriously reflected. Owing to the prevailing fragmentation of studies, they are not challenged to decide responsibly on a life-purpose or equipped to make such a decision wisely. They are not incited to disentangle and examine critically the assumptions and emotional attitudes underlying the particular studies they pursue, the profession for which they are preparing, the ethical judgments they are accustomed to make and the political or religious convictions they hold. Fundamentally, they are uneducated.

I know this observation hardly applies to public affairs alone, but one can only wonder whether this comes closer to the truth than we would like to admit. More broadly, has the desire to professionalize education for public affairs inadvertently undermined the value of becoming a public social science?

The significance here is a serious one that cuts to the core of professional education; that is, the subtle abdication of our critical role in exploring issues as being interwoven with the economic, political, economic, and historical fabric of society iself. Is it any wonder, then, that there is an educational proclivity to view societal problems as chiefly an organizational rather than as a political phenomenon—issues that are regarded as a problem of individual and group adjustment rather than of political or societal rearrangement or with deep-seated historical and economic roots (Erie, 1979)? Or put in slightly different terms, should we really be surprised that there is an intellectual propensity in professional education to displace social and value conflicts issues into concerns of administrative reforms, human relations, and decision-making models (Ventriss, 1993)? But here is the rub: How can we educate students for public service without facing the stark reality that both fields stand in perennial tension between the broader instrumental values couched in modernity and the substantive values of promoting civic responsibility (Hummel, 2007)?

I know there has been much discussion about the relevance of public service values and citizen-administrators as major goals for professional education. As Terry Cooper so emphatically put it: students of public affairs should "study examine, and critically understand the tradition of democratic citizenship . . . and . . . find one's self within its broad and varied streams (1991, p. 202). As much as I am sympathetic to these approaches, there is a nagging issue that warrants confronting: How do we realistically encourage democratic citizenship in our curriculum? I propose that we should fundamentally rethink the way we educate future administrators and policy analysts congruent to my emphasis on publicness and critical democratic thought. My overall approach is based on this premise: that there should be a more concerted focus on those macrosocietal issues examining the historical, social, and economic milieu of social problems and the varying roles administrators/analysts play in the interstices of governmental institutions and civic associations in civil society.

The possibilities for a reinvigorated education in the theory and practice of public affairs are rich. A curriculum focused on critical and normative competencies alongside the appropriate managerial and analytical courses might include course work on such topics as democratic theory, the historical development of the state, administrative and/or policy ethics, bureaucracy and democracy, social equity, civic responsibility in a time of economic and political uncertainty, and the impact of the global economy on domestic affairs. Of course, these broad offerings are only suggestions. Even though this may be seen as an affront to many in both fields, the purpose of an education in public management/administration and public policy is not the mere mastery of technical skills, but in exploring the underlying assumptions behind policy choices, how problems are defined, and who are defining them. These subjects, I argue, should be viewed not as mere electives but as mandatory core courses in the curriculum. Students, for example, who take a budget/accounting or public finance course would be required to take a core course dealing with social equity issues that are not customarily raised in much depth in such courses. If nothing else, these core courses on macrosocietal issues will remind us of the important democratic consequences and responsibilities of our knowledge and expertise and the central value of publicness in these uncertain times. This implies, of course, that we examine more issues at the macro-societal level that we have largely ignored or been reluctant to address. Critics, I can only imagine, would argue that this pedagogical perspective essentially excoriates the most crucial aspects of what is commonly thought of professional education. Further, many will probably claim that this approach could undermine the intellectual and professional credibility of both fields in the eyes of other disciplines and professions. These reservations require a serious discussion on the implications of what I am proposing. But, in the end, whatever we think we might be sacrificing in how others view us will be more than made up for in providing a more robust, civically minded field of inquiry.

It is only fitting at this point that I conclude with the following quote from Dwight Waldo (1980, p. 98) that continues to stay with me after all these years: "My own judgment is that Public Administration [and Public Policy], seeking to solve problems in a very real world, is importantly involved in creating the political theory of our time. I am confident that this will be the verdict of history." All things considered, I hope this book leads us in the right direction toward what that political theory (or new conceptual perspective) might actually look like, or at least certain aspects of it, as we wrestle with the major social and political issues that lie before us in this era of political and economic uncertainty. What this new perspective eventually looks like will assuredly shape the meaning and purpose of what we do and think about in public affairs for many, many years to come.

Finally, I think it is worth noting that it was Socrates who argued that democracy was a noble but sluggish horse. Therefore, Socrates thought he should serve as a gadfly, waking up democracy with a sting. This explicitly implied being rigorous in critically examining one's underlying assumptions. I hope that I have moved us closer to recognizing the value of a gadfly, and in so doing, reclaiming the centrality of publicness and forever staying alert to those forces that might undermine its role in human affairs.

Notes

Foreword

1. See Baker, S. R., Bloom, N., & Davis, S. J. (2016). Measuring economic policy uncertainty, *Quarterly Journal of Economics, 131* (4), pp. 1593–1636. These authors have employed an Economic Policy Index (EPU) based on counting articles, newspaper stories, and research reports that contain a set of key phrases mentioning uncertainty in a searchword. This process of mapping uncertainty actually started in the 1990s, but it has gained recently more credibility in light of the Euro crisis, Brexit, the potential for trade wars, and the rise of populism in many countries. Presently, in 2020, the EPU is at an all-time high. But, as John Dewey and Hannah Arendt remind us, there will always be uncertainty and contingency in human affairs. The pivotal question (and concern), then, is whether this sea of uncertainty can sometimes morph—under particular historical conditions—into an ominous state of affairs wherein increasingly some citizens take political refuge in certain beliefs and norms that are fundamentally corrosive to the modern polity. That is to say, these beliefs and norms become ensconced in antipublic sentiments sympathetic, if not supportive, of exclusionary nationalism, the distrust of scientific knowledge and expertise, and the uncritical acquiescence to political demagoguery. At its worst, such antipublic sentiments become part of a herd mentality that results in political resentment and disenchantment with the political process itself.

Chapter 1

1. I mention this to some extent because Candler has argued that public affairs scholarship in Brazil, India, the Philippines, Australia, and Canada (2014) have simultaneously asserted that American scholarship may not be useful to them, while at the same time seeking to address administrative and social pathologies that the American literature and practice developed to combat. This, too, despite

Candler also having argued that the American, and broader Anglophone literatures are woefully parochial.

Chapter 2

1. Scott and Hart's (1979) point here is similar to Abraham Kaplan's (1964) observation on the extant orthodoxy of modern scientific communities. The following statement can be applied equally to contemporary training in policy analysis and public management/administration: "every scientific community is a society in the small, so to speak, with its own agencies of social control. Officers of the professional associations, honored elders, editors of journals, reviewers, faculties, committees on grants, fellowships, and prizes—all exert a steady pressure for conformity to professional standards, as their counterparts in the larger society provide sanctions for the more general norms. In certain respects, scientific training functions to produce not only competence but also a kind of respectability, essential to membership in the professional community. Doctoral examinations, most candidates agree, have much in common with the tortures of initiation rites—and with the added tribulation of fear of failure: no one has ever had to repeat his Bar Mitzvah" (Kaplan, 1964, p. 4).

2. Poulantzas (1975) defines this term as follows: "The state is not an instrumental entity, existing for itself, it is not a thing, but the condensation of a balance of forces." The correspondence in question is established rather in terms of organization and representation: "The hegemonic class . . . beyond its immediate economic interests . . . must undertake to define the overall political interests of the classes . . . that constitute the power bloc, and thus its own long-term political interest" (p. 98). This awkward phrasing basically means that the state has become a major political object of social struggle and conflict even as it promotes the overall concerns of certain economic interests.

I have selected Poulantzas for a brief discussion in this book because he incorporated trends that warrant our attention when discussing the modern state. These trends involve five features: (1) a transfer of power from the legislative branch to the executive with the power being increasingly concentrated in the latter; (2) the decline of political parties as a vehicle for political representation; (3) a fusion between the different branches of the state with a decline in the rule of law; (4) the proliferation of complex networks cross-cutting public organizations of the state exercising political influence without proper public accountability and oversight; and, (5) the increasing involvement of surveillance of its citizens (Jessop, 1990). I thought these trends are worthy of more discussion and debate in the field. While, I do not agree with Poulantzas's structuralist's view of the modern state, he raises critical arguments that require more attention in our examination of the role of the state. My own thinking on the role of the state, which I am presently pursuing in my research, is how to integrate the insights of Donald Schon's (1971) "learning system," which he develops in his book *Beyond the Stable State*, with Guerreiro Ramos's (1981) "para-economic paradigm" that he describes in *The New Science of Organizations*. Both these thinkers, I believe, provide interesting ideas on statecraft, especially in a post-Fordist economic environment.

3. It is important to note that Poulantzas (1978) borrows heavily from Foucault's distinction between specific and universal intellectuals and, more generally, from Foucault's discussion of power and knowledge. Poulantzas is equally influenced here by Gramsci's (1971) distinction between organic and traditional intellectuals. However, Poulantzas criticizes Foucault for not adequately explaining resistance to power.

4. The Regulation School has been accused of having an inadequate theory of the state. Among others, Swyngedouw (1996) and Jessop (1990) have attempted to fill this important theoretical void.

5. The mention of the legal monopoly of coercive power raises the issue of what the meaning of the state is. While the literature on the state is too numerous to mention here, according to Alexander Passerin d'Entreves (1967), the modern state can be best defined in one of the following three ways. The *political realists,* he argues, have defined the state as the monopoly of legitimate force within territorial boundaries. The *legalists*, on the other hand, view the state as a system of laws and rules that defines the parameters of the state's power. And finally, the *political philosophers* contend that although force and law are important characteristics of the state, the critical factor is the obligation the state commands. The state, according to this view, "is the sum total of the obligations that a collectivity of people voluntarily accept as their own."

In terms of the literature in public management/administration, sadly the discussion of the state has been rarely raised. The exceptions to this state of affairs are the following: Milward, B. H., Jensen, L., Roberts, A., Dussauge-Laguna, M. I., Junjan, V., Torenvlied, R., Boin, A., Colebatch, H. K., Kettl, D., & Durant, R. F. (2016). Is public administration neglecting the state? *Governance, 29*(3), 1–26. Hood, C. (1988). *The art of the state.* Clarendon; Scott, J. L. (1998). *Seeing like a state.* Yale University Press. For a different perspective, consult Durant, R., and Rosenbloom, D. (2016). The hollowing of American public administration. *American Review of Public Administration, 47*(7), 719–737.

Chapter 4

1. Lou Weschler brought to my attention long ago that specifically public administration, by definition, is inherently a conservative field of inquiry. Weschler maintained accordingly, that there are certain contentious questions about society and the economy that tend to be completely avoided because they involve the unsettled relationship between the state and both disciplines.

2. Some may be perplexed as to why I have included Arendt on the list, given that she does not fall into any easy political categorization. I include her on this list not only because of her strong emphasis on citizen involvement in the political process, but also because she mounts a devastating critique against the role of the market economy in modern life. Some may wonder why I have not mentioned the works of Dwight Waldo, Frederick Mosher, and Norton Long. Each of these thinkers, in his own specific way, has deeply influenced my thinking on most of the issues I have raised in this chapter. I discuss these other thinkers mainly because they are seldom mentioned in the literature of public administration and public policy and because they represent views rarely debated for their potential contribution to public affairs.

3. The French Regulation School, while controversial in its implications, is described more fully in chapter 2.

4. For more information on this concept, refer to the interesting works of Aglietta (1979), Dunford (1990), Lipietz (1986), and Jessop (1990).

5. For a view that is quite different on liberalism, consult the excellent works of Stephen Macedo (1990), *Liberal Virtues,* and Peter Berkowitz (1999), *Virtue and the Making of Modern Liberalism.*

Chapter 5

1. The argument here is not that the issues of power and the state are the only salient issues that Guerreiro Ramos did not emphasize enough in his analysis. I acknowledge that Guerreiro Ramos did not put enough emphasis on intersubjectivity and dialogue as well. For purposes of space, however, I have focused only on the two factors I believed are essential in exploring some of his underdeveloped ideas. See Ventriss and Candler (2005) for another view on this subject.

2. Guerreiro Ramos admits openly the difficulty in defining substantive rationality. He tries to clarify its meaning, albeit in less than definitive terms, in his distinction between a formal and substantive theory of human associated life in chapter 2 of *The New Science of Organizations* (1981, p. 27).

3. Guerreiro Ramos would find most postmodern thought to be largely an example of what he called a "misplacement of concepts"—the notion that theoretical concepts developed in one discipline can be "misplaced" when employed uncritically in another discipline. But this is not to say that he would be entirely dismissive of all postmodern insights, particularly some of the insights of Michel Foucault. It is not claimed that Foucault provides a "better" framework for understanding the self, knowledge, and human relations, but rather that Foucault offers a perceptive understanding of some of the forces that are shaping the human condition, and thus can enrich the analysis of what Guerreiro Ramos was so eloquently trying to

expose. It is within this framework that I find Foucault interesting and intriguing. That is, as an opportunity to further expand Guerreiro Ramos's critique of public management/administration and public policy.

Chapter 6

1. The literature on the economic meltdown of 2008 seems to grow every day. Generally speaking, this vast literature seems to focus on the following broad criticisms: underpriced risk, greed, economic hubris, and debt. Specifically, the most mentioned factors include the abandonment of the Glass-Steagall Act; credit default swaps; the rise of shadow banking; predatory lending; unregulated trading in derivatives; reliance on the efficient market hypotheses; failure of private credit rating agencies; lax enforcement; mortgage-backed securities on real estate and how they impacted firms holding such securities. For those who want to examine this more closely, I have found these sources especially informative: Tooze, 2018; Akerlof and Shiller, 2009; Blinder, 2012; Barofsky, 2012; Financial Crisis Inquiry Commission, 2011; Krugman, 2009; Ahamed, 2009; Johnson & Kwak, 2010; Khademian, 2011; Kindleberger & Aliber, 2005; Harvey, 2010; Phillips, 2009; Posner, 2010;Reinhart & Rogoff, 2009; Soros, 2008; Stiglitz, 2010, 2012a, 2015, 2017; Nanto, 2009; Valencia & Laeven, 2008; O'Quinn, 2008; Wolf, 2008; Minsky, 1980; Rajan, 2006, 2010; Roubini & Mihn, 2011; Shiller, 2008; Sorkin, 2009; Quiggin, 2012. Of course, there is so much more, but these sources are a good place to begin.

2. Consult Richard Green's (2012a) perspective on public administration's role in the economic crisis and the very interesting reply by Lawrence Lynn (2012).

3. It should be noted that studies of income equality, as exemplified in Saez's analysis, have been questioned given that such studies largely focus on pretax incomes and tend to omit the myriad and availability of safety net programs in the United States (Hassett & Mathur, 2012, p. A17; Boudreaux & Perry, 2013). Hasset and Mathur (2012), writing in the *Wall Street Journal*, succinctly put it this way: "Over time, Americans have constructed a vast safety net that has adequately served the poor—as well as the middle class—to maintain significant consumption growth despite the apparent stagnation of cash incomes. The notion that a society is rigged or fundamentally unjust is ludicrous." Interestingly, there is no mention of underemployment or the issue of limited social mobility in this discussion. The real irony of this analysis is that those who read the data in this manner are often the ones calling for restricting the growth of government and many of its social programs.

4. Positional goods have also influenced the writings of Robert Frank (1985, p. 7), who has defined these goods as "goods that are sought after less because of any absolute property they possess than because they compare favorably with others in their own class." Frank (2005) argues that positional goods create externalities,

or, as he put it, an arms race for goods that try to boost one's status compared to others. For some specific intellectual influences on Hirsch's economic thinking, consult the works of Duesenbury (1949), Veblen (1954), and Arrow (1972).

5. Although Richard Freeman (1976, p. 129) did not mention positional goods when discussing social mobility and income distribution many years ago, his description is as timely as when he first penned these words:

> Competition for income and status may come to center more on place of employment and the job market than on the school system. The reduced role in social mobility could, depending on the type and efficacy of alternative routes of upward movement, *lead to greater class consciousness and conflict.* With the potentiality of exiting from one social stratum to another by formal education reduced, individuals may accord greater "loyalty" to their social group. The importance of college as a social melting pot, yielding contacts and friendships across groups, will be diminished. More importantly, if, as some believe, education has served as a "safety valve," helping to maintain social stability in the same manner as was alleged of the frontier years ago, *the narrowing of the valve may diminish an important force for stability.* The discontent of individuals and families experiencing downward generational mobility and of those from the lower strata who looked upon schooling as their "ticket to the middle class" could have destabilizing political consequences. (my emphasis)

In the aftermath of the financial meltdown, one need only observe the growing social conflict that occurred in such countries as France, Spain, Italy, and Greece (among others).

6. These normative considerations have also been elucidated by Fukuyama (1996) and Putnam (2001).Another aspect of this issue is the importance of "trust" and the evidence showing that it is a crucial factor to economic growth itself (Arrow, 1972).Jon Hilsenrath (2013, p. A2) put it this way summarizing Justin Wolfers research concerning how damaging a decline in trust can be to the health of the economy: "A longer-term decline of public trust in government might have been particularly damaging during the financial crisis because it prevented the government from pursuing more aggressive fiscal-stimulus programs to revive the economy, says Justin Wolfers, a University of Michigan economist. 'The government's ability to fight the recession was substantially constrained by the fact that its credibility was in tatters.' " Some conservative thinkers have also raised some objections on the erosion of normative constraints to limit market values on society. For example, see the works of Russell Kirk (1964), Paul Viereck (1956), Richard Weaver (1948), Jacques Ellul (1967), and John Gray (1993).

7. As I mentioned in another chapter, Ramos (1981, p. 80) characterizes cognitive politics as "a set of epistemological rules inherent in the prevailing political framework of advanced industrial countries, rules which are uncritically intended by the common citizen through the socialization process and/or through his/her exposure to systemically contrived influences."

8. On February 4, 2013, the Justice Department sued Standard & Poor's Rating Services for ignoring its own professional standards and consequently costing investors billions of dollars. The government asked for penalties of more than $1 billion dollars. The Financial Crisis Inquiry Commission concluded in its report that credit rating firms were major enablers of the economic crisis of 2007–08. As of yet, no single individual has been indicted for what happened in 2008.

9. For a lively discussion of Samuelson's contributions in this area see Justin Fox's (2011) interesting book. It is also worth reading a recent biography on Samuelson's life and the intellectual influences on his thinking (Szenberg, Gottesman, Ramrattan, 2005).

10. To get a thumbnail idea of what Krugman is referring to, see the works of Fama (1965, 1970) and Samuelson (1973). Consult Quiggin (2012); Patterson (2010) and, more recently, Weatherall (2013) for views that generally agree with Krugman's analysis.

11. Mouzelis's argument is that certain levels of analysis are more amenable to particular methodologies than others. The warning Mouzelis offers here is somewhat related to Giovanni Sartori's (1970) idea of conceptual stretching; that is, a methodological approach that is not inherently designed to conceptually handle issues at a particular level of analysis. The implications of Mouzelis's insight is his attempt to draw attention to the erroneous empirical belief that certain analytical approaches can be equally applied to any level of analysis irrespective of context (Ventriss, 2010). Raadschelders and Lee (2011) have made a similar argument along this line of thinking.

12. Notwithstanding the paucity of historical inquiry in public administration, there has been some insightful historical writing in field. Spicer (2004), for example, suggests that today's scholars have failed to consider the founding concepts by which scholars of public management/administration sought to frame their ambitions; or, where such attempts were made, a defensive posture against the bureaucratic bashing of the late 1970s and 1980s romanticized this understanding of history. In forgetting the field's history of ideas, Spicer claims, scholars in public affairs run the risk of losing touch with the meaning of public administration's founding moral and political beliefs. Raadschelders and Lee (2011), perhaps more than anyone else in the field, have tried to identify a number of distinguishing concepts, defining each according to its historical function, chronological context, and major themes and authors. Some public administration scholars have also sought to improve their understanding of the relationship between public administration (and public

policy) and the state from a historical perspective: Chandler, 1987; Fesler, 1982; Keller, 1979; McCraw, 2007; Mosher, 1983; Stillman, 1990; Gulick, 1990; Keller, 1989; Martin, 1987; Raadschelders, 2000; Van Riper, 1958; White, 1948. From a different theoretical angle, consult Skocpol and Ikenberg (1983) for their important analysis of the growth of the welfare state. Box and King (2000), on the other hand, have contended that what is crucial to the field is the degree to which scholars are critical of the historical method. Here, Box and King are, unknowingly perhaps, drawing upon ideas presented by the Annales School, suggesting the need for a more comprehensive approach to historical inquiry (Ventriss and Barney, 2006).

13. In many respects, I found Lynn's (2012) arguments rather interesting and as representative of what most scholars in public management/administration and public policy would have argued concerning any role we may have played in the economic crisis of 2008.

Chapter 7

1. Some may wonder why the concept of time is omitted here. I recognize the importance of the relationship between these two concepts—a relationship well documented in the literature of geography. I am not trying to wield, so to speak, a theoretical guillotine between these two concepts; rather, I have made an empirical judgment to emphasize the saliency of sociospatial factors. Moreover, to include temporal issues—which I have done to a certain extent in this chapter—would have taken more space to develop. Having said this, as my discussion unfolds in this chapter one can clearly see how the changing meaning of space is related to the changing nature of time.

2. The empirical literature is vast in documenting this trend. I have only cited those works that I think are the most interesting empirical studies in relation to public policy and public management/administration. On another note, a few words are in order about the meaning of "production of space." While this term is closely associated with Henri Lefebvre (1976, 1990; Smith, 1990), a process in which the market economy reproduces itself, I am also referring to how the global economy is restructuring the spatial order of cities and regions in terms of shifting patterns of investment and production and the concomitant political responses in reaction to these economic changes.

3. Those who wish to more fully examine what is called locality studies should consult some of these publications: Massey (2009, 1991); Cooke (1989); Cox & Mair (1988); Warde (1989); and Duncan & Savage (1989). The journal *Antipode* has been the theoretical outlet where some of the best debate on this subject has taken place.

4. Economic restructuring, according to Robert Beauregard (1989), can be understood along three dimensions: functional, temporal, and structural. How-

ever, he goes on to argue, in a convincing manner,that only two terms exist. One refers, he writes, to "transformations in mix of goods and services being produced within the economy . . . and the other to a broader set of changes in the nature of the economy, not only in its products and the distribution of employment, but also in the social relations of production. . . . [Finally,] structural changes involve long-term shifts in composition of demand, production and occupational patterns; new technology; an changing international division of labor; shifts in relative prices; and evolving location patterns (both migration and industrial spatial restructuring)" (1989, p. 211). In my search for a precise definition of this term, Beauregard's summary of the literature related to economic restructuring, while made several decades ago, has provided still one of the best interpretations of its varied meanings.

5. This view, in part, is drawn from the classic work of Robert Keohane and Joseph Nye's (1972) analysis that the rise of interdependence between national economies has essentially transformed international relations among states. In a later book, Keohane and Nye (1977) update their argument to assert that states exist in a world of "complex regimes," that is, states coexisting with nonstate actors. In short, transnational actors, to some extent, have limited the ability of states to exercise their full sovereignty. Historically, it is claimed that this new interdependency among nation-states has been the result of the following developments: (1) the oil crisis of 1973 that highlighted the dependence of other economies on oil; (2) the decline of U.S. prominence in the international economy; (3) the growing influence and the role of multinational corporations and financial institutions; (4) the global ecological problems that can only be successfully solved by international action; and, finally, (5) the effects of economic interdependency in the global economy. This view has hardly gone uncontested. Some have argued that the effects of interdependency have ironically led to more rather than less reliance on the nation-state, since it is the state that must ultimately manage the effects of interdependency. For example, nation-states still define their own macroeconomic policies, which can influence their competitive advantages compared to others. I acknowledge that it is naive to claim the decline of the nation-state. My point is that there is growing "internationalization of the state," which has transformed the conditions of political and economic decision making and has altered the context of national politics. To paraphrase Roy Mellor (1989), the nation-state is in a new, widening horizon of the organization of space—a space being perpetually bombarded by new global forces.

6. John Thompson, a one-time colleague of Giddens at Cambridge University, has described Giddens's theory as an attempt to grasp the dynamic relationship between social action and social structure. According to Thompson, what is important to keep in mind about Giddens's approach "is not how structure determines action, but rather how action is structured in everyday contexts and how the structured features of action are, by the very performance of action, thereby reproduced. The theory of structuration is thus inseparable from an account of social reproduction, that is, from an account of the ways in which societies, or specific organization, are

reproduced by the activities of individuals pursuing their everyday lives" (1989, p. 56). While the complexities associated with this theory cannot be outlined here, some scholars, such as Peter Saunders (1989), have wondered how his concept of space fits with the theory of structuration. Leaving this issue to the side for the moment, Giddens introduces other concepts in his analysis of space such as contextualitv (the situated character of interactions in time-space), locale (a physical region as part of the setting of interactions); and regionalization (the differentiation of time-space within or between locales in regions). It is important to note that Giddens draws on certain geographers in the development of his ideas dealing with spatiality, particularly that of Hagerstrand's (1974, 1975, 1985) well-cited time-geography and other geographers who have tried to apply Giddens's ideas to geographical space (Gregory, 1978; Pred, 1981).

7. As I have discussed in another chapter, this argument appears closely aligned to the approach of the French Regulation school (Lipietz, 1986). This school of thought has also been attributed to how it integrates the so-called mode of regulation (state action, political practices, and behavior norms) to what is termed a regime of accumulation. There is, it should be pointed out, much debate about just how widespread this new development actually is and whether this post-Fordist model is predicated upon some rather sweeping historical and empirical generalizations (Gambino, 1996; Gertler, 1988). A final note: my discussion concerning the reasons behind this spatial dispersion of capital is hardly exhaustive. For the purpose of brevity, I could only outline the major trends associated with this line of argument. Some of the best classical works, in my opinion, still can be found in Scott & Storper (1986), Storper & Walker (1989), and Bluestone & Harrison (1982).

8. I have tried to choose my words carefully here. I am referring to how the concept of space is socially constructed, a point made by Durkheim (1915) in his book *The Elementary Forms of the Religious Life*. As such, the concept of space ultimately involves how social relations are constructed and mediated. This understanding of space, and the purpose and meaning that different publics attach to their social spaces, is something that public management/administration and public policy have sadly neglected. This focus on space is an attempt on my part to draw attention to how publicness is impacted by new spatial arrangements that are hardly politically neutral. An attachment to a certain concept of space, as David Harvey (1990, 2010) tells us, inevitably implies a political decision. However, such decisions are becoming increasingly captive, among other social and political forces, of the "normal outcome of the expansion of the market system" (Ramos, 1981, p. 141). In essence, I reiterate that Ramos might indeed be accurate when he claims that the recovery of space for community life demands a qualified delimitation of the market system.

References

Foreword

Adorno, T. (1976). Education after Auschwitz, trans. Pickford, H. W. In *Critical models: interventions and catchwords*. Columbia University Press.

Bartels, L. M. (2016). *Unequal democracy: The political economy of the new guilded age*. Princeton University Press.

Goodwin, G., & Eatwell, R. (2018). *National populism: The revolt against liberal democracy*. Pelican.

Harvey, D. (2020). The anti-capitalist politics in a time of COVID-19. *Jacobin*, March 20, 1–9.

Mounk, Y. (2018). *The people vs. democracy: Why our freedom is in danger and how to save it*. Harvard University Press.

Polanyi, K. (1944). *The great transformation*. Farrar-Rinehart.

Thompson, D. (2020). The coronavirus will be a catastrophe for the poor. *Atlantic*, March 21.

Wall Street Journal (2020). Review Section, March 28–29. C1.

Chapter 1

Andreski, S. (1972). *Social science as sorcery*. St. Martin's Press.

Arendt, H. (1973). *The origins of totalitarianism*. Houghton Mifflin Harcourt.

Bachrach, P. (1967). *The theory of democratic elitism: A critique*. Little Brown.

Barber, B. R. (1984). *Strong democracy: Participatory politics for a new age*. University of California Press.

Bartels, L. M. (2016). *Unequal democracy: The new political economy of the gilded age*. Princeton University Press.

Barnes, M., Newman, J., Knops, A., & Sullivan, H. (2003). Constituting "the public" in public participation. *Public Administration*, *81*(2), 379–399. https://doi.org/10.1111/1467-9299.00352.

Bozeman, B., & Bretschneider, S. (1994). The "publicness puzzle" in organization theory: A test of alternative explanations of differences between public and private organizations. *Journal of Public Administration Research and Theory, 4*(2), 197–224. https://doi.org/10.1093/oxfordjournals.jpart.a037204.

Brown, W. (2015). *Undoing the demos: Neoliberalism's stealth revolution.* MIT Press.

Candler, G. G. (2014). The study of public administration in India, the Philippines, Canada and Australia: The universal struggle against epistemic colonization, and toward critical assimilation. *Revista de Administração Pública, 48*(5), 1073–1093. https://doi.org/10.1590/0034-76121716.

Crouch, C. (2004). *Post-democracy.* John Wiley & Sons.

Crouch, C. (2011). *The strange non-death of neo-liberalism.* John Wiley & Sons.

Crouch C. (2008). What will follow the demise of privatised Keynesianism? *The Political Quarterly, 79*(4), 476–487. https://doi.org/10.1111/j.1467-923X.2008.00970.x.

Dean, J. (2009). *Democracy and other neoliberal fantasies: Communicative capitalism and left politics.* Duke University Press.

Dryzek, J. S. (2000). *Deliberative democracy and beyond: Liberals, critics, contestations.* Oxford University Press.

Flake, J. (2017). *Conscience of a conservative: A rejection of destructive politics and a return to principle.* Random House.

Flathman, R. E. (1989). Citizenship and authority: A chastened view of citizenship. In *Toward a liberalism* (pp. 65–108). Cornell University Press. Retrieved from http://www.jstor.org/stable/10.7591/j.ctt207g5mh.7.

Frederickson, H. G. (1997). *The spirit of public administration.* John Wiley & Sons.

Goodsell, C. T. (2014). *The new case for bureaucracy.* Sage.

Gouldner, A. W. (1970). *The coming crisis of Western sociology.* Basic Books.

Gow, J. (1993). Les problématiques changeantes en administration publique (1965–1992). *Politique* (23), 59–105. https://doi.org/10.7202/040748ar.

Haque, M. S. (2001). The diminishing publicness of public service under the current mode of governance. *Public Administration Review, 61*(1), 65–82.

Harvey, D. (1996). *Justice, nature, and the geography of difference.* Blackwell.

Howe, I. (1984). *A margin of hope: An intellectual autobiography.* Harcourt, Brace, Jovanovich.

Ku, A. S. (2000). Revisiting the notion of "public" in Habermas's theory—Toward a theory of politics of public credibility. *Sociological Theory, 18*(2), 216–240. https://doi.org/10.1111/0735-2751.00096.

Lynd, R. S. (1939). *Knowledge for what? The place of social science in American culture.* Princeton University Press.

Layzer, J. A. (2015). *The environmental case: Translating values into policy.* CQ Press.

Low, S., & Smith, N. (2005). *The politics of public space.* Routledge.

Lustig, R. J. (1982). *Corporate liberalism: The origins of modern American political theory, 1890–1920.* University of California Press.

Macpherson, C. B. (2011). *The political theory of possessive individualism: Hobbes to Locke.* Oxford University Press.

Macpherson, C. B. (1973). *Democratic theory: Essays in retrieval.* Clarendon.

Mayer, J. (2016). *Dark money: The hidden history of the billionaires behind the rise of the radical Right.* Doubleday.

McGregor, E. B. (1984). The great paradox of democratic citizenship and public personnel administration. *Public Administration Review, 44,* 126–135. https://doi.org/10.2307/975552.

Moffitt, B. (2016). *The global rise of populism: Performance, political style, and representation.* Stanford University Press.

Montaigne, M. de. (1976). *The complete essays of Montaigne.* Stanford University Press.

Mouffe, C. (2005). *The return of the political.* Verso.

Moulton, Stephanie. (2009). Putting together the publicness puzzle: A framework for realized publicness. *Public Administration Review, 69*(5), 889–900. https://doi.org/10.1111/j.1540-6210.2009.02038.x.

Nabatchi, T. (2010). The (re)discovery of the public in public administration. *Public Administration Review, 70,* S309–S311.

Nabatchi, T., & Leighninger, M. (2015). *Public participation for 21st century democracy.* Jossey-Bass.

Nabatchi, T., Goerdel, H., & Peffer, S. (2011). Public administration in dark times: Some questions for the future of the field. *Journal of Public Administration Research and Theory, 21*(suppl. 1), i29–i43. https://doi.org/10.1093/jopart/muq068.

Nye, J. S., Zelikow, P., & King, D. C. (1997). *Why people don't trust government.* Harvard University Press.

Passos, J. D. (1936b). *The big money.* Harcourt Brace.

Pesch, U. (2005). *The predicaments of publicness: An inquiry into the conceptual ambiguity of public administration.* Eburon Uitgeverij BV.

Pesch, U. (2008). The publicness of public administration. *Administration & Society, 40*(2), 170–193.

Purcell, M. (2008). *Recapturing democracy: Neoliberalization and the struggle for alternative urban futures.* Routledge.

Pynchon, T. (1973). *Gravity's rainbow.* Viking.

Ramos, A. G. (1955). *Patologia social do "branco" brasileiro.* Jornal do Commercio.

Ramos, A. G. (1958). *A Reducao Sociologia.* Rio de Janeiro: MEC/ISEB.

Ramos, A. G. (1981). *The new science of organizations: A reconceptualization of the wealth of nations.* University of Toronto Press.

Rancière, J. (1999). *Disagreement: Politics and philosophy.* University of Minnesota Press.

Simon, J. K. (1971). A conversation with Michel Foucault. *Partisan Review, 38*(2), 196–201.

Somers, M. R. (2008). *Genealogies of citizenship: Markets, statelessness, and the right to have rights.* Cambridge University Press.

Stephens, B. (2017, January 20). Opinion: The dying art of disagreement. *The New York Times*. Retrieved from https://www.nytimes.com/2017/09/24/opinion/dying-art-of-disagreement.html.

Stivers, T. (2010). Democratic knowledge: The task before us. *Administration and Society, 42*(2), 248–259. https: 10.1177/0095399710365484.

Stone, D. (2012). *Policy paradox: The art of political decision making*. W. W. Norton.

Sullivan, W. M. (1986). *Reconstructing public philosophy*. University of California Press.

Swyngedouw, E. (2011). *Designing the post-political city and the insurgent polis*. Bedford.

Thompson, D. (2010, April 19). 80 percent of Americans don't trust the government. Here's why. *The Atlantic*. Retrieved from https://www.theatlantic.com/business/archive/2010/04/80-percent-of-americans-dont-trust-the-government-heres-why/39148/.

Ventriss, C. (1985). Emerging perspectives on citizen participation. *Public Administration Review, 45*(3), 433–440. https://doi.org/10.2307/3109973.

Ventriss, C. (1987). Two critical issues of American public administration: Reflections of a sympathetic participant. *Administration & Society, 19*(1), 25–47. https://doi.org/10.1177/009539978701900102.

Ventriss, C. (2007). A substantive view of ethical citizenship in public affairs. *Public Performance & Management Review, 31*(1), 38–53. https://doi.org/10.2753/PMR1530-9576310102.

Villa, D. R. (2001). *Socratic citizenship*. Princeton University Press.

Will, G. F. (1983). *Statecraft as soulcraft: What government does*. Touchstone.

Williams, L., & Shearer, H. (2011). Appraising public value: past, present and futures. *Public Administration, 89*(4), 1367–1384.

Chapter 2

Adams, G. B., & Balfour, D. L. (2014). *Unmasking administrative evil.* 4th edition, New York: Routledge.

Adams, G. B., & Balfour, D. L. (2012). Toward restoring integrity in "praetorian times." *Public Integrity, 14*(4), 325–339. https://doi.org/10.2753/PIN1099-9922140401.

Amenta, E., Nash, K., & Scott, A. (2016). *The Wiley-Blackwell companion to political sociology*. John Wiley & Sons.

Arendt, H. (1958). *The human condition*. University of Chicago Press.

Barber, B. R. (1984). *Strong democracy: Participatory politics for a new age*. University of California Press.

Barzelay, M. (2001). *The new public management: Improving research and policy dialogue*. University of California Press.

Beauregard, R. (1978). Planning in an advanced capitalist state. In Burchell, R., and Steinlieb, G., *Planning theory in the 1980's*. Transaction.

Benn, S. I., & Gaus, G. F. (1983). *Public and private in social life*. Croom Helm.

Bevir, M. (2011). *The Sage handbook of governance*. Sage.

Block, F., & Somers, M. R. (2014). *The power of market fundamentalism*. Harvard University Press.

Box R. C. (2008). *Making a difference: Progressive values in public administration*. M. E. Sharpe.

Box, R. C. (2014). *Public administration and society: Critical issues in American governance*. Routledge.

Boyer, R. (1990). *The Regulation School: A critical introduction*. Columbia University Press.

Brown, M., & Erie, S. (1979). *Power and administration: Alternative paradigms for the analysis of bureaucratic autonomy*. Unpublished manuscript.

Caiden, G. (1983). The need for a theory of public administration. Unpublished paper.

Calhoun, C. (2011). Civil society and the public sphere. In M. Edwards (Ed.), *The Oxford handbook of civil society*. Oxford University Press.

Calhoun, C., Gerteis, J., Moody, J., Pfaff, S., & Virk, I. (2002). *Contemporary sociological theory*. John Wiley & Sons.

Candler, G. G. (2014). The study of public administration in India, the Philippines, Canada and Australia: the universal struggle against epistemic colonization, and toward critical assimilation. *Revista de Administração Pública, 48*(5), 1073–1093. https://doi.org/10.1590/0034-76121716.

Carnoy, M. (1984). *The state and political theory*. Princeton University Press.

Castoriadis, C. (1997). *The imaginary institution of society*. MIT Press.

Clarke, J. (2005). Performing for the public: Doubt, desire, and governance of public services. In P. DuGay (Ed.), *The Values of Bureaucracy*. Oxford University Press.

Clarke, J., & Newman, J. (1997). *The managerial state: Power, politics, and ideology in the remaking of social welfare*. Sage.

Cox, K. R., & Mair, A. (1991). From localised social structures to localities as agents. *Environment and Planning A: Economy and Space, 23*(2), 197–213. https://doi.org/10.1068/a230197.

Dahl, A., & Soss, J. (2014). Neoliberalism for the common good? Public value governance and the downsizing of democracy. *Public Administration Review, 74*(4), 496–504. https://doi.org/10.1111/puar.12191.

Danziger, S., & Gottschalk, P. (1995). *America unequal*. Harvard University Press.

Denhardt, J., & Denhardt, R. (2015). *The new public service*. New York: Routledge.

Denhardt, R. B. (1981). Toward a critical theory of public organization. *Public Administration Review, 41*(6), 628–635. https://doi.org/10.2307/975738.

D'Entreves, A. P. (1967). *The notion of the state*. Oxford University Press.

Dewey, J. (1929). *The public and its problems*. Swallow Press.

Dryzek, J. (2008). The ecological crisis of the welfare state. *Journal of European Social Policy*. https://doi.org/10.1177/0958928708094890.

Dryzek, J. S. (2000). *Deliberative democracy and beyond: Liberals, critics, contestations*. Oxford University Press.

Dryzek, J. S. (2012). *Foundations and frontiers of deliberative governance*. Oxford University Press.

Dubnick, M. (2000). *Demons, spirits, and elephants*. Prepared for the American Society for Public Administration.

Dunn, W. N., & Miller, D. Y. (2007). A critique of the new public management and the neo-Weberian state: Advancing a critical theory of administrative reform. *Public Organization Review*, *7*(4), 345–358. https://doi.org/10.1007/s11115-007-0042-3.

Durkheim, E. (1964). *The division of labor in society*. Simon & Schuster.

Dyckman, J. (1978). Three crises of American planning. In R. Burchell and G. Steinlieb (Eds.), *Planning theories in the 1980s*. Rutgers University Press.

Easton, D. (1953). *The political system*. Knopf.

Erie, S. P. (1978). *Historical crisis of public administration*. Unpublished manuscript.

Evans, P. B. (1995). *Embeddedautonomy: States and industrial transformation*. Princeton University Press.

Fischer, F. (2003). *Reframing public policy: Discursive politics and deliberative practices*. Oxford University Press.

Forester, J. (1993). *Critical theory, public policy, and planning practice*. State University of New York Press.

Fox, C. J. (1996). Reinventing government as postmodern symbolic politics. *Public Administration Review*, *56*(3), 256–262. https://doi.org/10.2307/976449.

Fraser N. (1992). Rethinking the public sphere. *Social Text*, 25/26, 56–80.

Fraser, N. (2014). *Transnationalizing the public sphere*. John Wiley & Sons.

Frederickson, H. G., & Hart, D. K. (1985). The public service and the patriotism of benevolence. *Public Administration Review*, *45*(5), 547–553. https://doi.org/10.2307/3109929.

Fried, M. H. (1967). *The evolution of political society*. Random House.

Fung, A., & Wright, E. O. (2003). *Deepening democracy: Institutional innovations in empowered participatory governance*. Verso.

Gawthrop, L. C. (1998). *Public service and democracy: Ethical imperatives for the 21st century*. Chatham House.

Ghelardi, R. (1976). *Economics, culture, and society*. Dell.

Gooden, S. (2014). *Race and social equity*. Routledge.

Goodsell, C. T. (2014). *The new case for bureaucracy*. CQ Press.

Goodwin, R. (1975). *The American condition*. Doubleday.

Gulick, L. (1983). The dynamics of public administration today as guidelines for the future. *Public Administration Review*, *43*(3), 193–198. https://doi.org/10.2307/976327.

Habermas, J. (1962). *The structural transformation of the public sphere.* MIT Press.

Harmon, M. M. (1995). *Responsibility as paradox: a critique of rational discourse on government.* Sage.

Hart, D. K., & Scott, W. G. (1982). The philosophy of American management. *Southern Review of Public Administration, 6*(2), 240.

Harvey, D. (1982). *Justice, nature, and the geography of difference.* Blackwell.

Harvey, D. (2007). *A brief history of neoliberalism.* Oxford University Press.

Held, D. (1989). *Political theory and the modern state.* John Wiley & Sons.

Hummel, R. (2007). *The bureaucratic experience.* Routledge.

Isaac, J. C. (1992). *Arendt, Camus, and modern rebellion.* Yale University Press.

Jessop, B. (2014). *The state past, present, and future.* Polity.

Jessop, B (1994). Post-Fordism and the state. In Amin, A. (Ed.), *Post-Fordism reader.* Blackwell.

Jessop, B. (1983). The capitalist state and the rule of capital: Problems in the analysis of business associations. *West European Politics, 6*(2), 139–162. https://doi.org/10.1080/01402388308424417.

Jessop, B. (1985). *Nicos Poulantzas: Marxist theory and political strategy.* Macmillan. Retrieved from http://eprints.lancs.ac.uk/63366/.

Jessop, B. (1990). *State theory: Putting the capitalist state in its place.* Penn State University Press.

Jessop, B. (1993). Towards a Schumpeterian workfare state? Preliminary remarks on post-Fordist political economy. *Studies in Political Economy, 40*(1), 7–39. https://doi.org/10.1080/19187033.1993.11675409.

Jessop, B. (2007). *State power.* Polity.

Jessop, B. (2002). Liberalism, neoliberalism, and urban governance: A state-theoretical perspective. *Antipode, 34*(3), 452–472. https://doi.org/10.1111/1467-8330.00250.

Kaplan, A. (1964). *The conduct of inquiry.* Routledge.

Kariel, H. S. (1977). *Beyond liberalism, where relations grow.* Chandler & Sharp.

King, C. S., & Stivers, C. (1998). *Government is us: Strategies for an anti-government era.* Sage.

Latour, B. (2005). *Reassembling the social.* Oxford University Press.

Layzer, J. A. (2015). *The environmental case: Translating values into policy.* CQ Press.

Lipietz, A. (1985). *The enchanted world: Inflation, credit, and the world crisis.* Routledge, Chapman & Hall.

Lowi, T. (1979). *The end of liberalism: The second republic of the United States.* W. W. Norton.

Lynch, K. (2014). New managerialism, neoliberalism, and ranking. *Ethics in Science and Environmental Politics, 13*(2), 141–153. https://doi.org/10.3354/esep00137.

Lynn, L (2006). *Public management: Old and new.* Routledge.

Macpherson, C. B. (1962). *The political theory of possessive individualism: Hobbes to Locke.* Oxford University Press.

Macpherson, C. B. (1973). *Democratic theory: Essays in retrieval.* Clarendon Press.

Mannheim. K. (1956). *Essays on the sociology of culture.* Routledge & Kegan Paul.

Mannheim, K. (1948). *Man and society in an age of reconstruction.* Routledge & Kegan Paul.

McCurdy, H. E. (1978). Selecting and training public managers: Business skills versus public administration. *Public Administration Review, 38*(6), 571–578. https://doi.org/10.2307/976040.

Meier, K. J., & O'Toole, L. J. (2006). *Modeling public management.* Prepared for the Empirical Study of Organizations and public Management, Texas A&M University.

Miliband, R. (1969). *The state in capitalist society.* Basic Books.

Mouffe, C. (2005). *The return of the political.* Verso.

Muller, H. J., & Ventriss, C. (1985). *Public health in a retrenchment era: An alternative to managerialism.* State University of New York Press.

Nabatchi, T., & Leighninger, M. (2015). *Public participation for 21st century democracy.* John Wiley & Sons.

Nabatchi, T., & Amsler, L. B. (2014). Direct public engagement in local government. *The American Review of Public Administration, 44*(4). 63s-83s.

Network of Schools of Public Policy, Affairs, & Administration. (2009). *Public service values, mission-based accreditation.* Washington, DC.

Neiman, M. (2000). *Defending government: Why big government works.* Prentice-Hall.

Nettl, J. P. (1969). Power and the intellectuals. In C. C. O'Brien & W. D. Vanech (Eds.), *Power and consciousness.* New York University Press.

Nisbet, R. (1953). *The quest for community.* Oxford University Press.

Oldfield, K., & Conant, R. F. (2001). Professors, social class, and affirmative action: A pilot study. *Journal of Public Affairs Education, 7*(3), 171–185.

Osborne D., & Gaebler, T. (1992). *Reinventing government.* Scott Foresman.

Osborne, D., & Plastrik, P. (1997). *Banishing bureacracy.* Addison-Wesley.

Panitch, L. (1980). Recent theorizations of corporatism: Reflections on a growth industry. *The British Journal of Sociology, 31*(2), 159–187. https://doi.org/10.2307/589686.

Pateman, C. (2012). Participatory democracy revisited. *Perspectives on Politics, 10*(1), 7–19. https://doi.org/10.1017/S1537592711004877.

Peck, J., & Tickell, A. (2002). Neoliberalizing space. *Antipode, 34*(3), 380–404. https://doi.org/10.1111/1467-8330.00247.

Perrow, C. (1986). *Complex organizations: A critical essay,* 2nd edition. Scott & Foresman.

Piereson, J., & Riley, N. S. (2013). The problem with policy schools. Opinion Section, *Washington Post,* December, 6th.

Poggi, G. (2012). *The state: Its nature, development, and prospects.* Stanford University Press.

Polanyi, K. (1944). *The Great Transformation.* Beacon Press.

Pollitt, C. (1993). *Managerialism and the public services: Cuts or cultural change in the 1990s?* Blackwell Business.

Poulantzas, N. (1973). On social classes. *New Left Review, 78*, 27–54.

Poulantzas, N. (1975). *Classes in contemporary capitalism.* New Left Books.

Poulantzas, N. (1978). *State, power, and socialism.* London: Verso.

Ramos, A. G. (1981). *The new science of organizations: A reconceptualization of the Wealth of Nations.* University of Toronto Press.

Rancière, J. (1995). *On the shores of politics.* Verso.

Ranciere, J. (2010). *Dissensus: On politics and aesthetics.* New York: Continuum.

Rosenbloom, D. (2005). Taking social equity seriously in MPA education. *Journal of Public Affairs Education, 11*(3), 247–252.

Rosenbloom, D. H. (1986). *Public administration: understanding management, politics, and law in the public sector.* Random House.

Schaar, J. H. (1970). Legitimacy in the modern state. In P. Green and S. Levinson (Eds.). *Power and community.* Vintage.

Scott, W., & Hart, D. (1979). *Organizational America.* Houghton Mifflin.

Sheller, M., & Urry, J. (2003). Mobile Transformations of "public" and "private" Life. *Theory, Culture & Society, 20*(3), 107–125. https://doi.org/10.1177/0263276 4030203007.

Skocpol, T. (1979). *States and social revolutions: A comparative analysis of France, Russia, and China.* Cambridge University Press.

Somers, M. R. (2008). *Genealogies of citizenship.* Cambridge University Press.

Swyngedouw, E. (1996). Reconstructing citizenship, the re-scaling of the state and the new authoritarianism: Closing the Belgian mines. *Urban Studies, 33*(8), 1499–1521. https://doi.org/10.1080/0042098966772.

Swyngedouw, E. (2010). Impossible sustainability and the post-political condition. In *Making strategies in spatial planning.* Springer. https://doi.org/10.1007/978-90-481-3106-8_11.

Terry, L. D. (1998). Administrative leadership, neo-managerialism, and the public Management movement. *Public Administration Review, 58*(3), 194–200. https://doi.org/10.2307/976559.

Terry, L. D. (2003). *Leadership of public bureaucracies.* M. E. Sharpe.

Tussman, J. (1960). *Obligation and the body politic.* Oxford University Press.

Ventriss, C. (1982). The coming crisis of public administration education. *Southern Review of Public Administration, 6*(2), 137–150.

Ventriss, C. (1985). Emerging perspectives on citizen participation. *Public Administration Review, 45*(3), 433–440. https://doi.org/10.2307/3109973.

Ventriss, C. (1991). Contemporary issues in American public administration education: The search for an educational focus. *Public Administration Review, 51*(1), 4–14. https://doi.org/10.2307/976631.

Ventriss, C. (2015). The troubling implications of the great divide. *Public Administration Review,* 75(6), 892–900.

Ventriss, C. (2000). New public management: An examination of its influence on contemporary public affairs and its impact on shaping the intellectual agenda of the field. *Administrative Theory & Praxis, 22*(3), 500–518. https://doi.org/10.1080/10841806.2000.11643468.

Vincent, A. (1991). *Theories of the state.* Wiley-Blackwell.

Wagenaar, H. (2011). *Meaning in action.* M. E. Sharpe.

Wald, E. (1973). Toward a paradigm of future public administration. *Public Administration Review, 33*(4), 366–372. https://doi.org/10.2307/975117.

Waldo, C. D. (1971). *Public administration in a time of turbulence.* Chandler.

Waldo, C. D. (1968). Scope of the theory of public administration, In J. C. Charlesworth (Ed.), *Theory and practice of public administration.* American Academy of Political and Social Science.

Warner, M. (2002). *Publics and counterpublics.* Zone Books.

Weber, M. (1948). *From Max Weber: Essays in sociology.* Routledge & Kegan Paul.

Wills, G. (1969). *Nixon Agonistes: The crisis of the self-made man.* Mentor Books.

Wolfe, A. (1977). *The limits of legitimacy.* Free Press.

Wolin, S. S. (1960). *Politics and vision: Continuity and innovation in Western political thought.* Princeton University Press.

Wolin, S. S. (2008). *Democracy incorporated: Managed democracy and the specter of inverted totalitarianism.* Princeton University Press.

Chapter 3

Barber, B. (1984). *Strong democracy: Participatory democracy for a new age.* University of California Press.

Benhabib, S., Cameron, D., Dolidze, A., Halmai, G., Pishchikova, K., & Youngs, R. (2013). *The Democratic Disconnect.* Transatlantic Academy.

Barnett, C. (2008). Convening publics: The parasitical spaces of public action. *The Sage Handbook of Political Geography,* 403–418.

Berger, P. L. (1976). In praise of particularity: The concept of mediating structures. *The Review of Politics, 38*(3), 399–410.

Berger, P. L., & Neuhaus, R. J. (1977). *To empower people: The role of mediating structures in public policy.* American Enterprise Institute.

Bernstein, R. J. (1976). *The restructuring of social and political theory.* University of Pennsylvania Press.

Biller, R. P. (1979). Toward public administration rather than an administration of publics. In R. Clayton & W. Storm (Eds.). *Agenda for public administration.* University of Southern California Press.

Bozeman, B., & Johnson, A. (2014). The political economy of public values: A case for the public sphere and progressive opportunity. *American Review of Public Administration, 44*(1), 61–85.

Bozeman, B. (1987). *All organizations are public: Bridging public and private organizational theories*. Jossey-Bass.

Bozeman, B. (2007). *Public values and public interest: Counterbalancing economic individualism*. Georgetown University Press.

Bozeman, B., & Bretschneider, S. (1994). The "publicness puzzle" in organization theory: A test of alternative explanations of differences between public and private organizations. *Journal of Public Administration Research and Theory*, *4*(2), 197–224.

Calhoun, C. (1993). Civil society and the public sphere. *Public Culture*, *5*(2), 267–280.

Coglianese, C. (2005). *Expanding regulatory pluralism: The role for Information Technology in rulemaking*. Working paper.

Dahl, A., & Soss, J. (2014). Neoliberalism for the common good? Public value democracy and the downsizing of democracy. *Public Administration Review*, *74*(2), 496–504.

de Sola Pool, I. (1973). *Talking back: Citizen feedback and cable technology*. The MIT Press.

de Tocqueville, A. (1956) [1835]. *Democracy in America*. New American Library, 1956.

Denhardt, R. B., & Denhardt, J. V. (2000). The new public service: Serving rather than steering. *Public Administration Review*, *60*(6), 549–559.

Dewar, T. R. (1978). Professionalization of client. *Social Policy*, *8*(4), 4–9.

Dewey, J. (1927). *The public and its problems*. Henry Holt.

Dewey, J. (1930). *Human nature and conduct*. Southern Illinois University Press.

Fraser, N. (1990). Rethinking the public sphere: A contribution to the critique of actually existing democracy. *Social Text* (25/26), 56–80.

Friedmann, J., and Abonyi, G. (1976). Social learning: A model for policy research. *Environment and Planning, 8*, 927–940.

Friedmann, J. (1973). *Retracking America; A theory of transitive planning*. Anchor Press.

Gaus, G. F. (1983). Public and private interests in liberal political economy, old and new. *Public and Private in Social Life*, 183–221.

Gawthrop, L. C. (1985). Civis, civitas, and civilitas: A new focus for the year 2000. *Public Administration Review*, *44*, 101–107.

Gordon, E., Schirra, S., & Hollander, J. (2011). Immersive planning: A conceptual model for designing public participation with new technologies. *Environment and Planning B: Planning and Design*, *38*(3), 505–519.

Gottfried, P. (1999). *After liberalism. Mass democracy in the managerial state*. Princeton University Press.

Habermas, J. (1962). The structural transformation of the public sphere. MIT Press.

Haque, M. S. (2001). The diminishing publicness of public service under the current mode of governance. *Public Administration Review*, *61*(1), 65–82.

Hummel, R. P. (2007). *The bureaucratic experience: The post-modern challenge*. M. E. Sharpe.

Jacobs, H. R. (2014). The contested politics of public value. *Public Administration Review, 74*(4), 480–494.

Kammen, M. G. (1990). *People of paradox: An inquiry concerning the origins of American civilization.* Cornell University Press.

Kaplan, A. (1964). *The conduct of inquiry: Methodology for behavioral science.* Chandler.

Keane, J. (2000). Structural transformations of the public sphere. *Digital Democracy: Issues of Theory and Practice,* 70–89.

Kipnis, B. A., & Ventriss, C. (1984). *Operationalizing quality of life issues: from general goals toward workable objectives.* Unpublished paper.

Korten, D. C. (1980). Community organization and rural development: A learning process approach. *Public Administration Review,* 480–511.

Korten, D. C. (1981). The management of social transformation. *Public Administration Review, 41*(6), 609–618.

Korten, D. C., & Klauss, R. (Eds.). (1984). People-centered development; contributions toward theory and planning frameworks. Kumarian Press.

Krugman, P. (2012). Economics in crisis. *New York Times,* March 5, Opinion.

Lasch, C. (1995). *Haven in a heartless world: The family besieged.* W. W. Norton.

Lawson, G. (1994). The rise and rise of the administrative state. *Harvard Law Review, 107*(6), 1231–1254.

Leighninger, M. (2006). *The next form of democracy: How expert rule is giving way to shared governance—and why politics will never be the same.* Vanderbilt University Press.

Leighninger, M. (2012). Mapping deliberative civic engagement. In T. Nabatchi, T. Gurtil, M. Weiksner, & M. Leighninger (Eds.), *Democracy in Motion: Evaluating the Practice and Impact of Deliberative Civic Engagement* (pp. 19–39). Oxford University Press.

Levine, C. H. (1984). Retrenchment, human resource erosion, and the role of the personnel manager. *Personnel Administration, 13*(3), 249–263.

Lippmann, W. (1955). *Essays in the public philosophy.* Transaction Publishers.

Love, J. M., & Stout, M. (2015). Relational process ontology: A grounding for global governance. *Administration & Society, 47*(4), 447–481.

Lowi, T. J. (1979). The end of liberalism: The second republic of the United States. W. W. Norton.

Majone, G. (1989). *Evidence, argument, and persuasion in the policy process.* Yale University Press.

Mathews, D. (1985). The public in practice and theory. *Public Administration Review, 44,* 120–125.

Michael, D. N. (1983). Neither hierarchy nor anarchy: Notes on norms for governance in a systemic world. In W. Anderson (Ed.), *Rethinking Liberalism.* Avon Books.

Milakovich, M. E. (2010). The Internet and increased citizen participation in government. *Journal of EDemocracy and Open Government, 2*(1), 1–9.

Mills, C. W. (1963). *Power, politics, and people: The collected essays of C. Wright Mills*. Oxford University Press.

Moore, M. H., & Fung, A. (2012). Calling publics into existence: The political arts of public management. In M. H. Moore & R. Donahue (Eds.), *Ports in a storm: public management in a turbulent world* (pp. 180–210). Brookings Institute Press.

Moore, M. H. (1995). *Creating public value: Strategic management in government*. Harvard University Press.

Moore, M. H. (2013). *Recognizing public value*. Harvard University Press.

Morse, J., & Ventriss, C. (2018). *Reflecting on theory building: A call for empirical, interpretive, and confrontive theory in public and environmental affairs*. Administrative Theory & Praxis, *40*(3), 267–280.

Moulton, S. (2009). Putting together the publicness puzzle: A framework for realized publicness. *Public Administration Review*, *69*(5), 889–900.

Muller, H. J., & Ventriss, C. (1985). *Public health in a retrenchment era: An alternative to managerialism*. State University of New York Press.

Nabatchi, T., Gastil, J., Leighninger, M., & Weiksner, G. M. (2012). *Democracy in motion*. Oxford University Press.

Nabatchi, T. & Leighninger, M. (2015). *Public participation for 21st century democracy*. John Wiley & Sons.

Nabatchi, T. (2010). Addressing the citizenship and democratic deficits: The potential of deliberative democracy for public administration. *The American Review of Public Administration*, *40*(4), 376–399.

Newman, J., & Clarke, J. (2009). *Publics, politics, and power*. Sage

Pesch, U. (2005). *The predicaments of publicness: An inquiry into the conceptual ambiguity of public administration*. University of Chicago Press.

Pesch, U. (2008). The publicness of public administration. *Administration & Society*, *40*(2), 170–193.

Polat, R. K. (2005). The Internet and political participation: Exploring the explanatory links. *European Journal of Communication*, *20*(4), 435–459.

Ramos, A. G. (1981). *The new science of organizations: A reconceptualization of the wealth of nations*. University of Toronto Press.

Ringeling, A. (2013). Reflections on the distinctiveness of public administration as a discipline. *NISPAcee Journal of Public Administration and Policy*, *6*(2), 21–31.

Roberts, N. C. (2008). *The age of direct citizen participation*. Routledge.

Schon, D. (1971). *Beyond the stable state*. W. W. Norton.

Stoker, G. (2006). Public value management: A new narrative for networked governance? *The American Review of Public Administration*, *36*(1), 41–57.

Ventriss, C., & Luke, J. (1988). Organizational learning and public policy: Towards a substantive perspective. *The American Review of Public Administration*, *18*(4), 337–357.

Ventriss, C. (1985). Emerging perspectives on citizen participation. *Public Administration Review*, *45*(3), 433–440.

Ventriss, C. (1991). Contemporary issues in American public administration education: The search for an educational focus. *Public Administration Review*, 4–14.
Ventriss, C. (2016). Investing in people: Toward a co-possibility model for citizen engagement. *International Journal of Public Administration, 39*(13), 1020–1030.
Wagenaar, H. (2011). *Meaning in action: Interpretation and dialogue in policy analysis*. M. E. Sharpe.
Waldo, D. (1985). An agenda for future reflections: A conversation with Dwight Waldo. *Public Administration Review, July-August*, 459–467.
Wamsley, G. L., & Zald, M. N. (1973). *The political economy of public organizations: A critique and approach to the study of public administration*. Lexington Books.
Warner Jr., S. B. (1968). *The private city: Philadelphia in three stages of its growth*. University of Pennsylvania Press.
Warner, M. (2002). Publics and counterpublics. *Public Culture, 14*(1), 49–90.
Whitehead, A. N. (1929). *Process and reality*. Macmillan.
Williams, I., & Shearer, H. (2011). Appraising public value: past, present, and future. *Public Administration, 89*(4), 1367–1384.
Wilson, J., & Swyngedouw, E. (Eds.). (2014). *The post-political and its discontents*. Edinburgh University Press.
Wolin, S. S. (2008). *Democracy incorporated: Managed democracy at the specter of inverted totalitarianism*. Princeton University Press.
Young, I. M. (2000). *Democracy and inclusion*. Oxford University Press.
Zavestoski, S., Shulman, S., & Schlosberg, D. (2006). Democracy and the environment on the internet: Electronic citizen participation in regulatory rulemaking. *Science, Technology, & Human Values, 31*(4), 383–408.

Chapter 4

Adams, G. B., & Balfour, D. L. (2007). Leadership, administrative evil, and the ethics of incompetence: Lessons from Katrina and Iraq. In *Leading the future of the public sector: The Third Transatlantic Dialogue-Workshop Six: Ethical leadership in the context of globalization*. University of Delaware. May 31–June 2, 2007.
Adams, G. B., & Balfour, D. L. (2010). Market-based government and the decline of organizational ethics. *Administration & Society, 42*(6), 615–637.
Aglietta, M. (1979). *A theory of capitalist regulation: The US experience*. New Left Review.
Arendt, H. (1958). *The human condition*. University of Chicago Press.
Arendt, H. (1961). *Between past and future: Six exercises in political thought*. Viking Press.
Arendt, H. (1978). *The Jew as pariah: Jewish identity and politics in the modern age*. Grove Press.
Barber, B. R. (1984). *Strong democracy: Participatory politics for a new age*. University of California Press.

Behn, R. D. (1995). The big questions of public management. *Public Administration Review, 55*(4), 313–324.

Benhabib, S. (1992). Models of public space: Hannah Arendt, the liberal tradition and Jürgen Habermas. In C. Calhoun (Ed.), *Habermas and the Public Sphere* (Vol. *Studies in Contemporary German Social Thought*, pp. 73–98). MIT Press.

Berger, P. L. (1963). *Invitation to sociology: A humanistic perspective*. Doubleday.

Berkowitz, P. (1999). *Virtue and the making of modern liberalism*. Princeton University Press.

Best, S., & Kellner, D. (1991). *Postmodern theory: Critical interrogations*. Guilford Press.

Bobbio, N. (1979). Are there alternatives to representative democracy? *Telos, 1978*(35), 17–30.

Bowles, S., & Gintis, H. (1986). *Democracy and capitalism: Property, community, and the contradictions of modern social thought*. Basic Books.

Box, R. C. (2014). *Public administration and society: Critical issues in American governance*. Routledge.

Box, R. C. (2009). *Making a difference: Progressive values in public administration*. Routledge.

Box, R. C., Marshall, G. S., Reed, B. J., & Reed, C. M. (2001). New public management and substantive democracy. *Public Administration Review, 61*(5), 608–619.

Carnoy, M. (1984). *The state and political theory*. Princeton University Press.

Connolly, W. E. (2013). *The fragility of things: Self-organizing processes, neoliberal fantasies, and democratic activism*. Duke University Press.

Denhardt, J. V., & Denhardt, R. B. (2015). *The new public service: Serving, not steering*. Routledge.

Dryzek, J. S. (1987). Discursive designs: Critical theory and political institutions. *American Journal of Political Science, 31*(3), 656–679.

Dryzek, J. S. (1990). *Discursive democracy: Politics, policy, and political science*. Cambridge University Press.

Dunford, M. (1990). Theories of regulation. *Environment and Planning D: Society and Space, 8*(3), 297–321.

Evans, S. M., & Boyte, H. C. (1986). *Free spaces: The sources of democratic change in America*. Harper & Row.

Fischer, F. (2003). *Reframing public policy: Discursive politics and deliberative practices*. Oxford University Press.

Follett, M. P. (1965). *Dynamic administration: The collected papers of Mary Parker Follett*. Martino Fine Books.

Forester, J. (1989). *Planning in the face of power*. University of California Press.

Fox, C. J., & Cochran, C. E. (1990). Discretion advocacy in public administration theory: Toward a platonic guardian class? *Administration & Society, 22*(2), 249–271.

Fraser, N. (1990). Rethinking the public sphere: A contribution to the critique of actually existing democracy. *Social Text* (25/26), 56–80.

Fung, A., & Fagotto, E. (2009). *Sustaining public engagement: Embedded deliberation in local communities.* Everyday Democracy & Kettering Foundation.

Gawthrop, L. C. (1984). Civis, civitas, and civilitas: A new focus for the year 2000. *Public Administration Review, 44*, 101–111.

Gouldner, A. W. (1971). *The coming crisis of western sociology.* New York: Avon.

Gramsci, A. (1971). *Selections from the prison notebooks of Antonio Gramsci.* International Publishers.

Habermas, J. (1984). *The theory of communicative action: Reason and the rationalization of society.* Beacon Press.

Habermas, J. (1962). *The structural transformation of the public sphere: An inquiry into a category of bourgeois society.* (transl. by Thomas Burger). MIT Press.

Hansen, D. A. (1976). *An invitation to critical sociology.* Free Press.

Harvey, D. (1990). Between space and time: Reflections on the geographical imagination. *Annals of the Association of American Geographers, 80*(3), 418–434.

Harvey, D. (2005). *Spaces of global capitalism: Towards a theory of uneven geographical development.* Verso.

Harvey, D. (2007). *A brief history of neoliberalism.* Oxford University Press.

Harvey, D. (2010). *The enigma of capital.* Oxford University Press.

Held, D. (1987). *Models of democracy.* Polity Press.

Hirsch, F. (1976). *Social limits to growth.* Harvard University Press.

Hummel, R. P. (2007). *The bureaucratic experience: The post-modern challenge.* M. E. Sharpe.

Hummel, R. P., & Stivers, C. (1998). Government is us: The possibility of democratic knowledge in representative government. In *Government Is Us: Public Administration in an Anti-government Era* (pp. 28–48). Sage.

Jay, M. (1984). *Marxism and totality: The adventures of a concept from Lukács to Habermas.* University of California Press.

Jessop, B. (1990). *State theory: Putting the capitalist state in its place.* Penn State Press.

Jessop, B. (2009). The state and power. In *The Sage Handbook of Power* (pp. 367–382). Sage.

Johnston, R. J., & Taylor, P. J. (1992). *A world in crisis?: Geographical perspectives.* Blackwell.

Kass, H., & Catron, B. (1990). *Images and identities in public administration.* Sage.

Kirlin, J. J. (1996). The big questions of public administration in a democracy. *Public Administration Review, 56*(5), 416–423.

Laclau, E., & Mouffe, C. (1985). *Hegemony and socialist strategy: Towards a radical democratic politics.* Verso.

Leighninger, M. (2010). *Creating spaces for change: Working toward a "story of now" in civic engagement.* Deliberative Democracy Consortium and WK Kellogg Foundation.

Lindblom, C. E. (1982). Another state of mind. *The American Political Science Review, 76*(1), 9–21.

Lipietz, A. (1986). New tendencies in the international division of labor: Regimes of accumulation and modes of regulation. In Scott, A. & Storper, M. (Eds.), *Production, Work, Territory: The Geographical Anatomy of International Capitalism* (pp. 16–40). Allen & Unwin.

Luxemburg, R. (1961). *The Russian revolution, and Leninism or Marxism?* University of Michigan Press.

Luxemburg, R. (1971). The Russian revolution. In M.-A. Waters (Ed.), *Rosa Luxemburg Speaks*. Pathfinder.

Macedo, S. (1990). *Liberal virtues: Citizenship, virtue, and community in liberal constitutionalism*. Clarendon Press.

Macpherson, C. B. (1962). *The political theory of possessive individualism: Hobbes to Locke*. Clarendon Press.

McCarthy, T. (1992). Practical discourse: On the relation of morality to politics. In C. Calhoun (Ed.), *Habermas and the Public Sphere* (pp. 51–72). MIT Press.

Mills, C. W. (1959). *The sociological imagination*. Penguin.

Mills, C. W. (1963). *Power, politics, and people: The collected essays of C. Wright Mills*. Oxford University Press.

Mouffe, C. (1992). (Ed.). *Dimensions of radical democracy: Pluralism, citizenship, community*. Verso.

Mouffe, C. (1993). *The return of the political*. Verso.

Muller, H. J., & Ventriss, C. (1985). *Public health in a retrenchment era: An alternative to managerialism*. State University of New York Press.

Nabatchi, T., & Leighninger, M. (2015). *Public participation for 21st century democracy*. John Wiley & Sons.

Nabatchi, T., & Munno, G. (2014). Deliberative civic engagement: Connecting public voices to public governance. *Civic Studies*, 49–58.

Niebuhr, R. (1944). *The children of light and the children of darkness: A vindication of democracy and a critique of its traditional defense*. Scribner's.

O'Connor, J. R. (1987). *The meaning of crisis: A theoretical introduction*. Basil Blackwell.

Pateman, C. (1970). *Participation and democratic theory*. Cambridge University Press.

Pateman, C. (2012). Participatory democracy revisited. *Perspectives on Politics, 10*(1), 7–19.

Polanyi, K. (1944). *The great transformation*. Rinehart.

Posner, E., & Weyl, G. (2018). How economists became so timid. *The Chroncile Review*, June 8, Section B, 17–18.

Poulantzas, N. (1978). *State, power, socialism*. Verso.

Poulantzas, N. (1975). *Classes in contemporary capitalism*. New Left Books

Pranger, R. J. (1968). *The eclipse of citizenship: Power and participation in contemporary politics*. Holt, Rinehart, and Winston.

Putnam, R. D. (2000). *Bowling alone: The collapse and revival of American community*. Simon & Schuster.

Ramos, A. G. (1981). *The new science of organizations: A reconceptualization of the Wealth of Nations*. University of Toronto Press.

Roberts, N. (2004). Public deliberation in an age of direct citizen participation. *The American Review of Public Administration, 34*(4), 315–353.

Rohr, J. (1984). Reports from the Group. *Public Administration Review, 44*, 190–191.

Sandel, M. J. (1996). *Democracy's discontent: America in search of a public philosophy*. Harvard University Press.

Sandel, M. J. (2005). *Public philosophy: Essays on morality in politics*. Harvard University Press.

Sandel, M. J. (2013). *What money can't buy: The moral limits of markets*. Farrar, Straus and Giroux.

Silvert, K. H. (1977). *The reason for democracy*. Viking Press.

Smith, N. (1984). *Uneven development: Nature, capital, and the production of space*. Blackwell.

Smith, N. (1996). *The new urban frontier: Gentrification and the revanchist city*. Routledge.

Soja, E. W. (1989). *Postmodern geographies: The reassertion of space in critical social theory*. Verso.

Stiglitz, J. E. (2012). *The price of inequality: How today's divided society endangers our future*. W. W. Norton.

Sullivan, W. M. (1986). *Reconstructing public philosophy*. University of California Press.

Swyngedouw, E. (1996). Reconstructing citizenship, the re-scaling of the state and the new authoritarianism: Closing the Belgian mines. *Urban Studies, 33*(8), 1499–1521.

Taylor, M. (2007). Community participation in the real world: Opportunities and pitfalls in new governance spaces. *Urban Studies, 44*(2), 297–317.

Taylor, M. (2011). *Public policy in the community*. Macmillan International Higher Education.

Thompson, D. (1983). Bureaucracy and democracy. In G. C. Duncan (Ed.), *Democratic Theory and Practice* (pp. 235–250). Cambridge University Press.

Tussman, J. (1960). *Obligation and the body politic*. Oxford University Press.

Ventriss, C. (2015). The troubling implications of the great divide: The inequality crisis in an era of economic and political uncertainty. *Public Administration Review, 75*(6), 892–900.

Ventriss, C. (2016). Investing in people: Toward a co-possibility model for citizen engagement. *International Journal of Public Administration, 39*(13), 1020–1030.

Ventriss, C., & Luke, J. (1988). Organizational learning and public policy: Towards a substantive perspective. *The American Review of Public Administration, 18*(4), 337–357.

Waldo, D. (1948). *The administrative state: A study of the political theory of American public administration*. Ronald Press.

Waldo, D. (1981). *The enterprise of public administration: A summary view*. Chandler & Sharp.

Walzer, M. (1965). *The revolution of the saints: A study in the origins of radical politics.* Harvard University Press.

Walzer, M. (1983). *Spheres of justice: A defense of pluralism and equality.* Basic Books.

Wolin, S. S. (1960). *Politics and vision: Continuity and innovation in western political thought.* Little, Brown.

Chapter 5

Andrews, C. W. (2000). Revisiting Guerreiro Ramos's the new science of organizations through Habermasian lenses: A critical tribute. *Administrative Theory & Praxis, 22*(2), 246–272.

Arendt, H. (1958). *The human condition.* University of Chicago Press.

Arendt, H. (1968). *Men in dark times.* Houghton Mifflin Harcourt.

Barbash, F. (2018, January 26). Trump calls Mueller firing story "fake news." *Washington Post.* Retrieved from washingtonpost.com/news/morning-mix/wp/2018/01/26/trump-calls-mueller-firing-story-fake-news/.

Beck, U. (2000). *What is globalization?* John Wiley & Sons.

Best, S., & Kellner, D. (1981). *Postmodern theory.* Guilford Press.

Flax, J. (1993). *Disputed subjects: Essays on psychoanalysis, politics, and philosophy.* Routledge.

Foucault, M. (1972). *The archaeology of knowledge.* Pantheon Books.

Foucault, M. (1976). *Society must be defended: Lectures at the College de France.* Picador.

Foucault, M. (1977). *Discipline and punish: The birth of the prison.* Random House.

Foucault, M. (1980a). *Language, counter-memory, practice: Selected essays and interviews.* Cornell University Press.

Foucault, M. (1980b). *Power/knowledge: Selected interviews and other writings, 1972–1977.* Pantheon Books.

Foucault, M. (2008). The birth of biopolitics: Lectures at the College de France, 1978–1979. St. Martin's Press.

Gerth, H. H., & Mills, C. W. (1946). Introduction: The man and his works. In *From Max Weber: Essays in sociology* (pp. 2–74). Oxford University Press.

Hedges, C. (2011). *Death of the liberal class.* Knopf.

Held, D. (1989). *Political theory and the modern state: Essays on state, power, and democracy.* Stanford University Press.

Horkheimer, M. (1947). *The eclipse of reason.* Continuum.

Isaac, J. C. (1998). *Democracy in dark times.* Cornell University Press.

Leonard, S. T. (1990). *Critical theory in political practice.* Princeton University Press.

Leonhardt, D., & Thompson, S. A. (2017, June 23). President Trump's lies, the definitive list. *The New York Times.* Retrieved from nytimes.com/interactive/2017/06/23/opinion/trumps-lies.html.

MacLean, N. (2017). *Democracy in chains: The deep history of the radical right's stealth plan for America.* Penguin.

Mayer, J. (2016). *Dark money: The hidden history of the billionaires behind the rise of the radical right.* Doubleday.

Moffitt, B. (2016). *The global rise of populism: Performance, political style, and representation.* Stanford University Press.

Murphy, R. (1994). *Rationality and nature: A sociological inquiry into a changing relationship.* Westview Press.

Nietzsche, F. (1967). *On the genealogy of morals and ecce homo.* Knopf Doubleday.

Patton, P. (1987). *Creating culture: Profiles in the study of culture.* Allen & Unwin.

Poggi, G. (1978). *The development of the modern state: A sociological introduction.* Stanford University Press.

Ramos, A. G. (1981). *The new science of organizations: A reconceptualization of the Wealth of Nations.* University of Toronto Press.

Robertson, R. (1995). Glocalization: Time-space and homogeneity-heterogeneity. In M. Featherstone, S. Lash, & R. Robertson (Eds.), *Global Modernities* (pp. 24–44). Sage.

Somers, M. R. (2008). *Genealogies of citizenship: Markets, statelessness, and the right to have rights.* Cambridge University Press.

Ventriss, C., & Candler, G. G. (2005). Alberto Guerreiro Ramos, 20 years later: A new science still unrealized in an era of public cynicism and theoretical ambivalence. *Public Administration Review, 65*(3), 347–359.

Weber, M. (1968). *Economy and society: An outline of interpretive sociology.* New York: Bedminster Press.

Wolin, S. S. (2008). *Democracy incorporated: Managed democracy and the specter of inverted totalitarianism.* Princeton University Press.

Chapter 6

Adams, G. B. (1992). Enthralled with modernity: The historical context of knowledge and theory development in public administration. *Public Administration Review, 52*(4), 363–373.

Adams, G. B. (2011). The problem of administrative evil in a culture of technical rationality. *Public Integrity, 13*(3), 275–286.

Adams, G. B., & Balfour, D. L. (2009). *Unmasking administrative evil.* M. E. Sharpe.

Adams, G. B., & Balfour, D. L. (2010). Market-based government and the decline of organizational ethics. *Administration & Society, 42*(6), 615–637.

Adams, G. B., & Balfour, D. L. (2012). Toward restoring integrity in "praetorian times." *Public Integrity, 14*(4), 325–339.

Ahamed, L. (2009, September 17). The future of global finance. *The New York Times,* p. BR23.

Akerlof, G. A., & Shiller, R. J. (2009). *Animal spirits: How human psychology drives the economy, and why it matters for global capitalism.* Princeton University Press.

Anderson, E. (1990). The ethical limitations of the market. *Economics & Philosophy, 6*(2), 179–205.

Arrow, K. J. (1972). Gifts and exchanges. *Philosophy & Public Affairs, 1*(4), 343–362.

Bakunin, J. (1977, September 21). The Failure of Individualism. *Christian Century, 93*, 813–814.

Barber, B. R. (1984). *Strong democracy: Participatory politics for a new age.* University of California Press.

Barofsky, N. (2012). *Bailout: An inside account of how Washington abandoned Main Street while rescuing Wall Street.* Free Press.

Bartels, L (2016). *Unequal Democracy: The political economy of the new Gilded Age.* Princeton University Press.

Bell, D. (1976). *The cultural contradictions of capitalism.* Basic Books.

Bell, D., & Blanchflower, D. (2018). Underemployment in the U.S. and Europe. Working Paper 24927. Cambridge, MA: National Bureau of Economic Research.

Bencivenga, V. (2009). Understanding the financial crisis and comments on the ethical issues involved. Presented at the Ethical Society of Austin, Department of Economics, University of Texas.

Bevir, M. (2010a). *Democratic governance.* Princeton University Press.

Biggs, A. G. (2012, May 3). College grads need jobs, not a lower loan rate. *Wall Street Journal,* p. A13.

Blinder, A. S. (2012, January 19). Four deficit myths and a frightening fact. *Wall Street Journal.*

Block, F., & Somers, M. (2016). *The power of market fundamentalism.* Harvard University Press.

Boonstra, W. J., & Van Den Brink, A. (2007). Controlled decontrolling: Involution and democratisation in Dutch rural planning. *Planning Theory & Practice, 8*(4), 473–488.

Boudreaux, D. J., & Perry, M. J. (2013, January 23). The myth of a stagnant middle class. *Wall Street Journal,* p. A17.

Bourdieu, P. (1977). *Outline of a theory of practice.* Cambridge University Press.

Bowles, S., & Gintis, H. (1985). The labour theory of value and the specificity of Marxian economics. In S. Resnick & R. Wolff (Eds.), *Rethinking marxism: Struggles in marxist theory.* Autonomedia.

Bowles, S., & Gintis, H. (1986). *Democracy and capitalism: Property, community, and the contradictions of modern social thought.* Basic Books.

Box, R. C. (2010). Yearning for something better: How much change can we expect? *Administrative Theory & Praxis, 32*(3), 385–401.

Box, R. C., & King, C. S. (2000). The "T"ruth is elsewhere: critical history. *Administrative Theory & Praxis, 22*(4), 751–771.

Bureau of Labor Statistics Data. (2018). Labor Force Statistics from the Current Population Survey.

Burke, E. (1971). *A philosophical enquiry into the origin of our ideas of the sublime and beautiful, 1759*. Garland.

Caldwell, L. K. (1955). The relevance of administrative history. *Progress in Public Administration, 21*(3), 453–466.

Caldwell, L. K. (1996). The state as a work of art: Statecraft for the 21st century. *PS: Political Science and Politics, 29*(4), 657–664.

Camilleri, J. A. (1977). *Civilization in crisis: Human prospects in a changing world*. Cambridge University Press.

Candler, G. G. (2010). Toward a public-spirited public management economics: An essay in honor of John Kenneth Galbraith. *Administrative Theory & Praxis, 32*(3), 327–347.

Carvalho, L. F., & Rodrigues, J. (2006). On markets and morality: Revisiting Fred Hirsch. *Review of Social Economy, 64*(3), 331–348.

Cassidy, J. (2009). *How markets fail: The logic of economic calamities*. Farrar, Straus, and Giroux.

Cerny, P. G. (2008). Embedding neoliberalism: The evolution of a hegemonic paradigm. *The Journal of International Trade and Diplomacy, 2*(1), 1–46.

Chandler, R. C. (1987). *A Centennial history of the American administrative state*. Free Press.

Chetty, R., Hendren, N., Kline, P., Saez, E., and Turner, N. (2014). Is the United States still a land of opportunity? Working Paper 19844. National Bureau of Economic Research.

Clarke, C. (2009, June 18). An interview with Paul Samuelson, Part II. *The Atlantic*, 17.

Corak, M. (2010). *Chasing the same dream, climbing different ladders: Economic mobility in the United States and Canada*. The Pew Economic Mobility Project.

Cruikshank, B. (1999). *The will to empower: Democratic citizens and other subjects*. Cornell University Press.

Dewey, J. (1903). *Studies in logical theory*. University of Chicago Press.

Dewey, J. (1927). *The public and its problems*. Ohio University Press.

Dewey, J. (1935). The future of liberalism. *The Journal of Philosophy, 32*(9), 225–230.

Dougherty, C., & Mathews, A. W. (2012). Household income sinks to '95 level. *Wall Street Journal*, September 13, pp. A1, A6.

Duesenberry, J. S. (1949). *Income, saving, and the theory of consumer behavior*. Harvard University Press.

Dumont, L. (1977). *From Mandeville to Marx: The genesis and triumph of economic ideology*. University of Chicago Press.

Duncan, G. (1989). *Democracy and the capitalist state*. Cambridge University Press.

Durant, R. F. (2011). *Global crises, American public administration, and the "new interventionism" revisited*. Presented at the American Society for Public Administration, Baltimore, MD.

Durkheim, É. (1966). *The division of labor in society*. Free Press.

Dymski, G. A. (2006). Targets of opportunity in two landscapes of financial globalization. *Geoforum, 37*(3), 307–311.

Eichengreen, B. (2016). *Halls of mirrors: The great depression, the great recession, and the uses—and misuses—of history.* Oxford University Press.

Eliot, T. S. (1971). *T.S. Eliot: The complete poems and plays 1909–1950.* Harcourt Brace.

Ellul, J. (1967). *The political illusion.* New York: Vintage Books.

Erie, S. P. (1977). Political power and the problem of administrative theory. Presented at the Annual Conference of the American Society for Public Administration, Atlanta, GA.

Fama, E. F. (1965). The behavior of stock-market prices. *The Journal of Business, 38*(1), 34–105.

Fama, E. F. (1970). Efficient capital markets: A review of theory and empirical work. *The Journal of Finance, 25*(2), 383–417.

Farmer, D. J. (2010). Public administration in a world of economics. *Administrative Theory & Praxis, 32*(3), 373–384.

Federal Reserve Bank of New York. (2018, April 27). The Labor Market for Recent College Graduates. Retrieved July 11, 2018, from https://www.newyorkfed.org/research/college-labor-market/college-labor-market_underemployment_rates.html.

Fesler, J. W. (Ed.). (1982). *American public administration: Patterns of the past.* American Society for Public Administration.

Financial Crisis Inquiry Commission. (2011). *The financial crisis inquiry report: Final report of the National Commission on the Causes of the Financial and Economic Crisis in the United States.* U.S. Government Printing Office.

Fischer, F. (2003). *Reframing public policy: Discursive politics and deliberative practices.* Oxford University Press.

Fox, J. (2011). *The myth of the rational market: A history of risk, reward, and delusion on Wall Street.* Harper Collins.

Frank, R. H. (1985). *Choosing the right pond: Human behavior and the quest for status.* Oxford University Press.

Frank, R. H. (2005). Positional externalities cause large and preventable welfare losses. *American Economic Review, 95*(2), 137–141.

Frank, T. (2001). *One market under God: Extreme capitalism, market populism, and the end of economic democracy.* Anchor Books.

Freeland, C. (2012, October 14). The self-destruction of the 1 percent. *The New York Times*, p. SR5.

Freeman, R. (1976). *The overeducated American.* New York: Academic Press.

Friedman, B. M. (2012, May 25). Review of *The great divergence*, by T. Noah. *The New York Times*, p. 1,13.

Fukuyama, F. (1996). *Trust: the social virtues and the creation of prosperity.* New York: Free Press.

Galbraith, J. K. (2008). *The predator state: How conservatives abandoned the free market and why liberals should too.* New York: Free Press.

Gale, G. W., Gelfond, H., Fichtner, R., & Harris, B. H. (2020). The wealth of generations, special attention to the millennials. *Brookings Institution.*

Germain, R. (2009). Financial order and world politics: Crisis, change and continuity. *International Affairs, 85*(4), 669–687.

Giddens, A. (1971). *Capitalism and modern social theory: An analysis of the writings of Marx, Durkheim and Max Weber.* Cambridge University Press.

Giddens, A. (1981). *A contemporary critique of historical materialism. Vol. 1, Power, property and the state.* Macmillan.

Giddens, A. (1994). *Beyond left and right: The future of radical politics.* Stanford University Press.

Goodwin, R. N. (1992). *Promises to keep: A call for a new American revolution.* Times Books.

Gray, J. (1995). *Beyond the new right: Markets, government and the common environment.* Routledge.

Green, R. T. (2012a). Plutocracy, bureaucracy, and the end of public trust. *Administration & Society, 44*(1), 109–143.

Green, R. T. (2012b). Public administration's role in the financial crisis: How do we move forward, or should we? Reactions and response to Potter, Khademian, and Lynn. *Administration & Society, 44*(6), 766–775.

Greenhouse, S. (2013, January 13). Our Economic Pickle. *The New York Times,* p. SR5.

Grubel, H. G. (1978). Review of *Social limits to growth,* by Fred Hirsch. *The Canadian Journal of Economics, 11*(1), 151–154.

Gulick, L. H. (1990). Reflections on public administration, past and present. *Public Administration Review, 50*(6), 599.

Habermas, J. (1973). *Theory and practice.* Beacon Press.

Hacker, J. S., & Loewentheil, N. (2012, October 18). Growth and inequality: All will benefit if more are made secure. *The New York Times,* p. A3.

Hacker, J. S., & Pierson, P. (2011). *Winner-take-all politics: How Washington made the rich richer–and turned its back on the middle class.* Simon & Schuster.

Harvey, D. (2009). *Why the U.S. stimulus package is bound to fail.* Speech, City University of New York Lecture Series.

Harvey, D. (2010). *The enigma of capital and the crises of capitalism.* Oxford University Press.

Haskins, R., & Sawhill, I. V. (2009). *Creating an opportunity society.* Brookings Institution Press.

Hassett, K., & Mathur, A. (2012, October 25). Consumption and the myths of inequality. *The Wall Street Journal,* p. A17.

Henry, J. (1963). *Culture against man.* New York: Random House.

Hilsenrath, J. (2013, January 28). How a trust deficit is hurting the economy. *Wall Street Journal*, p. A2.

Hirsch, F. (1976). *Social limits to growth*. Harvard University Press.

Hummel, R. P. (2007). *The bureaucratic experience: The post-modern challenge*. M. E. Sharpe.

Jacobs, L., & King, D. (2009). America's political crisis: The unsustainable state in a time of unraveling. *PS: Political Science & Politics*, *42*(2), 277–285.

Jessop, B. (1993). Towards a Schumpeterian workfare state? Preliminary remarks on post-Fordist political economy. *Studies in Political Economy*, *40*(1), 7–39.

Johnson, S., & Kwak, J. (2010). *13 Bankers: The Wall Street takeover and the next financial meltdown*. Pantheon Books.

Judis, J. B. (2016). *The populist explosion: How the great recession transformed American and European politics*. Columbia Global Reports.

Judt, T. (2007b, December 6). The wrecking ball of innovation. *The New York Review of Books*, 22–25.

Karl, B. D. (1976). Public administration and American history: A century of professionalism. *Public Administration Review*, *36*(5), 489–503.

Keller, M. (1979). *Affairs of state: public life in late nineteenth century America*. Belknap Press of Harvard University Press.

Khademian, A. M. (2011). The financial crisis: A retrospective. *Public Administration Review*, *71*(6), 841–849.

Kindleberger, C. P., & Aliber, R. (2005). *Manias, panics, and crashes: A history of financial crises*. John Wiley & Sons.

Kirk, R. (1964). *The conservative mind from Burke to Santayana*. Regnery.

Kouzmin, A. (2009). Market fundamentalism, delusions, and epistemic failures in policy and administration. *Asia-Pacific Journal of Business Administration*, *1*(1), 23–39.

Kouzmin, A. (2010). The dismal (delusional and dangerous) "science" of economics and the "capture" of public administration. *Administrative Theory & Praxis*, *32*(3), 291–303.

Krugman, P. (2009). *The return of depression economics and the crisis of 2008*. W. W. Norton.

Kuttner, R. (1997). *Everything for sale: The virtues and limits of markets*. Alfred A. Knopf.

Lo, A. W. (2012). Reading about the financial crisis: A twenty-one-book review. *Journal of Economic Literature*, *50*(1), 151–178.

Lustig, R. J. (1982). *Corporate liberalism: The origins of modern American political theory, 1890–1920*. University of California Press.

Luton, L. S. (1999). History and American public administration. *Administration & Society*, *31*(2), 205–221.

Lynn, L. E. (2012). Rick Green has seen the enemy: Guess who? *Administration & Society*, *44*(6), 754–765.

Macartney, H. (2009). Disagreeing to agree: Financial crisis management within the "logic of no alternative." *Politics, 29*(2), 111–120.

Macpherson, C. B. (1962). *The political theory of possessive individualism: Hobbes to Locke.* Oxford University Press.

Mandel, E. (1976). *Late capitalism: translated [from the German] by Joris De Bres.* Humanities Press.

Mangan, K. (2012). Employers lack educators' optimism about jobs. *The Chronicle of Higher Education,* A21.

Martin, D. W. (1987). Déjà vu: French antecedents of American public administration. *Public Administration Review, 47*(4), 297–303.

Mason, R. (2000). Conspicuous consumption and the positional economy: policy and prescription since 1970. *Managerial and Decision Economics, 21*(3–4), 123–132.

Matthews, R. C. O. (1977). Review of *Social limits to growth,* by F. Hirsch. *The Economic Journal, 87*(347), 574–578.

Mayer, J. (2016). *Dark money: The hidden history of billionaries behind the Radical Right.* Doubleday.

McCraw, T. K. (2007). *Prophet of innovation.* Harvard University Press.

Merrifield, A. (2002). Dialectical urbanism: social struggles in the capitalist city. Monthly Review Press.

Minsky, H. P. (1980). Capitalist financial processes and the instability of capitalism. *Journal of Economic Issues, 14*(2), 505–523.

Morgenson, G. (2011). *Reckless endangerment; How outsized ambition, greed, and corruption led to the economic armageddon.* Times Books.

Mosher, F. C. (1983). *Basic documents of American public administration.* Holmes and Meier.

Mouzelis, N. P. (1973). *Organisation and bureaucracy an analysis of modern theories.* Aldine.

Muller, J. Z. (2002). *The mind and the market: Capitalism in modern European thought.* Alfred A. Knopf.

Nanto, D. K. (2009). *The global financial crisis: Analysis and policy implications.* Congressional Research Service.

Neustadt, R. E., & May, E. R. (1986). *Thinking in time: The uses of history for decision-makers.* Free Press.

Nisbet, R. A. (1988). *The present age: Progress and anarchy in modern America.* Harper & Row.

Noah, T. (2012). *The great divergence: America's growing inequality crisis and what we can do about it.* Bloomsbury.

O'Connor, J. (1987). *The meaning of crisis: A theoretical introduction.* Blackwell.

Offe, C. (1976). "Crisis of crisis management": Elements of a political crisis theory. *International Journal of Politics, 6*(3), 29–67.

O'Quinn, R. (2008). *The U.S. housing bubble and the global financial crisis: Vulnerabilities of the alternative financial system.* U.S. Joint Economic Committee Study.

Partnoy, F., & Eisenger, J. (2013, February). What's inside America's banks: How Wall Street could blow up the economy—again. *The Atlantic*, 60–71.

Patterson, S. (2010). *The quants: How a new breed of math whizzes conquered Wall Street and nearly destroyed it.* Crown.

Pauly, L. W. (2009). The old and the new politics of international financial stability. *Journal of Common Market Studies, 47*(5), 955–975.

Phillips, K. (2009). *Bad money: Reckless finance, failed politics, and the global crisis of American capitalism.* Penguin.

Piketty, T., Saez, E., & Zucman, G. (2016). *Distributional national accounts: Methods and estimates for the United States* (Working Paper No. 22945). National Bureau of Economic Research.

Polanyi, K. (1944). *The great transformation.* Rinehart.

Poltke, D. (1986). The limits to growth politics. *Contemporary Sociology* (45), 524–526.

Posner, R. A. (2010). *The crisis of capitalist democracy.* Harvard University Press.

Putnam, R. D. (2001). *Bowling alone: The collapse and revival of American community.* Simon and Schuster.

Quiggin, J. (2012). *Zombie economics: How dead ideas still walk among us.* Princeton University Press.

Raadschelders, J. C. N. (1998). *Handbook of administrative history.* Transaction.

Raadschelders, J. C. N. (2000). Administrative history of the United States: Development and state of the art. *Administration & Society, 32*(5), 499–528.

Raadschelders, J. C. N. (2005). Government and public administration: Challenges to and need for connecting knowledge. *Administrative Theory & Praxis, 27*(4), 602–627.

Raadschelders, J. C. N., & Lee, K.-H. (2011). Trends in the study of public administration: Empirical and qualitative observations from public administration review, 2000–2009. *Public Administration Review, 71*(1), 19–33.

Rajan, R. (2006). Has finance made the world riskier? *European Financial Management, 12*(4), 499–533.

Rajan, R. (2010). *Fault lines: How hidden fractures still threaten the world economy.* Princeton University Press.

Ramos, A. G. (1981). *The new science of organizations: A reconceptualization of the wealth of nations.* University of Toronto Press.

Reinhart, C. M., & Rogoff, K. S. (2009). *This time is different: Eight centuries of financial folly.* Princeton University Press.

Ritzer, G. (2004). *The McDonaldization of society.* Sage.

Roberts, A. (2010). The rise and fall of discipline: Economic globalization, administrative reform, and the financial crisis. *Public Administration Review, 70*(1), 56–63.

Roberts, A. (2011, July 10). A precipitous situation, not without precedent. *Boston Globe*, p. G4.

Roberts, A. (2012). *America's first great depression: Economic crisis and political disorder after the panic of 1837*. Cornell University Press.

Rogers, M. L. (2009). *The undiscovered Dewey: Religion, morality, and the ethos of democracy*. Columbia University Press.

Roubini, N., & Mihm, S. (2011). *Crisis economics: A crash course in the future of finance*. Penguin.

Rueschemeyer, D., & Evans, P. (1985). The state and economic transformation: Towards an analysis of the conditions underlying effective intervention. In P. Evans, D. Rueschemeyer, & T. Skocpol (Eds.), *Bringing the state back in*. Cambridge University Press.

Saez, E. (2012). *Striking it richer: The evolution of top incomes in the United States* (Updated with 2009 and 2010 estimates). University of California, Berkeley —Department of Economics.

Samuelson, P. A. (1973). Proof that properly discounted present values of assets vibrate randomly. *The Bell Journal of Economics and Management Science*, *4*(2), 369–374.

Sandel, M. J. (2013). *What money can't buy: The moral limits of markets*. Farrar, Straus and Giroux.

Sartori, G. (1970). Concept misformation in comparative politics. *The American Political Science Review*, *64*(4), 1033–1053.

Sawhill, I. & Pilliam, C. (June 25, 2019). *Six facts about wealth in the U.S.* Brookings Institution.

Schachter, H. L. (1998). History and identity in the field of public administration: An analysis from *Public Administration Review*. *Administrative Theory & Praxis*, *20*(1), 16–22.

Schmookler, A. B. (1984). *The parable of the tribes: The problem of power in social evolution*. Houghton Mifflin.

Schneider, M. (2007). The nature, history and significance of the concept of positional goods. *History of Economics Review*, *45*(1), 60–81.

Schoenberger, E. (1997). *The cultural crisis of the firm*. Oxford: Blackwell.

Schumpeter, J. A. (1942). *Capitalism, socialism, and democracy*. Harper.

Schumpeter, J. A. (1954). *History of economic analysis*. Oxford University Press.

Sen, A. K. (1999). Democracy as a universal value. *Journal of Democracy*, *10*(3), 3–17.

Shah, N. (2012, July 31). Which states have worst underemployment? *Wall Street Journal*, p. A4.

Shambaugh, J., & Nunn, R. (2017, October 24). Why wages aren't growing in America. *Harvard Business Review*.

Shermer, T. E. (2012). Banking on government. In S. Conn (Ed.), *To promote the general welfare: The case of big government* (pp. 65–84). Oxford University Press.

Shiller, R. J. (2008). *The subprime solution: How today's global financial crisis happened, and what to do about it.* Princeton University Press.

Skocpol, T., & Ikenberry, J. (1983). The political formation of the American welfare state in historical and comparative perspective. *Comparative Social Research, 6*, 87–148.

Smith, G. (2012). *Why I left Goldman Sachs: A Wall Street story.* Grand Central.

Sorkin, A. R. (2009). *Too big to fail: The inside story of how Wall Street and Washington fought to save the financial system from crisis—and themselves.* Viking.

Soros, G. (2008). *The new paradigm for financial markets: The credit crisis of 2008 and what it means.* PublicAffairs.

Spicer, M. (2004). Public administration, the history of ideas, and the reinventing government movement. *Public Administration Review, 64*(3), 353–362.

Stiglitz, J. E. (2010). *Freefall: America, free markets, and the sinking of the world economy.* W. W. Norton.

Stiglitz, J. E. (2012a). *The price of inequality.* W. W. Norton.

Stiglitz, J. E. (2012b). What's at stake in this election. *The New York Times*, October 21, pp. SR1, SR8.

Stillman, R. J. (1990). The peculiar "stateless" origins of American public administration and the consequences for government today. *Public Administration Review, 50*(2), 156–167.

Stivers, C. (1999). Translating out of time: Public administration and its history. *Public Administration Review, 59*(4), 362–366.

Stokes, B. (2017). Global publics more upbeat about the economy. Pew Research Center.

Sullivan, W. M. (1986). *Reconstructing public philosophy.* University of California Press.

Sum, A., & Khatiwada, I. (2010). *Underemployment problems in US labor markets in 2009: Predicting the probabilities of underemployment for key age, gender, race-ethnic, nativity, educational attainment, and occupational subgroups of US workers.* Center for Labor Market Studies, Northeastern University.

Szenberg, M., Gottesman, A. A., & Ramrattan, L. (2005). *Paul A. Samuelson: On being an economist.* Jorge Pinto Books.

Thompson, D. F. (1980). Moral responsibility of public officials: The problem of many hands. *American Political Science Review, 74*(4), 905–916.

Tong, R. (1986). *Ethics in policy analysis.* Prentice-Hall.

Tooze, A. J. (2018). *Crashed: How a decade of financial crises changed the world.* Viking.

Valencia, F., & Laeven, M. L. (2008). *Systemic banking crises: A new database.* (IMF Working Paper No. 08/224). International Monetary Fund.

Van Dam, A. (2020). The unluckiest generation in history. *Washington Post*, May 27.

Van Riper, P. (1958). *History of the United States Civil Service.* Row, Peterson.

Vanderburg, W. H. (2005). *Living in the labyrinth of technology.* University of Toronto Press.

Veblen, T. (1954). *The higher learning in America.* B. W. Huebsch.

Ventriss, C. (1998). Radical democratic thought and contemporary American public administration: A substantive perspective. *The American Review of Public Administration, 28*(3), 227–245.

Ventriss, C. (2000). New public management: An examination of its influence on contemporary public affairs and its impact on shaping the intellectual agenda of the field. *Administrative Theory & Praxis, 22*(3), 500–518.

Ventriss, C. (2010). The challenge for public administration (and public policy) in an era of economic crises . . . or the relevance of cognitive politics in a time of political involution. *Administrative Theory & Praxis, 32*(3), 402–428.

Ventriss, C. (2012a). Democratic citizenship and public ethics. *Public Integrity, 14*(3), 283–297.

Ventriss, C. (2012b). The future (and challenge) of policy analysis in an era of analytical and theoretical ambivalence: An essay. *Administrative Theory & Praxis, 34*(2), 287.

Ventriss, C., & Barney, S. (2006). At the altar of the state. Unpublished paper.

Viereck, P. (1962). *Conservatism revisited.* Collier.

Villa, D. (2001). *Socratic citizenship*. Princeton University Press.

Viner, J. (1954). Schumpeter's history of economic analysis. *The American Economic Review, 44*(5), 894–910.

Waldo, D. (1948). *The administrative state: A study of the political theory of American public administration.* Ronald Press.

Walzer, M. (1983). *Spheres of justice: a defense of pluralism and equality.* Blackwell.

Weatherall, J. O. (2013). *The physics of Wall Street: A brief history of predicting the unpredictable.* Houghton Mifflin Harcourt.

Weaver, R. M. (1948). *Ideas have consequences.* University of Chicago Press.

Weismann, J. (2012). Fifty-three percent of recent college graduates are jobless or unemployed—how? *Atlantic Monthly,* April 23.

Wessel, D. (2012, September 20). Race's role in economic fate. *Wall Street Journal,* A6.

White, L. D. (1948). *The Federalists: A study in administrative history.* MacMillan.

Wills, G. (1979). *Nixon agonistes: The crisis of the self-made man*. New American Library.

Wolf, M. (2008). *Fixing global finance*. Johns Hopkins University Press.

Wolin, S. S. (1994). Fugitive democracy. *Constellations, 1*(1), 11–25.

Wolin, S. S. (2008). *Democracy incorporated: Managed democracy and the specter of inverted totalitarianism.* Princeton University Press.

Zingales, L. (2012). Crony Capitalism and the Crisis of the West. *Wall Street Journal,* June 7, p. A19.

Chapter 7

Abers, R. (2000). *Inventing local democracy: Grassroots politics in Brazil.* Lynne Rienner.

Albrechts, L. (1991). Changing roles and positions of planners. *Urban Studies, 28*(1), 123–137.

Arendt, H. (1958). *The human condition.* University of Chicago Press.

Beauregard, R. A. (1989). Space, time, and economic restructuring. In *Economic Restructuring and Political Response.* Sage.

Bluestone, B., & Harrison, B. (1982). *The deindustrialization of America: plant closings, community abandonment, and the dismantling of basic industry.* Basic Books.

Bookchin, M. (1992). *Urbanization without cities: The rise and decline of citizenship.* Black Rose Books.

Brenner, N., Jessop, B., Jones, M., & Macleod, G. (2008). *State/space: A reader.* John Wiley & Sons.

Brenner, N., & Theodore, N. (2003). *Spaces of neoliberalism: Urban restructuring in North America and Western Europe.* John Wiley & Sons.

Casey, E. S. (1998). The production of space or the heterogeneity of place: A commentary on Edward Dimendberg and Neil Smith. In *Philosophy and Geography II: The Production of Public Space* (pp. 71–80). Rowman & Littlefield.

Castells, M. (1985). *High technology, space, and society.* Sage.

Child-Hill, R. (1984). Economic crisis and political response in the motor city. In L. Sawers & W. Tabb (Eds.), *Sunbelt/snowbelt* (pp. 313–338). Oxford University Press.

Clarke, J., & Newman, J. (2017). "People in this country have had enough of experts": Brexit and the paradox of populism. *Critical Policy Studies, 11*(1), 101–116.

Cochrane, A. (1991). The changing state of local government: Restructuring for the 1990s. *Public Administration, 69*(3), 281–302.

Combes, P., & Thisse, T. (2008) *Economic geography: The integration of regions and nations.* Princeton University Press.

Congressional Research Service. (2019). *The regional greenhouse gas initiative: Backgrounds, impacts, and selected issues.* Washington, DC.

Cooke, P. (1986a). Global restructuring, industrial change and local adjustment. In *Global restructuring, local response* (pp. 1–24). Economic and Social Research Council.

Cooke, P. (1986b). *Global restructuring, local response: A report commissioned by the Environment and Planning Committee of the ESRC.* Economic and Social Research Council.

Cooke, P. (1988). Flexible integration, scope economies, and strategic alliances: Social and spatial mediations. *Environment and Planning D: Society and Space, 6*(3), 281–300.

Cooke, P. (Ed.). (1989a). *Localities: The changing face of urban Britain.* Unwin Hyman.

Cooke, P. (1989b). Locality, economic restructuring and world development. In *Localities. The Changing Face of Urban Britain* (pp. 1–44). Unwin Hyman.

Courlet, C. (1989). Local industrial policies in favour of small and medium sized firms: The French case. In L. Albrechts, F. Moulaert, F. Roberts, & E. Swyngedouw (Eds.), *Regional policy at the crossroads: European perspectives* (pp. 180–190). Kingsley.

Cox, K. R. (1989). The politics of turf and the question of class. In J. Wolch & M. Dear (Eds.), *The power of geography: How territory shapes social life* (p. 61). Unwin Hyman.

Cox, K. R. (1997). Governance, urban regime analysis, and the politics of local economic development. In M. Lauria (Ed.), *Reconstructing urban regime theory: Regulating urban politics in a global economy* (pp. 99–121). Sage.

Cox, K. R., & Mair, A. (1988). Locality and community in the politics of local economic development. *Annals of the Association of American Geographers, 78*(2), 307–325.

Dear, M. (1990). Review of *Postmodern geographies: The reassertion of space in critical social theory,* by E. W. Soja. *Annals of the Association of American Geographers, 80*(4), 649–654.

Dicken, P. (2007). *Global shift, Fifth Edition: Mapping the changing contours of the world economy.* Guilford Press.

Dijck, van J., & Poell, T. (2015). Social media and the transformation of public space. *Social Media and Society, 1*(2), 1–5.

Dijck, van J., Poell, T., & de Waal, M. (2008). *The platform society: Public values in a connected world.* Oxford University Press.

Dikeç, M. (2012). Space as a mode of political thinking. *Geoforum, 43*(4), 669–676.

Domahidy, M. R., & Gilsinan, J. F. (1992). The back stage is not the back room: How spatial arrangements affect the administration of public affairs. *Public Administration Review, 52*(6), 588–593.

Duchacek, I. D. (1984). The international dimension of subnational self-government. *Publius: The Journal of Federalism, 14*(4), 5–31.

Duncan, S., & Savage, M. (1989). Space, scale and locality. *Antipode, 21*(3), 179–206.

Dunford, M., & Kafkalas, G. (Eds.). (1992). *Cities and regions in the new Europe: the global-local interplay and spatial development strategies.* Belhaven Press.

Durkheim, É. (1915). *The elementary forms of the religious life. A study in religious sociology. Translated from the French by J.W. Swain.* Allen & Unwin.

Elden, S. (2007). Rethinking governmentality. *Political Geography, 26*(1), 29–33.

Fainstein, S., & Fainstein, N. (1989). Technology, the new international division of labor and location: Continuities and disjunctures. In R. A. Beauregard (Ed.), *Economic restructuring and political response,* Vol. 34. Sage.

Fosler, R. S. (1988). *The New economic role of American states: Strategies in a competitive world economy.* Oxford University Press.

Foster, J. B., & Magdoff, F. (2009). *The great financial crisis: Causes and consequences.* New York University Press.

Fox, J. (2009). *The myth of the rational market: A history of risk, reward, and delusion on Wall Street.* Harper Collins.

Friedmann, J. (1986). The world city hypothesis. *Development and Change, 17*(1), 69–83.

Galbraith, J. K. (2008). *The predator state: How conservatives abandoned the free market and why liberals should too.* Simon and Schuster.

Gambino, F. (2007). A Critique of the fordism of the regulation school. *The Commoner, 12*, 39–62.

Gertler, M. S. (1988). The limits of flexibility: Comments on the post-Fordist vision of production and its geography. *Transactions of the Institute of British Geographers, 13*(4), 419–432.

Giddens, A. (1979). *Central problems in social theory: Action, structure, and contradiction in social analysis.* University of California Press.

Giddens, A. (1981). *A contemporary critique of historical materialism.* University of California Press.

Giddens, A. (1984). *The constitution of society: Outline of the theory of structuration.* University of California Press.

Giddens, A. (1985). Time, space and regionalisation. In Gregory & Urry (Eds.), *Social relations and spatial structures* (pp. 265–295). Springer.

Goodsell, C. T. (1988). *The social meaning of civic space: Studying political authority through architecture.* University Press of Kansas.

Gottdeiner, M., & Komninos, N. (Eds.). (1989). *Capitalist development and crisis theory: Accumulation, regulation and spatial restructuring.* Palgrave Macmillan UK.

Gregory, D. (1978). *Ideology, science, and human geography.* Hutchinson University Library.

Gregory, D. (1989). Presences and absences: Time-space relations and structuration theory. In D. Held & J. Thompson (Eds.), *Social theory of modern societies: Anthony Giddens and his critics* (pp. 185–214). Cambridge University Press.

Habermas, J. (1962). *The structural transformation of the public sphere.* MIT Press.

Hägerstrand, T. (1974). Ecology under one perspective. In E. Bylund, H. Linderholm, & O. Rune (Eds.), *Ecological problems of the circumpolar area: Papers from the International Symposium at Luleå, Sweden, June 28–29, 1971.* Norrbottens Museum.

Hägerstrand, T. (1975). Space, time, and human conditions. In A. Karlqvist, L. Lundqvist, & F. Snickars (Eds.), *Dynamic allocation of urban space.* Saxon House & Lexington Books.

Hägerstrand, T. (1985). Time-geography: Focus on the corporeality of man, society, and environment. In S. Aida (Ed.), *The science and praxis of complexity* (pp. 193–216). United Nations University Press.

Hall, E. T. (1966). *The hidden dimension: Man's use of space in public and private.* Doubleday.

Hall, P. (1984). *The world cities.* Weidenfeld and Nicolson.

Harvey, D. (1988). *The geographical and geopolitical consequences of the transition from Fordist to flexible accumulation.* Rutgers University Press.

Harvey, D. (1989). From managerialism to entrepreneurialism: The transformation in urban governance in late capitalism. *Geografiska Annaler: Series B, Human Geography, 71*(1), 3–17.

Harvey, D. (1990). Between space and time: Reflections on the geographical imagination. *Annals of the Association of American Geographers, 80*(3), 418–434.

Harvey, D. (1996). *Justice, nature, and the geography of difference.* Blackwell.

Harvey, D. (2006). *Spaces of capitalism: Towards a theory of uneven geographical development.* Verso.

Harvey, D. (2007). *A brief history of neoliberalism.* Oxford University Press.

Harvey, D. (2010). *The enigma of capital and the crises of capitalism.* Oxford University Press.

Harvey, D. (2012). *Rebel cities: From the right to the city to the urban revolution.* Verso.

Harvey, D. (2014). *Seventeen contradictions and the end of capitalism.* Oxford University Press.

Held, D. (1989). *Political theory and the modern state: Essays on state, power, and democracy.* Stanford University Press.

Henderson, J. W., & Castells, M. (1987). *Global restructuring and territorial development.* Sage.

Jessop, B. (1990). Fordism and post-Fordism: a critical reformulation. In A. J. Scott & M. J. Stroper, *Pathways to industrialization and regional development* (pp. 46–69). Routledge.

Jones, M. (2009). Phase space: Geography, relational thinking, and beyond. *Progress in Human Geography, 33*(4), 487–506.

Keohane, Robert O., & Nye, J. S. (1972). *Transnational relations and world politics.* Harvard University Press.

Keohane, Robert Owen, & Nye, J. S. (1977). *Power and interdependence: world politics in transition.* Little, Brown.

Kling, J. (1991). The geography of capitalism and the decentering of culture in the formation of the late capitalist city. Presented at the American Political Science Association, Washington, DC.

Komninos, N. (1987). Designing the post-Fordist city. In *UIA XVI World Congress, Contributed Papers* (pp. 140–143). Royal Institute of British Architects.

Krätke, S. (1992). Berlin: The rise of a new metropolis in a post-Fordist landscape. In M. Dunford & G. Kafkalas (Eds.), *Cities and regions in the new Europe* (pp. 213–238). Belhaven Press.

Lefebvre, H. (1976). Reflections on the politics of space. *Antipode, 8*(2), 30–37.

Lefebvre, H. (1991). *The production of space.* Basil Blackwell.

Lipietz, A. (1986). New tendencies in the international division of labor: Regimes of accumulation and modes of regulation. In A. J. Scott & M. Storper (Eds.), *Production, work, territory: The geographical anatomy of industrial capitalism* (pp. 16–40). Allen & Unwin.

Logan, J. R., & Molotch, H. L. (1987). *Urban fortunes: The political economy of place.* University of California Press.

Low, S. M., & Smith, N. (2006). *The politics of public space.* Routledge.

Luke, J., Ventriss, C., Reed, B. J., & Reed, C. (1988). *Managing economic development: a guide to state and local leadership strategies.* Jossey-Bass.

Manning, B. (1977). The congress, the executive, and intermestic affairs: Three proposals. *Foreign Affairs, 55*(2), 306–324.

Massey, A. (2009). Policy mimesis in the context of global governance. *Policy Studies, 30*(3), 383–395.

Massey, D. (2005). *For space.* Sage.

Massey, D. (1991). The political place of locality studies. *Environment and Planning A: Economy and Space, 23*(2), 267–281.

Massey, D. (1996). Politicising space and place. *Scottish Geographical Magazine, 112*(2), 117–123.

Mayer, M. (1992). The shifting local political system in European cities. In M. Dunford & G. Kafkalas (Eds.), *Cities and regions in the new Europe* (pp. 255–274). Belhaven Press.

Mazzucato, M. (2015). *The entrepreneurial state: Debunking public vs. private sector myths.* Anthem Press.

McNally, D. (2011). *Global slump: The economics and politics of crisis and resistance.* PM Press.

Mellor, R. E. H. (1989). *Nation, state, and territory: A political geography.* Routledge.

Merriman, P., Jones, M., Olsson, G., Sheppard, E., Thrift, N., & Tuan, Y.-F. (2012). Space and spatiality in theory. *Dialogues in human geography, 2*(1), 3–22.

Milanović, B. (2005). *Worlds apart: Measuring international and global inequality.* Princeton University Press.

Moffitt, B. (2016). *The global rise of populism: Performance, political style, and representation.* Stanford University Press.

Morgan, K. (1992). Innovating by networking: new models of corporate and regional development. In Dunford & Kafkalas (Eds.), *Cities and regions in the new Europe* (pp. 150–169). Belhaven Press.

Moulaert, F., & Willekens, F. (1987). Decentralization in industrial policy in Belgium. In W. Stöhr & H. Muegge (Eds.), *International economic restructuring and the regional community.* Avebury.

Muller, H., & Ventriss, C. (1985). *Public health in a retrenchment era.* State University of New York Press.

O'Brien, R. (1992). *Global financial integration: The end of geography.* Royal Institute of International Affairs.

Panitch, L., & Konings, M. (2008). *American empire and the political economy of global finance.* Springer.

Peet, R. (1987). *International capitalism and industrial restructuring: A critical analysis.* Allen & Unwin.

Phillips, K. (2009). *Bad money: Reckless finance, failed politics, and the global crisis of American capitalism.* Penguin.

Piketty, T. (2014). *Capital in the twenty-first century.* Harvard University Press.

Piore, M., & Sabel, C. (1984). *The second industrial divide : possibilities for prosperity.* Basic Books.

Porter, P. W., & Faust, D. R. (2009). *A world of difference: Encountering and contesting development.* Guilford Press.

Pred, A. (1981). Social reproduction and the time-geography of everyday life. *Geografiska Annaler. Series B, Human Geography, 63*(1), 5–22.

Ramos, A. G. (1981). *The new science of organizations: A reconceptualization of the wealth of nations.* University of Toronto Press.

Reich, R. B. (2016). *Saving capitalism: For the many, not the few.* Vintage.

Sassen-Koob, S. (1986). New York City: Economic restructuring and immigration. *Development and Change, 17*(1), 85–119.

Sassen-Koob, S. (1987). Issues of core and periphery: Labour migration and global restructuring. In J. M. Henderson & M. Castells (Eds.), *Global restructuring and territorial development* (pp. 60–87). Sage.

Sassen, S. (2014). *Expulsions: Brutality and complexity in the global economy.* Harvard University Press.

Saunders, P. (1989). Space, urbanism, and the created environment. In D. Held & Thompson (Eds.), *Social theory of modern societies: Anthony Giddens and his critics* (pp. 215–34). Cambridge University Press.

Sayer, A. (1989). On the dialogue between humanism and historical materialism in geography. In A. L. Kobayashi & S. Mackenzie (Eds.), *Remaking Human Geography* (pp. 206–226). Unwin Hyman.

Schneier, B. (2015). *Data and Goliath: The hidden battles to collect and control your world.* W. W. Norton.

Scott, A. J., & Storper, M. (1986). *Production, work, territory: The geographical anatomy of industrial capitalism.* Allen & Unwin.

Smith, M. P. (2008). *Power, community and the city.* Transaction.

Smith, M. P., & Feagin, J. R. (1987). *The capitalist city: Global restructuring and community politics.* Basil Blackwell.

Smith, N. (1989). Uneven development and location theory: Towards a synthesis. *New Models in Geography, 1*, 142–163.

Smith, N. (1990). *Uneven development: nature, capital, and the production of space.* Blackwell.

Soja, E., Morales, R., & Wolff, G. (1983). Urban restructuring: An analysis of social and spatial change in Los Angeles. *Economic Geography, 59*(2), 195–230.

Soja, E. W. (1985). The spatiality of social life: Towards a transformative retheorisation. In Gregory & Urry (Eds.), *Social Relations and Spatial Structures* (pp. 90–127). Palgrave.

Soja, E. W. (1989). *Postmodern geographies: The reassertion of space in critical social theory.* Verso.

Soja, E. W. (2010). Beyond post-metropolis. *Urban Geography, 32*(4), 451–469.

Soja, E. W. (2014). *My Los Angeles: From urban restructuring to regional restructuring.* University of California Press.

Sommer, R. (1969). *Personal space; the behavioral basis of design*. Prentice-Hall.

Steele, F. I. (1973). *Physical settings and organization development*. Addison-Wesley Longman.

Stiglitz, J. E. (2002). *Globalization and its discontents*. Penguin Books.

Stiglitz, J. E. (2010). *Freefall: free markets and the sinking of the global economy*. Penguin.

Stiglitz, J. E. (2013). *The price of inequality*. Penguin Books.

Stiglitz, J. E. (2015). *The great divide: Unequal societies and what we can do about them*. W. W. Norton.

Stöhr, W. B. (1990). *Global challenge and local response: Initiatives for economic regeneration in contemporary Europe*. United Nations University Press.

Storper, M., & Scott, A. J. (2016). Current debates in urban theory: A critical assessment: *Urban Studies, 53*(6), 1114–1136.

Storper, M., & Walker, R. (1989). *The capitalist imperative: Territory, technology, and industrial growth*. Basil Blackwell.

Sullivan, W. M. (1986). *Reconstructing public philosophy*. University of California Press.

Swyngedouw, E. A. (1992). The Mammon quest, "glocalisation," interspatial competition, and the monetary order: The construction of new scales. In Swyngedouw (Ed.), In *Cities and regions in the new Europe* (pp. 39–67). Bell Haven Press.

Swyngedouw, E. A. (1989). The heart of the place: The resurrection of locality in an age of hyperspace. *Geografiska Annaler: Series B, Human Geography, 71*(1), 31–42.

Thompson, J. B. (1989). The theory of structuration. In D. Held & J. B. Thompson (Eds.), *Social theory of modern societies: Anthony Giddens and his critics*. Cambridge University Press.

Thrift, N. J. (1987). *Class and space: The making of urban society*. Routledge & Kegan Paul.

Urry, J. (2004). *The sociology of space and place. The Blackwell companion to sociology*. Blackwell.

Ventriss, C. (1994). The impact of international trade and direct foreign investment on national and subnational levels: An overview. In R. Baker (Ed.), *Comparative public management* (pp. 9–22). Praeger.

Ventriss, C. (2000). New public management: An examination of its influence on contemporary public affairs and its impact on shaping the intellectual agenda of the field. *Administrative Theory & Praxis, 22*(3), 500–518.

Ventriss, C. (2010). The challenge for public administration (and public policy) in an era of economic crises . . . or the relevance of cognitive politics in a time of political involution. *Administrative Theory & Praxis, 32*(3), 402–428.

Vincent, R. J. (1986). *Human rights and international relations*. Cambridge University Press.

Warde, A. (1989). Recipes for a pudding: A comment on locality. *Antipode, 21*(3), 274–281.

Wei, Y. D. (2015). Spatial inequality. *Applied Geography*, Special Edition, 61, 1–116.

Wolfe, M. (2009). *Fixing global finance: How to curb financial crises in the 21st century*. Yale University Press.

Zieleniec, A. J. L. (2007). *Space and social theory*. Sage.

Chapter 8

Arendt, H. (1958). *The human condition*. University of Chicago Press.

Arendt, H. (1977). *Life of the mind*. Harcourt.

Barber, B. R. (1984). *Strong democracy: Participatory politics for a new age*. University of California Press.

Beck, U., Giddens, A., & Lash, S. (1994). *Reflexive modernization: Politics, tradition and aesthetics in the modern social order*. Stanford University Press.

Becker, D. (1983). *The new bourgeoisie and the limits of dependency*. Princeton University Press.

Beierle, T. C. (2002). *Democracy in practice: Public participation in environmental decisions*. Routledge.

Block, F. (1987). *Revising state theory: Essays in politics and postindustrialism*. Temple University Press.

Bohman, J. (1998). Survey article: The coming of age of deliberative democracy. *Journal of Political Philosophy*, *6*(4), 400–425. https://doi.org/10.1111/1467-9760.00061.

Bohman, J. (2007). Political communication and the epistemic value of diversity: Deliberation and legitimation in media societies. *Communication Theory*, *17*(4), 348–355. https://doi.org/10.1111/j.1468-2885.2007.00301.x.

Bryan, F. M. (2004). *Real democracy*. University of Chicago Press.

Bryson, J. M., Quick, K. S., Slotterback, C. S., & Crosby, B. C. (2013). Designing public participation processes. *Public Administration Review*, *73*(1), 23–34. https://doi.org/10.1111/j.1540-6210.2012.02678.x.

Burrell, G. (1980). Radical organization theory. In D. Dunkerley & G. Salaman (Eds.), *The International Yearbook of Organization Studies*. Routledge.

Carpini, M. X. D., Cook, F. L., & Jacobs, L. B. (2004). Public deliberation, discursive participation, and citizen engagement: A review of the empirical literature. *Annual Review of Political Science*, *7*, 315–344. https://doi.org/10.1146/annurev.polisci.7.121003.091630.

Clegg, H. A. (1975). Pluralism in industrial relations. *British Journal of Industrial Relations*, *13*(3), 309–316. https://doi.org/10.1111/j.1467-8543.1975.tb00613.x.

Clegg, S. (2013). *The theory of power and organization (RLE: Organizations)*. Routledge.

Cooke, B., & Kothari, U. (2001). *Participation: The new tyranny?* Zed Books.

Cooke, M. (2006). Five arguments for deliberative democracy. In M. d'Entreves, *Democracy as public deliberation* (p. 35). Routledge.

Deleon, S. D., & Ventriss, C. (2010). Diamonds, land use, and indigenous peoples: The dilemmas of public participation and multi-national diamond corporation. *Public Administration and Management, 15*(1), 98–137.

Dicken, P. (2007). *Global shift: Mapping the changing contours of the world economy.* Sage.

Dryzek, J. S. (2007). Theory, evidence, and the tasks of deliberation. In S. W. Rosenberg (Ed.), *Deliberation, participation, and democracy* (pp. 237–250). Palgrave Macmillan.

Farrell, J. (2016). Corporate funding and ideological polarization about climate change. *Proceedings of the National Academy of Sciences, 113*(1), 92–97. https://doi.org/10.1073/pnas.1509433112.

Forester, J. (1989). *Planning in the face of power.* University of California Press.

Fraser, N. (1990). Rethinking the public sphere: A contribution to the critique of actually existing democracy. *Social Text, 25*(26), 56–80.

Forester, J. (1999). *The deliberative practitioner: Encouraging participatory planning processes.* MIT Press.

Fung, A., & Fagotto, E. (2009). *Sustaining public engagement: Embedded deliberation in local communities.* Kettering Foundation.

Fung, A. (2006). Varieties of participation in complex governance. *Public Administration Review, 66*(1), 66–75. https://doi.org/10.1111/j.1540-6210.2006.00667.x.

Fung, A., & Wright, E. O. (2003). *Deepening democracy: Institutional innovations in empowered participatory governance.* Verso.

Gibson-Wood, H., & Wakefield, S. (2012). "Participation," white privilege, and environmental justice: Understanding environmentalism among Hispanics in Toronto. *Antipode, 45*(3), 641–662. https://doi.org/10.1111/j.1467-8330.2012.01019.x.

Giddens, A. (1999). *The third way: The renewal of social democracy.* John Wiley & Sons.

Görgens, T., & Van Donk, M. (2011). *From basic needs toward socio-spatial transformation: Coming to grips with the "Right to City" for the urban poor in South Africa.* Islandia Institute.

Gottlieb, R. (1993). *Forcing the spring: The transformation of the American environmental movement.* Island Press.

Gutmann, A., & Thompson, D. (2004). *Why deliberative democracy?* Princeton University Press.

Habermas, J. (1984). *The theory of communicative action.* Beacon Press.

Habermas, J. (1996). *Between facts and norms.* MIT Press.

Harvey, D. (1996). *Justice, nature, and the geography of difference.* Blackwell.

Harvey, D. (2000). *Spaces of hope.* University of California Press.

Harvey, D. (2007). Neoliberalism as creative destruction. *The ANNALS of the American Academy of Political and Social Science, 610*(1), 21–44. https://doi.org/10.1177/0002716206296780.

Harvey, D. (2010). *Social justice and the city.* University of Georgia Press.

Hickey, S., & Mohan, G. (2004). *Participation—From tyranny to transformation?: Exploring new approaches to participation in development.* Zed Books.

Hirst, P. (2000). Democracy and governance. In *Debating governance: Authority, steering, and democracy* (pp. 13–35). Oxford University Press.

Hornik, K., Cutts, B., & Greenlee, A. (2016). Community theories of change: Linking environmental justice to sustainability through stakeholder perceptions in Milwaukee (WI, USA). *International Journal of Environmental Research and Public Health, 13*(10), 979. https://doi.org/10.3390/ijerph13100979.

Hummel, R. P. (2007). *The bureaucratic experience: The post-modern challenge.* M. E. Sharpe.

Hummel, R. P., & Stivers, C. (1998). Government is us: The possibility of democratic knowledge in representative government. In C. S. King & C. Stivers (Eds.), *Government is us: Public administration in an anti-government era* (pp. 28–48). Sage.

Jessop, B. (1990). *State theory: Putting the capitalist state in its place.* Penn State Press.

Jessop, B. (2007). *State power.* Polity Press.

Kasemir, B., Jager, J., Jaeger, C. C., & Gardner, M. T. (2003). *Public participation in sustainability science: A handbook.* Cambridge University Press.

Lipschutz, R. D. (2004). Globalisation and global governance in the twenty-first century: The environment and global governance. In *Global governance in the twenty-first century* (pp. 143–144). Palgrave Macmillan.

Marsden, R. (1993). The politics of organizational analysis. *Organization Studies, 14*(1), 93–124. https://doi.org/10.1177/017084069301400107.

Mead, G. H. (2010). Mind, self, and society. In J. Margolis & J. Catudal, *Quarrel between invariance and flux: A guide for philosophers and other players.* Penn State Press.

Merrifield, A. (2002). *Metromarxism: A Marxist tale of the city.* Routledge.

Moffitt, B. (2016). *The global rise of populism: Performance, political style, and representation.* Stanford University Press.

Morgan, G. (1986). *Images of organization.* Sage.

Muller, H. J., & Ventriss, C. (1985). *Public health in a retrenchment era: An alternative to managerialism.* State University of New York Press.

Nabatchi, T., & Leighninger, M. (2015). *Public participation for the 21st century democracy.* Jossey-Bass.

Parsons, T. (1971). *The system of modern societies.* Prentice-Hall.

Pateman, C. (2012). Participatory democracy revisited. *Perspectives on Politics, 10*(1), 7–19. https://doi.org/10.1017/S1537592711004877.

Poulantzas, N. (1978). *State, power, and socialism.* Verso.

Rahman, M. A. (1995). Participatory development: Toward liberation of co-optation? In G. Craig & M. Mayo (Eds.), *Community empowerment: A reader in participation and development.* Zed Books.

Ramos, A. G. (1981). *The new science of organizations: A reconceptualization of the wealth of nations.* University of Toronto Press.

Roberts, N. C. (2008). *The age of direct citizen participation.* New York: Routledge.

Saward, M. (2000). A critique of Held. In B. Holden, *Global democracy: Key debates*. Routledge.

Scott, W. G., & Hart, D. K. (1989). *Organizational values in America*. Transaction.

Smith, M. J. (2000). *Rethinking state theory*. Routledge.

Sørensen, E. (2012). Measuring the accountability of collaborative innovation. *The Innovation Journal; Ottawa, 17*(1), 2–18.

Thomas, J. C. (1995). *Public participation in public decisions: New skills and strategies for public managers*. Jossey-Bass.

Unger, R. M. (1987). *Social theory, its situation and its task*. CUP Archive.

Van der Meer, T., & Hakhverdian, A. (2016). Political trust as the evaluation of process and performance: A cross-national study of 42 European countries. *Political Studies, 65*(1), 81–102. https://doi.org/10.1177/0032321715607514.

Van der Meer, T. (2017). Democratic input, macroeconomic output, and political trust. In S. Zmerli (Ed.), *Handbook on political trust* (pp. 270–284). Edward Elgar.

Ventriss, C. (1985). Emerging perspectives on citizen participation. *Public Administration Review, 45*(3), 433–440. https://doi.org/10.2307/3109973.

Ventriss, C. (1998). Swimming against the tide: Reflections on some recent theoretical approaches of public administration theory. *Administrative Theory & Praxis, 20*(1), 91–101.

Ventriss, C. (2002). The need and relevance for public rationality: Some critical reflections. *Administrative Theory & Praxis, 24*(2), 287–298. https://doi.org/10.1080/10841806.2002.11029362.

Ventriss, C. (2016). Investing in people: Toward a co-possibility model for citizen engagement. *International Journal of Public Administration, 39*(13), 1020–1030. https://doi.org/10.1080/01900692.2016.1190747.

Weber, M. (1978). *Economy and society: An outline of interpretive sociology*. University of California Press.

Wondolleck, J. M., & Yaffee, S. L. (2000). *Making collaboration work: Lessons from innovation in natural resource managment*. Island Press.

Young, I. M. (1990). *Justice and the politics of difference*. Princeton University Press.

Chapter 9

Adams, G. (1992). Enthralled with modernity: The historical context of knowledge and theory development in public administration. *Public Administration,* 52(4), 363–373.

Adams, G., & Balfour, D. (2014). *Unmasking administrative evil*. Sage.

Arendt, H. (1958). *The human condition*. University of Chicago Press.

Arendt, H. (1997). *On revolution*. Penguin Books.

Arendt, H. (1998). *Men in dark times*. Harcourt Brace & World.

Bailey, S. K. (1976). *The purpose of education*. Phi Delta Kappa Educational Foundation.

Barnett, C. (2007). Publics in markets: What's wrong with neo-liberalism. In S. Smith (Ed.), *The handbook of social geography* (187–205). Sage.

Bok, D. (1975). The presidential report, 1973–1975. *Harvard Today*, 18, 4–10.

Boyte, H. C., & Fretz, E. (2011). Civic professionalism. *Journal of Higher Education Outreach and Engagement, 14*(2), 67–90.

Box, R. C. (2008). *Critical public administration*. M. E. Sharpe.

Box, R. C. (2014). *Public service values*. Routledge.

British Broadcast News. (2020). The worst economic crisis since 1930s depression, IMF says. April 10.

Brint, S. (1994). *In an age of experts*. Princeton University Press.

Bryson, J., & Eissweiller, P. (Eds.). (1987). *Shared power*. University Press of America.

Cooper, T. (1991). *An ethic of citizen participation for public administration*. Prentice-Hall.

Dryzek, J. (2000). *Deliberative democracy and beyond*. Oxford University Press.

Dryzek, J. (2006). *Deliberative global politics*. Polity.

Dyckman, J. W. (1978). Three crises of American planning. In R. Burchell & G. Sternlieb (Eds.), *Planning theory in the 1980s* (285–297). Rutgers University Press.

Dzur, A. W. (2008). *Democratic professionalism*. Pennsylvania State University Press.

Erie, S. (1979). *Historical crisis of public administration*. Unpublished manuscript.

Evett, J. (2011). A new professionalism: Challenges and opportunities. *Current Sociology, 59*(4), 406–422.

Felts, A. (1994). *Critical theory and public administration theory*. Presented at the Seventh National Symposium on Public Administration Theory, Akron, OH.

Fischer, F. (2009). *Democracy and expertise*. Oxford University Press.

Fox, C. (1993). Alternatives to orthodoxy. *Administrative Theory & Praxis, 15*(2), 52–70.

Fung, A. (2006). Varieties of participation in complex governance. *Public Administration Review, 66*, 66–75.

Gitlin, T. (1989). *The sixties: Years of hope, days of rage*. Bantam Books.

Hummel, R. (2007). *The bureaucratic experience*. M. E. Sharpe.

Isaac, J. C. (1998). *Democracy in dark times*. Cornell University Press.

Joshi, A., & Moore, M. (2004). Institutionalized co-production: Unorthodox public service delivery in challenging environments. *Journal of Development Studies, 40*, 31–49.

Kiljn, E., & Kopperjan, J. (2000). Public management and policy networks. *Public Management, 2*, 135–158.

Kirlin, J. (1979). Adapting the intergovernmental fiscal system to the demands of an advanced economy. In G. Tobin, *The changing structure of the city* (77–104). Sage.

Kolbert, E. (2020). Pandemic and the shape of human history. *The Atlantic*, March 20.

Larson, M. S. (1984). The production of expertise and the constitution of expert power. In T. Haskell (Ed.), *The authority of experts*. Indiana University Press.

Laudan, L. (1978). *Progress and its problems: Towards a theory of scientific growth*. University of California Press.

Levine, C. H. (1984). Citizenship and service delivery: The promise of co-production. *Public Administration Review, 44*, 178–187.

Mayer, J. (2016). *Dark money: The hidden history of billionaires behind the rise of the radical right*. Doubleday.

Moberly, W. (1949). *The crisis in the university*. S. C. M. Press.

Mosher, F. C. (1968). *Democracy and the public service*. Oxford University Press.

Muller, H., & Ventriss, C. (1985). *Public health in a retrenchment era*. State University of New York Press.

Newman, J., & Sullivan, H. (2004). Public participation and collaborative governance. *Journal of Social Policy, 33*, 203–223.

Perrow, C. (1979). *Complex organizations*. Random House.

Perry, J. L. (2007). Democracy and the new public service. *American Review of Public Administration, 27*(1), 3–16.

Pesch, U., Spekkink, W., & Quist, J. (2018). Local sustainability initiatives: Innovation and civic engagement in societal experiments. *European Planning Studies, 27*, 300–317.

Pinsler, J. (2020). The pandemic will cleave America in two. *The Atlantic*, April 10.

Pugh, D. L. (1989). Professionalism in public administration: Problems, perspectives, and the role of ASPA. *Public Administration Review, 49*, 1–8.

Ramos, A. G. (1981). *The new science of organizations: A reconceptualization of the wealth of nations*. University of Toronto Press.

Reitter, P., & Wellmon, R. (2020). Max Weber invited the crisis of humanities. *The Chronicle of Higher Education,* February 14.

Salamon, L. (1987). Of market failure and third party government. *Nonprofit and Voluntary Quarterly, 16*, 29–49.

Sandel, M. J. (1996). *Democracy's discontent: America in search of a public philosophy*. Harvard University Press.

Schon, D. (1971). *Beyond the stable state*. W. W. Norton.

Schon, D. (1984). *The reflective practitioner*. Doubleday.

Schon, D. (2001). The crisis of professional knowledge and pursuit of an epistemology of practice. In J. Raven & J. Stephenson (Eds.), *Competence in the learning society* (183–207). Peter Lang.

Sorrensen, E. (2012). Governance networks as a frame for inter-demoi participation and deliberation. *Administrative Theory& Praxis, 14*, 509–532.

Stever, J. A. (1988). *The end of public administration*. Transactional Publishers.

Toozer, A. (2020). The normal economics is never coming back. *Foreign Affairs*, April 8.

Ventriss, C. (1991). Contemporary issues in American public administration education: The search for an educational focus. *Public Administration Review, 51*, 4–14.

Ventriss, C. (2000). New public management: An examination of its influence on contemporary public affairs and its impact on shaping the intellectual agenda of the field. *Administration Theory & Praxis, 22*(3), 500–518.

Ventriss, C. (2002). The need and relevance for public rationality: Some critical reflections. *Administrative Theory & Praxis, 24*(2), 287–298. https://doi.org/10.1080/10841806.2002.11029362.

Ventriss, C., & Luke, J. (1988). Organizational learning and public policy: Towards a substantive perspective. *The American Review of Public Administration, 18*(4), 337–357. https://doi.org/10.1177/027507408801800402.

Ventriss, C. (2016). Investing in people: Towards a co-possibility model of citizen engagement. *International Journal of Public Administration, 39*(15), 1020–1030.

Villa, D. R. (2001). *Socratic citizenship*. Princeton University Press.

Waldo, D. (1980). *The enterprise of public administration: a summary view*. Chandler & Sharp.

Whitehead, A. N. (1963). *Science in the Modern World.* Mentor Books.

Wills, G. (1979). *Confessions of a conservative.* Doubleday.

Wolin, S. (1960). *Politics and vision: Continuity and innovation in Western political thought*. Princeton University Press.

Index

www.ingramcontent.com/pod-product-compliance
Lightning Source LLC
LaVergne TN
LVHW050150080826
844660LV00002B/141

* 9 7 8 1 4 3 8 4 8 1 2 5 8 *